FOURTH

Directory of Periodicals

Publishing Articles on English
and American Literature and Language

FOURTH
DIRECTORY of PERIODICALS

*Publishing Articles on
English and American
Literature and Language*

DONNA GERSTENBERGER
and GEORGE HENDRICK

THE **SWALLOW PRESS** INC.
CHICAGO

Published by
The Swallow Press Incorporated
1139 South Wabash Avenue
Chicago, Illinois 60605

ISBN (clothbound edition) 0-8040-0675-X
ISBN (paperbound edition) 0-8040-0676-8
LIBRARY OF CONGRESS CATALOG CARD NUMBER 74-21506

INTRODUCTION

This *Fourth Directory of Periodicals* is offered as a result of the growing evidence that the *Directory* has become an institution in the world of academic publishing. Its usefulness in the placing of manuscripts has long been established; it is in the subsidiary uses that the surprises have come. A number of university graduate classes in bibliography have, for example, used the *Directory* as an introduction to the whole concept of scholarly publishing, and librarians and book stores have been among those to testify to the *Directory*'s usefulness. The format we adopted for the first *Directory* in 1959 has proved its worth in successive updates, and it has become so familiar that it seems to provide the basic pattern for specialized directories by other scholars.

In undertaking this revision of the *Directory*, we have faced the most difficult task since organizing the first book fifteen years ago, for the situation in periodical publication is probably more fluid now than at any time in the last two decades. Journals are coming into existence almost as rapidly as they are departing. The new emphasis on interdisciplinary approaches and on new facets of language study account in part for the proliferation of journals as does the sheer numerical increase in academic institutions. On the other hand, the financial difficulties of American universities and the high cost of printing have resulted in the death of a number of journals, while a number of others have emigrated to Canada. Those journals whose death or temporary suspension or absorption we report since the *Third Directory* (1970) include *Alaska Review, Alphabet, American-German Review, Arkham Collector, Auction of the Mind, Barat Review, Bennington Review, Buffalo Studies, Cabellian, Count Dracula Society Quarterly, Critical Survey, Discours, Duquesne Review, Journal of the Catch Society, Language and Automation, Laurel Review,*

Menckeniana, Midway, Minnesota Review, Stony Brook, Trace, Uma-nesimo, and *Word Watching*. Other journals are on our uncertain list, and if a user of the *Directory* wants to try his luck, he might start with the addresses in the last *Directory*, although all our queries have gone unanswered. These include *Blackmore Studies, American Dialogue, Approach, Catholic World, Comment, Dialogist, Eikon, International Language Reporter, Modern Age, New England Review, Stephen Crane Newsletter, Theology, Tolkien Journal*, and *Wallace Stevens Newsletter*. One journal, *New Letters* (formerly *The University Review*, formerly *The University of Kansas City Review*), has forbidden its inclusion; therefore the editor should definitely be queried before sending a manuscript (to University of Missouri-Kansas City, 5100 Rockhill Road, Kansas City, Mo. 64110).

We have generally not listed special limited periodicals such as alumni magazines, state historical society bulletins or quarterlies, or undergraduate magazines restricted to on-campus contributors. Folklore and linguistic periodicals and those journals which might be of interest in the history of ideas have been included, as have several periodicals in the modern foreign languages since these journals at times publish comparative literature articles. We list several of the film journals and a sampling of "little magazines" that carry occasional critical articles.

Although many periodicals which do not desire unsolicited manuscripts did not answer our queries, those that did are listed on the grounds that their presence makes the *Directory* more complete and answers the question of the scholar considering these magazines as possible places of publication. In a few instances, even though the journal did not answer our requests for information, we have listed its address for those who might find it useful.

A subject index has been provided as a bibliographic guide to fields of scholarly interest, although entry under any one category should not be considered exclusive in any way.

Through paragraphing, we have attempted to indicate the major blocks of information for each journal. Thus, the reader desiring to locate quickly a certain type of information about a certain journal (e.g., major fields of interest) can, if familiar with our system, find it without reading the complete contents of each entry. (The key to information selected for each journal precedes the first page of entries.)

Information on the preparation of manuscripts is thoroughly covered in the latest edition of the MLA style sheet, which should be consulted unless the journal in question specifies the University of Chicago style manual. All manuscripts must, of course, be typed and double-spaced and include a stamped self-addressed envelope for return. In the case of foreign periodicals, enclose International Reply Coupons.

While the *Directory* will serve as a guide to periodicals, whenever possible, a prospective contributor should consult a recent issue of the journal under consideration.

The *Fourth Directory* has been made possible through the financial aid of the Graduate School of the University of Washington, and special thanks are due to Ms. Sherry Laing for her part in compiling the materials of this book.

D. G.
University of Washington
Seattle

G. H.
University of Illinois
Urbana-Champaign .

KEY TO ENTRIES

Entries are arranged alphabetically, excluding *The*. Thus, *The Evelyn Waugh Newsletter* will be found under *E*. Each entry contains the following information: TITLE, editorial address, price on a yearly basis unless otherwise specified, frequency of publication, year of founding, and sponsor; major fields of interest; manuscript information; payment; copyright policy.

Unless specifically indicated within the entry, the periodicals do not:

(1)   Restrict contributions to subscribers or members.
(2)   Desire solicited manuscripts only.
(3)   Have special religious or political bias.
(4)   Carry creative, non-scholarly material.
(5)   Desire more than one manuscript copy of an article.
(6)   Have bibliographical issue.

ABERDEEN UNIVERSITY REVIEW, Department of Mathematics, King's College, Aberdeen AB9 2UB, Scotland. 2 issues a year; £1.50. Founded 1913; sponsored by Aberdeen University.

Major fields of interest: Articles of literary and general interest. Creative material also used.

Manuscript information: Articles of 3000-5000 words preferred. Footnotes should be placed at foot of each page, denoted by superscript. Report within 1 month.

Payment: 12 offprints.

Republication allowed with permission and acknowledgment.

ADAM INTERNATIONAL REVIEW, a Literary Journal in English and French, 28 Emperors' Gate, London SW7 4H5. $9 for 4 issues.

Major fields of interest: Contemporary writing, occasional studies of comparative literature, literary history, but chiefly introductions to foreign literatures. Also bio-bibliographical material. Literary criticism, especially dealing with neglected writers, contemporary or even "ancient" ones, is welcome. Recently the magazine has also become an "international journal of the theatre, architecture, visual arts, music." Creative work is preferred.

Manuscript information: 2000-3000 words. A moderate number of footnotes accepted "if they are really necessary."

Payment: By agreement; 50 offprints.

Copyright remains with author.

AEGIS, Box 267, Moorhead State College, Moorhead, Minnesota 56560. $3; twice yearly (spring and fall). Founded 1973.

Major fields of interest: "The editors of AEGIS encourage the submission of all kinds of articles on literature and language: criticism, scholarship, linguistics, bibliography and comparative literature." Creative, non-scholarly work also published. "Finally, the editors welcome pieces of any type which are satirical or irreverent, providing they are well-informed and graced with wit."

Manuscript information: 12-15 pages in manuscript. MLA style sheet. One copy needed. Footnotes at end of article. Report in 1-3 months.

Payment: Either offprints of articles or copies of journal or both.

Copyright held by editors; released to authors upon request.

AFRICAN LITERATURE TODAY, Professor Eldred Jones, Department of English, University of Sierra Leone. $6; once yearly. Founded 1968.

Major fields of interest: African literary criticism. Critical articles preferred.

Manuscript information: 2000-5000 words. Oxford house style; minimal footnotes; if essential place at end of chapters. 2 copies of Ms. desired. Report time up to 3 months.

Payment: £3.3.0 per thousand words; 1 free copy.

Copyright remains with the author.

AGENDA, 5 Cranbourne Court, Albert Bridge Road, London, S.W.11, 4PE, England. $6, quarterly. Founded 1959.

Major fields of interest: Poetry and criticism. Special issues on individual writers and painters. Not limited to poets. Creative work preferred but critical articles also published.

Manuscript information: Articles of 3000 words, but no fixed limit.

Payment: £1 per page, "when we can afford it!" 6 complimentary copies.

AGORA, S.U.N.Y. College at Potsdam, Potsdam, N.Y. 13676; $4; twice yearly. Founded 1969; sponsored by S.U.C. Potsdam.

Major fields of interest: Humanities and the social sciences: a philosophical or critical approach.

Manuscript information: Articles should be 15-20 pp. MLA Style Sheet. Report in 2 months.

Payment: 12 issues of journal.

Indexed in *Philosopher's Index* and *MLA Abstracts*.

THE ALABAMA REVIEW, University, Alabama 35486. $6; quarterly. Founded 1948; sponsored by the Alabama Historical Association.

Major fields of interest: Alabama and Southern history. Scholarly articles preferred. Creative non-scholarly material also published.

Manuscript information: 5000-10,000 words preferred. Study of format suggested. 3-6 months required for decision.

Payment: None.

No copyright.

THE AMERICAN BOOK COLLECTOR, 1434 S. Yale Avenue, Arlington Heights, Illinois 60005. $7.50; bi-monthly. Founded 1950.

Major fields of interest: Bibliographical subjects; articles on book collecting, autographs, ex libris.

Manuscript information: 1000-5000 words with illustrations preferred if possible. Footnotes must be kept to a minimum and should be typed on a separate sheet. Report within 1 to 2 weeks.

Payment: 6 to 12 copies of the issue.

Copyright for protection of contributors.

AMERICAN DOCUMENTATION, c/o Arthur W. Elias, Information Co. America, 225 S. 15th Street, Philadelphia, Pennsylvania 19102. $18.50; bi-monthly (Jan., March, May, July, Sept., Nov.). Founded 1950; sponsored by the American Society for Information Science.

Major fields of interest: Critical approaches to bibliography, librarianship, linguistics, the history of ideas, the organization of knowledge, literature notes, and reviews.

Manuscript information: No specific length. Additional copies of the Ms. expedite report. Footnotes may be either at the bottom of the page or cumulated at the end of the Ms. Report usually within 1 month.

Payment: 25 offprints.

Copyright by American Society for Information Science.

AMERICAN IMAGO, 46 East 73rd St., New York, New York 10021. $10; quarterly with occasional extras. Founded in 1939. (IMAGO founded by Freud in 1912.)

Major fields of interest: Applied psychoanalysis: literature, art, culture, philosophy. Articles must be psychoanalytical but not necessarily written by a professional psychoanalyst.

Manuscript information: Articles should be 30 pages or less. Footnotes may be placed at the bottom of the page or at the end of the article. Report in 1-3 months.

Payment: 2 copies of the issue; writer pays for reprints.

Copyright by magazine; liberal policy toward reprinting.

AMERICAN JOURNAL OF PHILOLOGY, Johns Hopkins University Press, Homewood, Baltimore, Maryland 21218. $10.00 for individuals, $18.00 for institutions; quarterly. Founded 1880.

AJP is presently devoted to the publication of articles on all aspects, except the purely archaeological, of Graeco-Roman antiquity and closely contiguous fields.

AMERICAN LITERARY REALISM, 1870-1910, Department of English, University of Texas at Arlington, Arlington, Texas 76010. $5 domestic, $6 other; quarterly. Founded 1967; sponsored by the Department of English, University of Texas at Arlington. Most contributions are invited, but unsolicited materials are welcome, especially if they have a bibliographical or textual slant.

Major fields of interest: American Literature, 1870-1910.

Manuscript information: Length of article should rarely exceed 5000 words; notes normally not over 1000 words. ALR style. Footnotes should be kept to minimum; relevant material should be included in the body of the text. Return postage required. Report usually within 4 weeks.

Payment: 2 copies of issue; 5 to 10 tear sheets. Additional copies at production cost.

Copyright by The Department of English, University of Texas at Arlington; permission to reprint is required.

AMERICAN LITERATURE, Duke Unversity Press, 6667 College Station, Durham, North Carolina 27708. $7, $3.50 for students; quarterly. Founded 1929; sponsored by the American Literature Section of MLA.

Major fields of interest: Historical, critical, and bibliographical articles on American literature; book reviews. Articles should represent additions to knowledge or fresh critical appraisals based upon scholarly study.

Manuscript information: Articles may be as long as 25 pages; brief notes also used. MLA style sheet, supplemented by University of Chicago style manual. Length of time for report varies — ordinarily 2 months.

Payment: 50 offprints; additional at cost.

Copyright by Duke University Press.

Bibliography of "Articles on American Literature Appearing in Current Periodicals" published in each issue.

AMERICAN NOTES & QUERIES, 31 Alden Road, New Haven, Connecticut 06515. $6.50; monthly, except July and August. Founded in 1962; sponsored by Lee Ash, Editor and Publisher.

Major fields of interest: Minor notes of scholarly interest, especially historical, bibliographical, and biographical in all fields; literature, history, books about books, folklore, lexicography, discovery and exploration, history of science, etc. Avoid purely subjective analyses or interpretations of literature or literary passages. Includes scholarly book reviews by specialists of out-of-the-way books.

Manuscript information: Notes, up to 2000 words; Queries are generally shorter. MLA style sheet. Report immediately; publication within three years, depending upon relevance.

Payment: 4 copies of the issue to authors of Notes; additional copies at cost: 50 for $3, 100 for $6.

Not copyrighted.

AMERICAN QUARTERLY, Box 1, Logan Hall, University of Pennsylvania, Philadelphia, Pennsylvania 19104. $10 for 5 issues. Founded 1951; sponsored by American Studies Association and University of Pennsylvania.

Major fields of interest: Interdisciplinary studies of areas of American culture, past and present.

Manuscript information: Articles should be about 20 pages or shorter. MLA style sheet. Footnotes should be held to a minimum. 6 month wait for decision.

Payment: 25 offprints; 1 free copy of journal.

Copyright by the Journal; permission to reprint required.

Bibliographical issue published in Summer number.

AMERICAN REVIEW, 666 Fifth Avenue, New York, New York 10019. $5.95; tri-quarterly. Founded 1967; sponsored by Bantam Books.

Major fields of interest: Contemporary Literature, Politics, Society and Culture. Articles must be written in clear, expressive, jargon-less prose. Critical and biographical articles used but with a strong contemporary interest. Creative material used.

Manuscript information: Articles may be from 4000-7000 words. Footnotes are discouraged. Report in 1 month.

Payment: 6¢ per word.

THE AMERICAN-SCANDINAVIAN REVIEW, 127 East 73rd Street, New York, New York 10021. $7.50; quarterly. Founded 1913; sponsored by The American-Scandinavian Foundation.

Major fields of interest: All the Scandinavian countries, their history, culture, literature, art, current events; also Scandinavians in America. Creative work also used.

Manuscript information: Articles of 2000-3000 words preferred; MLA style sheet; report within a few weeks.

Payment: On acceptance; reprints at author's expense.

Copyright by The American-Scandinavian Foundation.

THE AMERICAN SCHOLAR, 1811 Q Street, N.W., Washington, D.C. 20009. $6.50; quarterly. Founded 1932; published by Phi Beta Kappa.

Major fields of interest: Articles on subjects of substantial general interest in clear and unpedantic language; nontechnical articles and essays on current affairs, the cultural scene, politics, the arts, religion, and science. Poetry also used.

Manuscript information: Articles of 4000 words preferred; generally no footnotes accepted. Report usually in 2-4 weeks.

Payment: $150 on acceptance; three copies of issue.

Copyright is held by THE AMERICAN SCHOLAR until the author wishes to have the copyright transferred so that he can include the article in a book of his own.

AMERICAN SPEECH, c/o John Algeo, Park Hall, University of Georgia, Athens, Georgia 30602. $6; quarterly. Founded 1925; sponsored by American Dialect Society.

Major fields of interest: Scholarly studies of the English language, especially in the western hemisphere — current usage, dialectology, history and structure of English; also articles on other languages influencing English or influenced by it and on general linguistic theory. The Miscellany section publishes short notes.

Manuscript information: Articles normally do not exceed 9000 words; Miscellany notes do not exceed 1500 words. MLA style sheet usually used; footnotes should be on separate page at end of Ms. 2 copies of Ms. required. Report within 4 months.

Payment: 1 to 10 copies of issue; offprints may be bought in multiples of 50 if ordered beforehand. No offprints of Miscellany notes.

Copyright by Columbia University Press, whose permission must be gained before any matter is reprinted.

Bibliographies published occasionally.

AMERICAN STUDIES: An International Newsletter (formerly AMERICAN STUDIES NEWS), 2101 Constitution Avenue, N.W., Washington, D.C. 20418. Free; tri-annually (Spring, Fall, Winter). First published 1962; sponsored by Advisory Committee on American Studies of the Committee on International Exchange of Persons, Conference Board of Associated Research Councils. Unsolicited Mss. not desired.

Major fields of interest: American Studies broadly defined, but "the magazine is neither a journal for arcane research nor a journal of opinion; rather, a service to the international American Studies academic community." Prefer articles on "current status of American Studies programs internationally, bibliographical essays on important topics in American studies."

Manuscript information: Articles may be 3000-5000 words, bibliographical essays from 5000-6000 words. Chicago style sheet. If required, explanatory footnotes are included; all footnotes and bibliographic entries according to Chicago 15.1 and 16.45. 3 Ms. copies needed. Report usually in 1 month.

Payment: No offprints.

Not copyrighted.

AMERICAN STUDIES (formerly MIDCONTINENT AMERICAN STUDIES JOURNAL), 1135 Maine Street, 163 Oread Hall, University of Kansas, Lawrence, Kansas 66044. Subscription rates: Institutions, $5; General, $3; Students, $1.50; back issues, $4; Bulk orders for textbook use, $2; semi-annual at present. Founded 1960 (supplanting the Bulletin, CMVSA); sponsored by MASA and the University of Kansas.

Major fields of interest: Studies of American culture through its arts, history, or institutions. Articles of purely literary interest not accepted.

Manuscript information: 8-12 pages preferred; 18 pages maximum. MLA style sheet, footnotes at end. Submit two copies; best not to put name on each page. Report within 45 days when possible. "We urge contributors to nag us if more than 2 months go by."

Payment: 6 copies of the journal; offprints at $25 per 100.

Copyright by MASA.

AMERICAN STUDIES IN SCANDINAVIA, Sitlarsg. 2, S-752 20 Uppsala, Sweden. $1.50; twice yearly. Founded 1968, sponsored by Nordic Association for American Studies.

Major fields of interest: American studies in History, Social Sciences, Political Science, Linguistics, Economics, etc.

Manuscript information: Articles should be 10-30 pp. A4 style sheet; 2 copies needed for readers. Report in 1 month.

Payment: 25 offprints.

Each issue contains a bibliography on books in the field of American Studies published in the Nordic countries.

AMERICAN TRANSCENDENTAL QUARTERLY, Drawer 1080, Hartford, Connecticut 06101. $14, $15 foreign; quarterly. Founded 1969; sponsored by The Emerson Society.

Major fields of interest: American 19th Century, especially the New England writers; interest is in all aspects of American life as it is reflected in literature. Creative non-scholarly material also published

Manuscript information: No prescribed length; any standard style sheet, footnotes preferably at the end of the article. Conciseness of material requested. Report in 1 week.

Payment: None.

Bibliographical issue published occasionally.

ANGLIA. Zeitschrift für Englische Philologie. c/o Professor Dr. H Gneuss, 8 München 40, W. Germany, Schellingstr. 3; Professor Dr H. Käsmann, 69 Heidelberg, W. Germany, Augustinergasse 15; Professor Dr. E. Wolff, 852 Erlangen, W. Germany, Bismarckstr. 1; Professor Dr. Th. Wolpers, 34 Göttingen, W. Germany, Nikolausberger

Weg 15. Articles on language and medieval literature should be sent to Professor Gneuss or Professor Käsmann. Articles on modern English and American literature should be sent to Professor Wolff or Professor Wolpers. DM 88; quarterly. Founded 1878.

Major fields of interest: English and American language and literature. Critical articles, editions of short unpublished texts, as well as articles on historical and descriptive linguistics.

Manuscript information: Articles of 16-20 pages preferred. MLA style sheet. Report in 3 months.

Payment: 50 offprints for articles, 20 for reviews.

Copyright held by Max Niemeyer Verlag, Tübingen.

THE ANGLO-WELSH REVIEW, Deffrobahi, Maescelyn, Brecon, Wales. £1.50 or $5 for 3 issues. Founded 1949; sponsored by Dock Leaves Press.

Major fields of interest: Anglo-Welsh literature, i.e., writing in English by Welshmen or about Welshmen or Wales or by people who have visited Wales. Also contemporary Welsh painting, sculpture, and music. Exclusive of theological and political material, the whole range of contemporary Welsh life and culture, so far as it is expressed, translated, or interpreted through the medium of English, constitutes the field of this journal. Some creative non-scholarly material; poetry, and more rarely, short stories.

Manuscript information: 1200-3000 words the preferred length. Report within 2 months.

Payment: 2 copies of the issue; also cash payments.

Copyright retained by contributor.

ANNUALE MEDIAEVALE, Duquesne University Press/Humanities Press, Inc., 450 Park Avenue South, New York 10016. $10; annually. Founded 1959; published jointly by Duquesne University Press and Humanities Press, Inc. Manuscripts are sent to the Editor, Dept. of English, Duquesne University, Pittsburgh, Pa. 15219.

Major fields of interest: Mediaeval studies. All types of articles accepted.

Manuscript information: No length restrictions. MLA style sheet; footnotes following article. Reports usually within 2 to 3 months.

Payment: None; offprints charged for.

Copyright by the journal.

ANTHROPOLOGICAL LINGUISTICS, Anthropology Department, Indiana University, Bloomington, Indiana 47401. $4 for 9 issues. Founded 1959; sponsored by Archives of Languages of the World, Indiana University.

Major fields of interest: Anthropological linguistic studies of any language. Problems on technical parts of grammars published, as well as whole grammars published in parts.

Manuscript information: Articles of 20-40 pages preferred. Check previous issues for style; cited (native) terms in Roman; glosses in italics. Footnotes should be typed on a separate sheet and numbered consecutively.

Payment: 50 reprints; additional obtainable for cost of paper and postage.

ANTHROPOS, Anthropos Institut, D-5205 St. Augustin, W-Germany. 120 Swiss Frcs for 3 issues a year. Founded 1906; sponsored by Anthropos Institut.

Major fields of interest: Ethnography (field reports), ethnology, linguistics, prehistory, archaeology, history of religion.

Comprehensive bibliography in each issue.

Payment: 25 offprints; additional copies at cost.

Length of time between submission of an article and notification of the decision: maximum 3-5 months.

THE ANTIGONISH REVIEW, St. Francis Xavier University, Antigonish, N.S., Canada. $5; quarterly. Founded 1970; sponsored by St. Francis Xavier University.

Major fields of interest: Literature of the English-speaking world, philosophy, French Canadian studies, the short story, poetry. Titles in the first issue included: "The Beardsley Foreground," "More Light on Rolfe's 'Hadrian the Seventh,' " and "Melville's 'Redburn: His First Voyage.' "

Manuscript information: Articles of 3000-4000 words preferred. Footnotes should be placed on separate sheet at end of typescript.

Payment: By arrangement.

Copyright remains the authors'.

THE ANTIOCH REVIEW, P.O. Box 148, Yellow Springs, Ohio 45387. $6; quarterly. Founded 1941; sponsored by Antioch College.

Major fields of interest: A national independent quarterly of critical and creative thought which prints articles of interest to both the liberal scholar and the educated layman. Regular issues feature resourceful and lively articles on social and cultural problems, politics and the arts, as well as new short fiction, poetry and discussions. Special issues (about two per year) bring together a number of writers all exploring a particular problem or condition of broad contemporary concern. Viewpoint is independent, inquiring and committed; editorial policy is liberal but not dogmatic, disciplined but not pedantic, imaginative but not mystical; aims at assimilating the best of spirited academic expression and educated literary journalism.

Manuscript information: Articles of 2000-8000 words preferred. University of Chicago style manual, but footnotes should be held to a minimum; report in 2 to 6 weeks.

Payment: $8 per printed page; reprints at cost.

Copyright by The Antioch Review, Inc.

APPALACHIAN JOURNAL, Box 536, Appalachian State University, Boone, N.C. 28607. $4; twice yearly. Founded 1972; sponsored by Appalachian State University.

Major fields of interest: A broad spectrum of studies dealing directly with the entire region of the Appalachian mountains, from New York to Alabama; the mountain people, their history, culture, folklore, religion, attiudes; Appalachian geology and ecology. Scholarly articles, short stories and poetry *about* the Appalachian region.

Manuscript information: MLA style sheet. Report in 1 to 3 months.

Payment: 6 copies of the *Journal.*

Copyright: Author assigns all rights to the *Journal.* The *Journal* will, in turn, grant republication provided the *Journal* is acknowledged as prior and original publisher of the material.

ARCADIA, Horst Rüdiger, Universität Bonn, Germanistisches Seminar, 53 Bonn 1, West Germany. 56 DM; 3 times yearly. Founded 1966; sponsored by Deutsche Forschungsgemeinschaft.

Major fields of interest: Restricted to themes falling into the field of comparative literature, including translation problems, characteristics of comparative literature as a discipline, etc.; English, French, and German languages acceptable.

Manuscript information: No length restrictions in principle but articles should be approximately 20 printed pages. MLA style sheet, laxly; footnotes to follow text in Ms., at bottom of page in print. Report in 1 to 2 months.

Payment: 12 DM ($4) per page, possibly; 20 free offprints, more at cost.

Copyrighted by Walter de Gruyter, Berlin.

ARCHIV FÜR DAS STUDIUM DER NEUEREN SPRACHEN UND LITERATUREN, English articles c/o Professor Dr. Rudolph Sühnel, Anglistisches Seminar der Universität, Augustinergasse 75, D-6900 Heidelberg, West Germany. DM 72; biannually. Founded 1838.

Major fields of interest: Philology, literary studies, and comparative literature.

ARIEL, A Review of International English Literature. Editor, George Wing, ARIEL, The University of Calgary, 2920 — 24 Avenue N.W. Calgary, Alberta, Canada T2N 1N4. $6; quarterly. Founded 1970.

Major fields of interest: The journal succeeds A REVIEW OF ENGLISH LITERATURE, "but will have an increased coverage of literature. While writing from Britain and North America will be its main concern, it will also include criticism of literature written in English in other parts of the world. It will include review articles, reviews and poems, as well as translations."

Manuscript information: Articles should be between 2400 and 4000 words, and verse not longer than 2 pages. MLA style sheet; footnotes at end of article. Report in 3 months.

Copyrighted.

ARION, Boston University, 270 Bay State Road, Rm. 512, Boston, Massachusetts 02215. $6, $7 foreign; quarterly. Founded 1962; sponsored by Department of University Professors, Boston University, Boston.

Major fields of interest: The classical era and the classical tradition. Critical essays, translations, reviews preferred. Creative material published occasionally.

Manuscript information: 5-40 journal pages preferred. Chicago or MLA style sheets. Report in 6 months.

Payment: "In exceptional cases."

Copyrighted by the Trustees of Boston University.

ARIZONA QUARTERLY, The University of Arizona, Tucson, Arizona 85721. $2; quarterly. Founded 1945; sponsored by The University of Arizona.

Major fields of interest: All fields that might appeal to a literate audience, except Western history. Creative writing also published.

Manuscript information: Articles are 3000-3500 words. MLA style sheet. Use footnotes sparingly, incorporating as many as possible in the text. 4-6 weeks for report — longer in summer.

Payment: 20 copies of the issue.

Copyright by magazine, but permission to reprint given freely.

THE ARLINGTON QUARTERLY, Box 366, University Station, Arlington, Texas 76010. $5; quarterly. Founded 1967; sponsored by the Department of English, The University of Texas at Arlington.

Major fields of interest: Writing of quality in poetry, short fiction, personal essays and scholarly essays. All good writing considered regardless of subject matter. Critical articles of impressionistic and analytical type preferred; some "heavy scholarship" published. Short stories and poetry also published.

Manuscript information: Not more than 10 double-spaced typewritten pages. MLA style sheet; footnotes appear at bottom of printed page. Report generally within 30 days.

Payment: None; 10 copies of the magazine.

Copyright by the Department of English of the University of Texas at Arlington; assigned to authors when requested for inclusion of essays, poems, or short stories in collected works.

ARTS IN SOCIETY, Room 728, Lowell Hall, 610 Langdon St., University of Wisconsin, Madison, Wisconsin 53706. $7.50; tri-annually. Founded 1958; sponsored by University of Wisconsin.

Major fields of interest: Those fields relating to the status, function, and role of the arts in society. Critical, expository, and polemical articles and essays preferred. Creative, non-scholarly material also published.

Manuscript information: Average article is 15 to 25 typewritten pages; any length will be considered. Footnotes to be included with text at bottom of page. Report within 1 month.

Payment: Honorarium.

Copyright by the University of Wisconsin.

THE ARYAN PATH, c/o Mrs. Sophia Wadia, 40 New Marine Lines, Bombay 400 020, India; London office: 62 Queen's Gardens, W.2.3AH, England. $5.50; monthly. Founded 1930; sponsored by Theosophy Co. (India) Private Ltd.

Major fields of interest: The journal's aims are "to give unprejudiced expression to the idealistic, humanitarian and progressive thought of the day; to present the ideals inherent in the Literatures, Philosophies, Religions, Arts and Sciences of all peoples, ancient and modern." Representative titles: "The Nature of Meaning in Poetry: an Indian Approach and an English Approach," "Religious Aspects of Contemporary English Poetry," "The Alleged Silence of the Buddha," "Science and Faith," "The Doctrine of Reincarnation in Persian Thought." Only original contributions are published.

Manuscript information: Articles of about 2000 words preferred. Documentation desirable.

Payment: Possible only in India or Britain, by arrangement; 6 offprints when requested.

Copyright reserved by First Rights.

ASOMANTE, P.O. Box 1142, San Juan, Puerto Rico 00902. $5.50 in Puerto Rico, Cuba, and U.S.; $6 other countries; quarterly. Founded 1945; sponsored by Asociación de Graduadas de la Universidad de Puerto Rico.

Major fields of interest: Literature, philosophy, art. Creative writing also published. ASOMANTE is a Spanish-language publication, publishing original papers in Spanish, and first translations from English, French, and Italian. Book reviews and list of new books in Spanish, English, and French.

Manuscript information: Articles should be from 5 to 20 pages in length.

Payment: $10-$25, according to number of pages; no offprints given.

Copyright by the Journal; permission must be obtained for reproducing articles.

ASPEN LEAVES, Box 3185, Aspen, Colorado 81611. Semiannually. Founded 1973; sponsored by Aspen Magazine, Inc.

Major fields of interest: Poetry, fiction, non-fiction, critical essays, and reviews. "*Aspen leaves* is the publication of a non-profit educational corporation, and the monies earned will be directed towards grants and awards for writers and poets. We seek quality material from both published and unpublished authors, . . . faculty and students."

Manuscript information: Typed, regular submission style. 2 copies needed. Report in 6 to 8 weeks. Deadlines are biannual: December 1 and April 1. Submissions must have a self-addressed stamped envelope in order to be returned.

Payment: "We offer no financial remuneration to contributors other than what they might earn through awards and grants offered in future issues." 2 copies of the magazine.

THE ATLANTIC MONTHLY, 8 Arlington Street, Boston, Massachusetts 02116. $10.50; monthly. Founded 1857.

Major fields of interest: THE ATLANTIC is a general, national magazine of high quality; it publishes fiction, poetry, and articles.

Manuscript information: Articles are 2000-8000 words; average length is 4500 words. Footnotes generally not used. Time before report varies; rejection is relatively quick but borderline cases take longer.

Payment on acceptance.

The magazine buys first serial rights, and reassigns copyright upon request.

AUMLA, Department of Romance Languages, University of Canterbury, Christchurch, New Zealand. $NZ2 per single copy; 2 a year, normally. Founded 1953; sponsored by Australasian Universities Language and Literature Association.

Major fields of interest: The whole field of Classical Studies and of English, Romance, Germanic, Slavonic, Oriental, Polynesian, and Semitic Languages. Uses articles on literary criticism, philology, and linguistics.

Manuscript information: Articles of 4000-7000 words preferred. Use standard British notations for references; notes should be held to minimum and numbered consecutively. Report within 2-3 months.

Payment: 15 offprints to contributors of articles; 2 offprints to contributors of book reviews.

AUSTRALIAN LITERARY STUDIES, Department of English, University of Tasmania, Box 252C, GPO Hobart 7001, Australia. $4.50 Aus. overseas rate; $3 Aus. within Aus. and NZ; twice each year. Founded 1963; sponsored by University of Tasmania and Australian Government through the Commonwealth Literary Fund.

Major fields of interest: Australian literature and its relation to other literature, including commonwealth literature. All types of articles used.

Manuscript information: Prefer 5000-7500 words for articles; 2000 to 3000 words for the Notes & Document Section. MLA style sheet; footnotes are numbered consecutively and grouped at end of article; single inverted commas are used for quotations that are not inset. Report in approximately 4 weeks.

Payment: Approximately $20-30 Aus. per article. No free offprints, but reduction given to an order of 6 or more copies of issue.

Author of article retains copyright, but permission for reprinting and acknowledgment requested by *Australian Literary Studies*.

Bibliography of Australian literature in May issue each year.

BACONIANA, Canonbury Tower, Islington, London N. 1, England. £1; published periodically. Founded 1886; sponsored by The Francis Bacon Society, Inc.

Major fields of interest: Philosophy of Francis Bacon and Bacon's connection with authorship of plays commonly ascribed to Shakespeare, and other contemporary works. Relevant creative material also published.

Manuscript information: Articles of 1500-2000 words preferred, but longer articles may be printed or serialized. Any style sheet acceptable; 2 copies of Ms. Report within 3 to 4 weeks.

Payment: 6 copies of the issue.

All articles copyrighted, but permission to reproduce will be given.

THE BAKER STREET JOURNAL, Julian Wolff, Editor, 33 Riverside Drive, New York, New York 10023. $4; quarterly. Founded 1946; sponsored by The Baker Street Irregulars.

Major fields of interest: Sherlockiana only. Critical, exegetical analyses used. Light verse also used occasionally.

Manuscript information: Articles of 1000-2000 words preferred; footnotes should be on same page with text, numbered consecutively. Report in about 2 weeks.

Payment: 2 copies of the issue.

Copyright by The Baker Street Irregulars.

BALL STATE UNIVERSITY FORUM, Ball State University, Muncie, Indiana 47306. $5; 4 issues yearly. Founded 1960; sponsored by Ball State University.

Major fields of interest: Articles on language, literature, history, education, social sciences, sciences, fine arts. Poetry, short stories, one-act plays also used.

Manuscript information: Articles should be between 400 and 6000 words. MLA style sheet. Report in 3 months.

Payment: 10 offprints.

BERKSHIRE REVIEW, Williams College, Williamstown, Massachusetts 01267. $1; semi-annually (Fall and Spring). Founded 1965; sponsored by Williams College.

Major fields of interest: Articles, poems, stories of general interest, and reviews involving a discussion and comparison of several works.

Manuscript information: Articles and stories of 3000-5000 words. See recent issue for style; footnotes discouraged, but run at end of article when unavoidable. Report in 1 month.

Payment: $50-$75 for prose according to length; $20-$25 per poem; 10 copies of the issue.

Copyright by the journal but permission to republish given on request.

THE BIBLIOTHECK, The University Library, Stirling, FK9 4LA, Scotland. £1.50 ($4.50); semi-annually. Founded 1956; sponsored by Scottish Group of the University & Research Section of the Library Association.

Major fields of interest: Scottish bibliography and allied topics.

Manuscript information: Not over 6000 words. Use style of THE LIBRARY, TRANSACTIONS OF THE BIBLIOGRAPHICAL SOCIETY. Report in a few weeks.

Payment: 6 offprints.

"Normal copyright provisions apply."

BIBLIOTHEQUE D'HUMANISME & RENAISSANCE, Librairie Droz S. A., 11 r. Massot, Geneva, Switzerland. $13.60; 3 issues yearly. Founded 1933.

Major fields of interest: History of ideas, religion, and literature of the 16th century. Source studies and bibliographies published. Articles in French, Italian, German, and English.

Manuscript information: Articles of 20 pages preferred.

Payment: 30 offprints.

BLACKWOOD'S MAGAZINE, 32 Thistle Street, Edinburgh EH2 1HA, U.K. $10; monthly. Founded 1817; sponsored by William Blackwood.

Major fields of interest: Original work of all kinds; fiction, adventure, travel, history and biography.

Manuscript information: Articles of between 3000 and 9000 words (average 5000). Report in 2-3 days.

Payment: £8 per thousand words for first 3000, £5 per 1000 thereafter; 1 complimentary copy of journal.

No copyright.

Index published in June and December.

BLAKE NEWSLETTER, AN ILLUSTRATED QUARTERLY, Morris Eaves, Managing Editor, Department of English, University of New Mexico, Albuquerque, N.M. 87131. $5; individuals, $4; if overseas by air is desired, $8; quarterly. Founded 1967; sponsored by Department of English, University of New Mexico.

Major fields of interest: William Blake. Bibliographical issue in the fall; also frequent special bibliographical issues.

Manuscript information: Under 20 typed pages; MLA style sheet; 2 manuscript copies needed by readers. Report in 60 days.

Payment: 2-5 complimentary copies, depending on kind of article.

Copyright held by journal editors.

BLAKE STUDIES, Department of English, Illinois State University, Normal, Illinois 61761. $7.50; 2 issues yearly. Founded 1968; sponsored by Kay Parkhurst Easson and Roger R. Easson.

Major fields of interest: William Blake, his time, his circle. Critical essays, book reviews, scholarly articles, and notes accepted. Brief notices of important but minor publications.

Manuscript information: 12-20 typewritten pages desired. MLA style sheet; footnotes to follow text. Report in 6-8 weeks.

Payment: None (privately supported); any number of offprints given on request of author, and paid for by author.

Copyright by the publishers, Kay Parkhurst Easson and Roger R. Easson.

BODLEIAN LIBRARY RECORD, Bodleian Library, Oxford OX1 3BG, England. 50p per issue; irregular, 1 or 2 per year. Founded 1938; sponsored by Bodleian Library.

Major fields of interest: Articles on books, manuscripts, and bibliography. Articles should preferably have some connection with the Library, either its history or its contents.

Manuscript information: Articles of 1000-5000 words, "but no strong line." Footnotes should be placed at foot of each page. Report time is variable.

Payment: 25 offprints.

Copyright by the Bodleian Library and contributors.

BONNIERS LITTERÄRA MAGASIN, Sveavägen 56, Box 3159, 103 63 Stockholm 3, Sweden. 28 Swedish Crowns for 5 issues. Founded 1932; sponsored by Albert Bonniers Förlag.

Major fields of interest: Belles lettres.

Manuscript information: Articles of 2-10 pages preferred. Articles are in Swedish. Report in 4 weeks.

BOOK COLLECTOR, 58 Frith Street, London WIV 6BY, England. £5 ($17.50); quarterly. Founded 1952.

Major fields of interest: Bibliography, bibliophily, book collecting in all aspects of interest to collectors, bibliographical scholars, antiquarian booksellers, librarians of Rare Book Collections. Bibliographical articles (including history of libraries, biographies of collectors, reminiscences and profiles of collectors) are published.

Manuscript information: Articles of 2500-5000 words preferred. Footnotes should be placed at bottom of page and numbered consecutively.

Payment: 50 offprints (more by arrangement); payment for book reviews.

BOOKS ABROAD, University of Oklahoma, Norman, Oklahoma 73069. $8, $14.50 for 2 years; quarterly. Founded 1927; published by the University of Oklahoma.

Major fields of interest: BOOKS ABROAD is an international literary quarterly devoted to comment on trends and developments of contemporary foreign literatures and to reviewing recently published foreign books in practically all languages. Particular emphasis is placed on contemporary creative writing, literary criticism, and related topics within the framework of the humanities. Articles should be critical, biographical, or comparative in nature.

Manuscript information: 3000 words maximum for articles; 300 words for book reviews; 1500 words for articles in Commentaries section. MLA style sheet, but footnotes are discouraged and usually integrated into text. 2 to 3 weeks for acceptance or rejection.

Payment: 25 offprints for articles; 1 tearsheet for reviews.

Original (hitherto unpublished in any language) articles are copyrighted through the University of Oklahoma Press. Articles may be reprinted if credit for original publication is given to BOOKS ABROAD.

BOOKS AT BROWN, Friends of the Library, Brown University, Providence, Rhode Island 02912. Distributed to Friends of the Library; published irregularly. Founded 1938; sponsored by Friends of the Library of Brown University. Articles are written by University faculty or alumni; unsolicited Mss. not desired.

Major fields of interest: Literary, special collections, and rare books in Brown University; historical, biographical, bibliographical studies.

Manuscript information: Articles of 3000-5000 words preferred. Footnotes should be placed at the bottom of the page or at the end of the article. Report in 4-6 weeks.

Payment: 12 copies of the issue.

Copyright held by Brown University.

BOUNDARY 2: A JOURNAL OF POSTMODERN LITERATURE, boundary 2, SUNY-Binghamton, Binghamton, N.Y. 13901. $5; 3 times a year. Founded 1972; sponsored by English Department of SUNY-Binghamton.

Major fields of interest: Though the editors are uncertain about the directions postmodern literature is taking, they feel that the age of Mallarmé, Eliot, Joyce, Yeats, Pound, etc. has more or less run its course. They believe that since World War II a new imagination has been struggling to be born and these last twenty years (like the thirty or so before World War I) represent another period of transition. The function of *boundary 2* is therefore to publish criticism and scholarship that attempt to clarify its direction as well as creative writing that explores its possibilities.

Other related concerns: re-evaluation of "modernism" (c. 1880-1940) and criticism of earlier periods, writers, or individual works from a "postmodern" critical perspective; criticism in related postmodern areas: especially cinema, the plastic and graphic arts, and philosophy.

Type of articles preferred: Critical and scholarly, though we are open to experimental critical prose. We are not interested in *explication de texte, per se*.

Manuscript information: No restriction on length; MLA style sheet; footnotes at end of article. Report in approximately 3 months.

Payment: Small honorarium; 10 offprints plus 3 copies of the journal.

Copyright held by journal unless other arrangements are made.

BRIGHAM YOUNG UNIVERSITY STUDIES, A-283 JKB, Brigham Young University, Provo, Utah 84601. $7 for 4 issues. Founded 1958; sponsored by Brigham Young University.

Major fields of interest: Latter-Day Saint thought and general knowledge. Creative work also welcomed.

Manuscript information: Mss. not to exceed 4000 words. Chicago style manual should be followed in all matters, including footnote treatment. Report within 3 months.

Payment: 20 offprints and 3 copies of the full issue.

BRITISH BOOK NEWS, 65 Davies Street, London WC 1A 1BP, England. $6 including annual index; monthly. Founded 1940; published by The British Council. BRITISH BOOK NEWS commissions its articles; unsolicited Mss. are not desired.

Major fields of interest: BRITISH BOOK NEWS consists mainly of reviews of new books and new editions on all subjects published in the United Kingdom and the Commonwealth. Fiction and children's books are included. The reviews are preceded by one or more articles either surveying the literature of a particular subject over a period or dealing with a subject of general interest to bookmen. Each issue is classified under the Dewey system and indexed; an annual cumulative index is published.

THE BRITISH JOURNAL OF AESTHETICS, 90A St. John's Wood High Street, London, N.W.8, England. Free to members of The British Society of Aesthetics (membership £2. 2. 0 yearly; application forms from The Secretary, c/o Department of Philosophy, Birkbeck College, Malet Street, London, W.C.1, England); £3 or equivalent in foreign currencies for non-members; quarterly. Founded 1960; published for The British Society of Aesthetics by Thames & Hudson Ltd., 30 Bloomsbury Street, London, W.C.1.

Major fields of interest: Philosophy of art; theory and principles of criticism and appreciation. Philosophical, psychological, sociological, scientific, educational aesthetics.

Manuscript information: Preferred length 5000-9000 words.

Payment: 20 bound offprints; additional offprints at 25p each subject to prior notice.

Copyright by The British Society of Aesthetics.

BRONTË SOCIETY TRANSACTIONS, Brontë Parsonage Museum, Haworth, Keighley BD22 8DR, England. £1; annually. Founded 1895; sponsored by the The Brontë Society.

Major fields of interest: The Brontë family. Articles are mainly biographical and source studies. Creative material also used.

Manuscript information: Articles of 2000-2500 words preferred. Footnotes used when necessary. Report in 1 month.

Payment: Copies provided; also annual essay competition with prize of £25.

Copyrighted by The Brontë Society, but permission is given to publish elsewhere.

BROWNING INSTITUTE STUDIES, Department of English, University of Maryland, College Park, Maryland 70742. Free to members of the Browning Institute, $15 to new subscribers; annual. Founded 1973; sponsored by the Browning Institute.

Major fields of interest: Robert and Elizabeth Barrett Browning, and other literary and artistic figures associated with them. Biographical, critical, and bibliographical articles preferred. Long articles; no brief explications of individual poems.

Manuscript information: MLA style sheet. 2 copies needed. Footnotes on separate page. Self-addressed stamped envelope for return. Report in 3 months.

Payment: 25 offprints, 1 copy of journal.

Copyright by The Browning Institute.

BROWNING SOCIETY NOTES, 29 Southmoor Rd., Oxford, England OX2 6RF. £1.25 in U.K., $4 abroad; 3 times annually. Founded 1970; sponsored by The Browning Society of London.

Major fields of interest: Life and works of Robert and Elizabeth Barrett Browning (and *related* studies regarding their families, contemporaries, and period).

Type of articles preferred: Biographical, critical, and source study, reports of work in progress in the United Kingdom; first appearance of letters. No creative non-scholarly work, but does review poetic and dramatic renderings of Browning works in public and sometimes art work of other forms as well.

Manuscript information: 10-20 pages double spaced. If the article is of outstanding brilliance, will accept up to 30 pages. Brief notes published as well. MLA style sheet; footnotes kept to a minimum, placed at end of article. Report in approximately 3 weeks.

Payment: 1 copy of issue.

Copyright remains with the author.

BUCKNELL REVIEW, Bucknell University, Lewisburg, Pennsylvania 17839. $7.50 for 3 issues. Founded 1940; sponsored by Bucknell University.

Major fields of interest: The editors are especially interested in intellectual essays on subjects of scholarly, general interest; in criticism and in literary history, the editors will accept technical articles, which should be of general interest. The magazine will publish philosophical and exegetical essays in criticism. Articles on comparative literature, on problems in aesthetics and philosophy, on science and society, and on the philosophy of science are welcome.

Manuscript information: Articles of 12-25 typewritten pages preferred. MLA style sheet. Report in 2-4 weeks.

Payment: 2 copies of the issue and 5 reprints.

Copyrighted.

BULLETIN DE L'ASSOCIATION GUILLAUME BUDE, 95 Boulevard Raspail, Paris, 6 eme, France. 30 Fr. in France and foreign; 4 times a year. Founded 1923; sponsored by Association Guillaume Bude.

Major fields of interest: General culture, centered on humanism, particularly classical humanism.

Manuscript information: Depending upon the importance of the subject, 5-40 pages.

Payment: 25 offprints.

Copyrighted.

BULLETIN OF BIBLIOGRAPHY AND MAGAZINE NOTES, 15 Southwest Park, Westwood, Massachusetts 02090. $10; quarterly (January-March, April-June, July-September, October-December). Founded 1897; published by F.W. Faxon Co., Inc.

Major fields of interest: Publishes bibliographies, checklists, and research studies useful to students, librarians, and all library users.

A record of new, changed, and discontinued periodical titles is a regular feature.

Manuscript information: Author notified of Ms. acceptability within 2 months. A Ms. should conform to the second edition of the MLA style sheet. Space is limited as each issue is about 44 pages.

Payment: None.

No copyright.

BULLETIN OF HISPANIC STUDIES, The University, P.O. Box 147, Liverpool, L69 3BX, England. $10; quarterly. Founded 1923; sponsored by Liverpool University. Editor: Geoffrey Ribbans; Assistant Editor, H. B. Hall.

Major fields of interest: Hispanic languages and literatures. Representative titles: "Modernismo: A Contribution to the Debate," "Towards a Definition of Calderonian Tragedy."

Manuscript information: Articles should not be more than 6000 words in length. Footnotes should be kept to a minimum. Report in 1 to 2 months.

Payment: 25 offprints.

Copyrighted; material may not be reproduced in whole or in part without permission of the editor.

BULLETIN OF THE JOHN RYLANDS UNIVERSITY LIBRARY OF MANCHESTER, The John Rylands University Library of Manchester, Deansgate, Manchester M3 3EH, England. £3; twice yearly, Autumn and Spring. Founded 1903; sponsored by the Library.

Major fields of interest: Theology, the humanities, and arts in general.

Manuscript information: Articles of about 10,000 words preferred. Footnotes are numbered at the foot of each page. Report within 2 to 3 weeks.

Payment: 15 copies free; 15 additional copies at cost.

Copyright by the Library.

BULLETIN OF THE MIDWEST MODERN LANGUAGE ASSOCIATION, University of Iowa, Iowa City, Iowa 52240. $4 for one year; $7.50 for 2 years; $10.50 for 3 years. Founded 1968; sponsored by MMLA. Published as a service to members of MMLA, who are invited to submit articles of general scholarly and professional interest. Essays on the study and teaching of language and literature, particularly in relation to political, cultural, and historical issues, are especially welcome, as are studies in critical methodology, literary history, and the theory of language. Submitted essays should not exceed 8000 words in length, and should follow the format described in the MLA style sheet.

BULLETIN OF THE NEW YORK PUBLIC LIBRARY, New York Public Library, Fifth Ave. and 42nd St., New York, New York 10018. $7.50; quarterly. Founded 1897; sponsored by New York Public Library. Order from Readex Books, 101 Fifth Avenue, New York, N.Y. 10003.

Major fields of interest: Publishes critical studies of "anything in, about, or in back of books and manuscripts and useful bibliographical tools for such study, from check-lists to annotated bibliographies" (if of "monograph length, the Library will consider separate publication"). Studies of new or neglected materials in the Library are especially desirable, but the BULLETIN publishes articles and notes of general interest to scholars and bookmen, provided they relate in some way to the Library's holdings. "Essays impressively useful to librarians or to readers of books are suitable; not of interest are essays in criticism or explications of familiar texts or surveys of well-trodden ground. Technical terms or foreign language terms should be handled in such a way as to leave no essential communications obscure to the intelligent non-specialist or monoglot."

Manuscript information: MLA style sheet with some exceptions; consult copy of Bulletin or send sample entries to Editor before typing major projects. 2-3 months for decision.

Payment: 6 copies of the issue; offprints at cost.

Copyrighted.

BULLETIN OF THE ROCKY MOUNTAIN MODERN LANGUAGE ASSOCIATION, 409 Woodbury, University of Colorado, Boulder, Colorado 80302. $2 for members, $6 for non-members; quarterly. Founded 1968; sponsored by RMMLA. Contributors must be subscribers.

Major fields of interest: Critical and descriptive articles concerning language, literature, and pedagogy.

Manuscript information: 2000-6000 words. MLA style sheet; footnotes at end of article. 2 copies of Ms. needed. Report in 6-8 weeks.

Payment: None; minimum order of 25 offprints may be purchased.

CALAMUS: An International Whitman Quarterly, c/o Professor William L. Moore, Toho Gakuen University of Music, Sengawa, Chofu, Tokyo, Japan. $3, tri-annually. Founded 1969; sponsored by Taizo Shinozaki, Taibundo, Tokyo.

Major fields of interest: Walt Whitman — attitudes toward him, research on him, applications of his ideas. Will reprint articles on Whitman which have appeared elsewhere and excerpts from dissertations. "We welcome articles by students as well as by professors." Dramas or fiction on Whitman also published.

Manuscript information: No restrictions on length. No specified style sheet. Not particular about footnote form. Immediate report.

Payment: "A piece of Japanese calligraphy which may be framed — an art piece; 5 copies of magazine."

Copyright may be retained by author.

CALIFORNIA ENGLISH JOURNAL, P.O. Box 4427, Whittier, California 90607. $9 (membership in CATE); 4 times a year (Feb., Apr., Oct., Dec.). Founded 1965; sponsored by the California Association of Teachers of English.

Major fields of interest: The teaching of English (elementary through graduate school) and the preparation of English teachers. Teaching of literature, writing, language, reading, speech, etc. Content must relate closely to stated purposes of CATE. Creative work also published (a poetry section in each issue). The Journal is read in most states of the US, but emphasis is on material of particular California interest whenever possible.

Manuscript information: General articles of 1500-2500 words; shorter pieces of 250-1000 (includes reviews). Include 50-word Vita and background on article. Keep footnotes to minimum; reference list at end of article if necessary. Report in several weeks.

Payment: None; 2 copies of the issue; reprints may be purchased direct from printers.

Copyright by CATE.

CALIFORNIA QUARTERLY, Jack Hicks, Editor, Department of English, 100 Sproul Hall, University of California at Davis, Davis, California 95616. $5; quarterly. Founded 1972; sponsored by Department of English and Associated Students of University of California.

Major fields of interest: Contemporary fiction and poetry, graphic art. Very limited non-fiction on recent fiction, poetry, arts.

Manuscript information: Manuscripts up to 10,000 words. MLA or University of Chicago style sheet. One copy needed. Report in 4-6 weeks.

Payment: None; 6 copies of journal.

Copyright policy: "We copyright contents of each issue; copyright transferred if needed."

THE CAMBRIDGE QUARTERLY, Newhayes, Huntingdon Road, Cambridge, CB3 OLH, England. 30/- ($5); quarterly (Spring, Summer, Autumn, Winter). Founded 1965.

Major fields of interest: General, literary criticism.

Manuscript information: No length restrictions. MLA style sheet; footnotes at bottom of page, numbered consecutively throughout article. Report in 2 months.

Payment: None; 6 offprints.

Copyright retained by editors on behalf of authors.

CAMBRIDGE REVIEW: A JOURNAL OF UNIVERSITY LIFE AND THOUGHT, 7 Green Street, Cambridge, England. £1.80 or $4; every 3rd and 6th week during the university term (6 issues per annum)

Major fields of interest: Contemporary issues of academic interest. Comment on literature, politics, education, theatre, science, etc. with emphasis on book reviews. Some creative writing.

Manuscript information: Maximum length 2500 words normally

Payment: Free copies of issue; offprints if requested.

For copyright, apply to the editor.

CANADIAN AUTHOR & BOOKMAN, 8726 — 116 St., Edmonton 82, Alberta, Canada. $3; quarterly. Founded 1936; sponsored by the Canadian Authors Association.

Major fields of interest: Canadian writing and authors, literature in any form (including poems).

Manuscript information: Articles not over 2500 words; poems any length.

Payment: 4-6 copies of magazine.

Not copyrighted.

THE CANADIAN FORUM, 56 Esplande E., Toronto, Canada, M5E 1A8. $7.50; monthly. Founded 1920; sponsored by Canadian Forum Ltd.

Major fields of interest: Politics; the arts. Critical articles of original research and opinion. Publishes creative non-scholarly material.

Manuscript information: 3000 to 6000 words. Report in 3 months.

Payment: Contributors' copies; 5 offprints.

Copyright policy: First serial rights.

Index in April issue.

THE CANADIAN JOURNAL OF LINGUISTICS/LA REVUE CANA-DIENNE DE LINGUISTIQUE (formerly THE JOURNAL OF THE CANADIAN LINGUISTIC ASSOCIATION), Canadian Linguistic Association, English Department, Queen's University, Kingston, Ontario, Canada. $6 a year for 2 issues. Founded 1954; sponsored by the Canadian Linguistic Association.

Major fields of interest: Linguistic studies. Source studies and critical articles on the languages of Canada.

Manuscript information: Articles of 2000-25000 words preferred. Articles may be in either French or English. Write for style sheet.

Payment: 25 offprints.

CANADIAN LITERATURE, University of British Columbia, Vancouver 8, Canada. $5.50; quarterly. Founded 1959; sponsored by the University of British Columbia.

Major fields of interest: Critical articles on Canadian literature.

Manuscript information: MLA style sheet, with footnotes held to a minimum. Articles of 4000 words or less preferred. Prompt report.

Payment: Payment for all articles. Copies of the issue available to authors at 25 per cent discount.

Bibliographical issue annually in winter.

THE CANADIAN MODERN LANGUAGE REVIEW, 34 Butternut Street, Toronto, Canada, M4K 1T7. $7 Can.; quarterly. Founded 1944; published by the Ontario Modern Language Teachers' Association.

Major fields of interest: Timely topics on foreign languages including literature, linguistics, methodology, critical studies, sample tests, lesson plans, helpful hints, dissent, book reviews (foreign languages only).

Manuscript information: maximum of 10 pages, typed, double-spaced, footnotes at end of article. Send original and copy; include self-addressed envelope and return postage. Report in 1 month.

Payment: None; 2 copies of CMLR.

Copyright by journal; reproduction by permission and with credit line.

Index in June issue.

CANADIAN REVIEW OF AMERICAN STUDIES, c/o Prof. Robert White, Stong College, York University, Downsview 463, Ontario, Canada. $5; semi-annually. Founded 1970; sponsored by Canadian Association for American Studies.

Major fields of interest: American Studies, in and among all relevant disciplines; cultural relations between Canada and the U.S. Interdisciplinary work, critical articles and review essays are of special interest.

Manuscript information: Articles of 3000-5000 words preferred. MLA style sheet; footnotes usually at end of article. 2 copies needed. Report in 3-8 weeks.

Payment: 25 offprints.

Copyright retained by journal, but permission to reprint granted freely.

CARAVEL MAGAZINE, 315 Kneale Avenue South, Thief River Falls, Minnesota 56701. $2 for 4 issues; irregularly. Founded 1957; edited and published by Ben Hagglund.

Major fields of interest: Prose accounts of the poet's relation to the world wanted; how he makes a living, what people think of poetry, etc. Verse submitted should deal with people and places, with what peoples of the world have in common.

Manuscript information: 1000 words the preferred length for prose. Report within 1 to 2 months.

Payment: 5¢ a line for poetry; $5 for prose accounts. Complimentary copies mailed to contributors.

First American magazine rights are purchased; permission to reprint readily obtained by writing the publisher.

THE CARLETON MISCELLANY, Carleton College, Northfield, Minnesota 55057. $3; twice a year. Founded 1960; sponsored by Carleton College.

Major fields of interest: General literary review — essays, poems, stories, and reviews.

Manuscript information: MLA style sheet. 7500 words the maximum length. Footnote treatment at author's discretion. Report within a month.

Payment: 2 copies of the magazine. $8 per page for prose; $10 for verse.

Copyright held by the magazine, but reprint rights granted or copyright transferred to the author.

CARLETON NEWSLETTER, University College, University of Florida, Gainesville, Florida 32601. $2; quarterly: July, October, January, April. Founded July 4, 1970; sponsored by the University of Florida.

Major fields of interest: Study of William Carleton's fiction. Type of articles preferred: Critical, biographical, *explication de texte*, source study, etc.

Manuscript information: MLA style sheet; one copy needed by readers.

Payment: 5 offprints.

CAROLINA QUARTERLY, Box 1117, Chapel Hill, North Carolina 27514. $4 (US), $5 (foreign); 3 issues a year. Founded 1948; sponsored by the University of North Carolina.

Major fields of interest: Contemporary fiction and poetry. Occasional articles of contemporary interest to general literate audience. Creative material used.

Manuscript information: Articles should be no longer than 7500 words. No style sheet preference; heavily annotated articles are not considered. Report in 6 to 8 weeks.

Payment: Approximately $5 magazine page; 3 copies of journal.

Copyrighted; may be transferred for collection purposes.

CASTRVM PEREGRINI, Postbox 645, Amsterdam, Netherlands. $17 plus postage for 5 issues. Founded 1950; sponsored by Lothar Helbing, W. Fraenger, and Karl August Klein. Editor: M.R. Goldschmidt.

Major fields of interest: General literature, history of literature, history of art, history of ideas, with the exception of political subjects, book reviews. Articles in German. Poetry also published.

Manuscript information: Maximum length for articles is 10,000 words. Footnotes should be avoided; if absolutely necessary, place at the end of the article. Report usually within 3 months; specialized subjects up to 6 months.

Payment: 3 offprints.

THE CEA CRITIC, Earle Labor, Editor, Centenary College, Shreveport, Louisiana 71104. $8 for 4 issues; bi-monthly (November through May); membership dues also include subscriptions to the CEA FORUM and occasional CEA Chap Books. Publication reserved to CEA members. Founded 1939; sponsored by The College English Association, Inc.

Major fields of interest: "usable" literary criticism — i.e., brief critical essays (under 2500 words) which cast new light on how literary materials can become more meaningful in the college English classroom. Creative work, especially poetry, included when related to the teaching of literature. Avoid scholarly overspecialization. Preference given to contributions distinguished by lucidity, brevity, wit, and grace of style.

Manuscript information: Short articles required, preferably 500-2000 words. Documentation should be embodied in the text itself; footnotes should be used only if less awkward than parenthetical documentation in text. Report usually within 2 months; publication within a year following acceptance.

Payment: 2 copies of publication, plus 5-10 tearsheets of article. Copyrighted.

THE CEA FORUM, Earle Labor, Editor, Centenary College, Shreveport, Louisiana 71104. $8 for 4 issues; bi-monthly (October through April); membership dues also include subscriptions to THE CEA CRITIC and occasional CEA Chap Books. Publication reserved to CEA members. Founded 1970; sponsored by The College English Association, Inc.

Major fields of interest: The teaching of college English; "News and Views" concerning timely academic issues; reports of national and regional CEA activities; poetry relating to the profession. Contributions should be lively, well-written, incisive, and informal. Humor and sensibility are particularly encouraged.

Manuscript information: Short articles required (under 1500 words); "mini-articles" (limited to 1 typewritten, double-spaced page) given special preference. Footnotes and other scholarly paraphernalia discouraged. Report within 2 months, sooner on "mini-articles"; publication usually within 6 months of acceptance.

Payment: 5 copies of the publication.

Copyrighted.

CEAA NEWSLETTER, c/o Professor M. J. Bruccoli, Director CEAA, Department of English, University of South Carolina, Columbia, South Carolina 29208. Free; occasionally, once a year. Founded 1968; sponsored by CEAA.

Major fields of interest: Texts of American literature; matters relating to the Center for Editions of American Authors; bibliographical notes and queries.

Manuscript information: Short notes and articles up to 5 typed pages. MLA style sheet. Report as soon as possible.

Payment: None; 10 offprints.

Not copyrighted.

THE CENTENNIAL REVIEW, 110 Morrill Hall, Michigan State University, East Lansing, Michigan 48823. $3, $5 for 2 years; quarterly. Founded 1957; sponsored by Michigan State College of Arts and Letters.

Major fields of interest: Articles in the principal disciplines of the sciences and arts — the natural and physical sciences, social sciences, humanities, and arts. Articles should avoid extremes of specialization and popularization, but should attempt to convey the results and implications of specialized study in a language understandable to persons in all fields of the liberal arts. Special interest is in providing a meeting ground for the liberal arts as a whole and in articles reviewing states of knowledge; articles may deal with particular scholarly methods, research techniques, or intellectual attitudes, elucidate interrelationships between established or chronically ex: clusive disciplines, set forth historical or critical perspective on current problems or ideas.

Manuscript information: Articles range from 5000-6000 words in length. MLA style sheet "followed approximately in regard to style." 2 copies of Ms. desired. Report in 2-3 months.

CENTRUM: Working Papers of the Minnesota Center for Advanced Studies in Language, Style, and Literary Theory, 207 Main Engineering Building, University of Minnesota, Minneapolis, Minnesota 55455. $2 per issue; twice yearly (Spring and Autumn). Founded 1973; sponsored by Minnesota Center for Advanced Studies in Language, Style, and Literary Theory.

Major fields of interest: Theory of language, style, and literature. Interested in computer-aided analysis of discourse and papers with interdisciplinary approach. Research, book reviews, review articles, surveys of recent work, annotated bibliographies, notes, and queries.

Manuscript information: MLA style sheet or *Language* style. Footnotes at end of text. Every Ms. reporting research should be accompanied by an abstract, maximum 100 words. Report in 1 month.

Payment: 5 copies of issue.

Copyright by Center, but reprint requests granted.

CHAUCER REVIEW, 42 South Burrowes, University Park, Pennsylvania 16802. $7.50; quarterly. Founded 1966; sponsored by Penn State Press, with cooperation of the Chaucer Group, MLA.

Major fields of interest: Chaucer and Medieval Studies and literary criticism; preference is for criticism, but almost any approach pertinent to Chaucer and medieval materials considered.

Manuscript information: Articles of 10-20 pages; MLA style sheet; footnotes on separate pages at end of article. Report in 3-6 months.

Payment: None; 25 offprints.

Copyright by Pennsylvania State University.

Bibliography in Summer issue.

CHELSEA, P.O. Box 5880, Grand Central Station, New York, N.Y. 10017. $3.50 for 2 issues. Founded 1958; published by Chelsea Associates.

Major fields of interest: Contemporary literature, art, and theater. Translation of foreign authors little known in U.S. a special interest. Creative material is the main part of every issue.

Manuscript information: No specified length. Report within 2 to 3 months.

Payment in copies, unless a grant specifies authors' payments.

Copyright obtained separately for each issue, remains at author's disposal in case of reprint elsewhere.

CHICAGO REVIEW, The University of Chicago, Chicago, Illinois 60637. $5, $9.50 for 2 years; quarterly. Founded 1946; sponsored by the University of Chicago.

Major fields of interest: Contemporary literature in general, experimental prose and poetry. Literary criticism and essays; articles should be critical in nature. Full-length drama.

Manuscript information: No length limit specified. Footnotes, if necessary, should be held to a minimum. Report within 2 to 5 weeks.

Payment: Copies of the magazine and subscription.

Copyright held by the magazine until transfer is requested by the author.

CHILDREN'S LITERATURE: THE GREAT EXCLUDED, the Journal of the MLA Seminar on Children's Literature and of the Children's Literature Association. For information on The Children's Literature Assn., write Anne Devereaux Jordan, Executive Secretary, P.O Box 2445, Kalamazoo, Michigan 49003. Vols. I and II are $4.25 each; for information on subscription rates for Vols. III and IV write UConn Bookstore, Storrs, Ct. 06268.

Major fields of interest: Children's literature. Recent articles include "Back to Pooh Corner," "Children's Reading in the Jewish Academy," "Milton's *Comus* as Children's Literature," "Medieval Songs of Innocence and Experience," "The Proper Bringing Up of Young Pip," "The Wizardess of Oz — and Who She Is," "Children's Theatre in East and West Germany," "Science Fiction and the Adolescent," "Prickles Under the Frock: Beatrix Potter," and "The Child in Shakespeare."

THE CHRISTIAN CENTURY, 407 South Dearborn Street, Chicago, Illinois 60605. $12; weekly. Founded 1884; published by The Christian Century Foundation. Editor: James M. Wall.

Major fields of interest: Political, religious, and social subjects. Critical articles of about 2500 words preferred. Report in about 2 weeks.

Payment: 2¢ per word; 3 copies given to authors.

Copyright by The Christian Century Foundation.

CHRONICA, James J. Murphy, Editor, Department of Rhetoric, University of California, Davis, California 95616. $4; twice yearly (Fall and Spring). Founded 1967; sponsored by Medieval Association of the Pacific. Unsolicited Mss. not desired. CHRONICA is the newsletter of MAP, published in journal format.

Major fields of interest: Middle Ages; 1 article each issue, solicited by the editor.

Manuscript information: Articles of 2000 words; MLA style sheet; treatment of footnotes variable. Report in 2 weeks.

Payment: None.

No copyright.

CITHARA: Essays in the Judeo-Christian Tradition, St. Bonaventure University, St. Bonaventure, New York 14778. $3.50; twice yearly. Founded 1961; sponsored by St. Bonaventure University.

Major fields of interest: Humanistic studies. Interdisciplinary articles, especially those that state or imply a relationship to the Judeo-Christian tradition, preferred.

Manuscript information: 3000-5000 words preferred. MLA style sheet; 2 copies if possible. Footnotes should be placed at the end of the text and double-spaced. Report usually within a month.

Payment: Copies of the issue.

Copyright: Use of material permitted on request.

CLA JOURNAL, Morgan State College, Baltimore, Maryland 21239. $6 for 4 issues in United States; $6.50 in Canada; $7 elsewhere in the world (September, December, March, and June). Founded 1957; sponsored by the College Language Association.

Major fields of interest: Any type of article dealing with languages and literature, including bibliographical articles.

Manuscript information: No specified length, although excessively long articles must be "unusually meritorious and timely." MLA style sheet. 2 copies of the Ms. desirable. Necessary and intelligent documentation encouraged; place footnotes at the bottom of the page. In some cases, after the main reference has been established in a footnote, later references to lines, pages, etc., may be given in parentheses in the text. Report within 2 months.

Payment: Extra copies of the journal are given to contributors; reprints available at a small cost only.

CLASSICA ET MEDIAEVALIA, c/o Franz Blatt, Statteager 6, Gevninge Pr., 4000 Roskilde C, Denmark. 60 Danish Crowns for annual issue. Founded 1938; sponsored by Societas Danica Indagationis Antiquitatis et Medii Aevi.

Major fields of interest: Classical antiquity (not archeology), classical languages and literature, history of the classical tradition, history of law, ecclesiastical history, medieval Latin literature. Critical articles or source studies preferred.

Manuscript information: 28 to 30 pages the preferred length for articles.

Payment: 30 offprints.

Bibliographical issue yearly.

THE CLASSICAL JOURNAL, H. D. Evjen, Editor, University of Colorado, Boulder, Colorado 80302. $6.50 for 8 issues (October-May). Founded 1905; published by the Classical Association of the Middle West and South, Inc.

Major fields of interest: Classical Greek and Latin literature, history, civilization, etc., and the classical tradition. Articles should be of general interest to college and high school teachers. Recent titles: "*Oedipus Tyrannus* and the Problem of Knowledge," "How Caesar Bridged the Rhine," "Some 'Metaphysical' Aspects of the Homeric Simile."

Manuscript information: No length preference, but not usually over 5-8 pages in print. Footnotes at the end of the Ms. Reports, based upon recommendations by Classics scholars, are normally issued within 3 months.

Payment: Complete issues for the author; offprints may be ordered.

CLIO, An Interdisciplinary Journal of Literature, History and the Philosophy of History, University of Wisconsin-Parkside, Kenosha, Wisconsin 53140. $12 (Institutions), $4.50 (Individuals); 3 times a year. Founded October, 1971; sponsored by University of Wisconsin-Parkside.

Major fields of interest: Literature, History, and the Philosophy of History. Critical articles.

Manuscript information: MLA style sheet, 2nd ed. Original and 1 carbon needed by readers. Length of articles varies: 15-60 Ms. pages (3500 to 13,500 words). Report within 3 months. Minimal footnotes.

Payment: 2 copies of journal and offprints at cost.

Copyright policy: Usual scholarly journal practice.

COLBY LIBRARY QUARTERLY, Colby College, Waterville, Maine 04901. $3; quarterly. Founded 1943; sponsored by Colby College.

Major fields of interest: Studies of Maine authors (i.e., Sarah Orne Jewett, Edwin Arlington Robinson, Jacob Abbott, Edna St. Vincent Millay, Kenneth Roberts) and Maine history as well as studies of books and authors from outside Maine (Henry James, Willa Cather, William Dean Howells, Ellen Glasgow, Thomas Hardy, A. E. and Laurence Housman, modern Irish writers, and others) who are well represented by special collections in the Colby College Library or who have exerted an influence on Maine life or letters. Articles should primarily be biographical, critical, bibliographical, or source studies, including first appearances of letters, etc. Complete issues on special authors published frequently.

Manuscript information: Articles should not exceed 20 double-spaced typewritten pages. Footnote material should be incorporated into the text as much as possible. Indispensable footnotes are acceptable and should be typed on a separate sheet. Editors will convert Ms. references into a simplified style acceptable to the journal. Report within 3 weeks.

Payment: 10 copies of the issue.

Issues not generally copyrighted except for special, restricted material.

COLLEGE AND RESEARCH LIBRARIES, Richard M. Dougherty, Editor, The General Library, University of California, Berkeley,

California 94720. $5 (including membership), otherwise $15; bi-monthly. Founded 1939; sponsored by the Association of College and Research Libraries, American Library Association.

Major fields of interest: Librarianship as related to the problems of college, university, and research libraries. Critical, biographical, historical, bibliographical, and other research findings used.

Manuscript information: Articles of 1500-2500 words in length. 2 copies of the Ms. desired. University of Chicago style manual. About 5 weeks or less for report.

Payment: None.

Material may be reproduced elsewhere with permission of the editor and author.

COLLEGE COMPOSITION AND COMMUNICATION, Department of English, Ohio State University, Columbus, Ohio 43210. $3; quarterly (February, May, October, and December). Founded 1950; an official publication of the National Council of Teachers of English.

Major fields of interest: Theory and teaching of composition; relationships of studies in literature, language, and linguistics to composition; rhetorical, stylistic, thematic, or critical analyses of non-fiction prose writers commonly studied in college composition courses; studies in usage, grammar, rhetoric, and the logic of composition. Articles should avoid highly specialized topics of limited interest to the instructor of undergraduate English courses.

Manuscript information: Desired length of articles 2500-3000 words; contributions for Staffroom Interchange, 1500-5000 words. Anything beyond these limits should justify itself by exceptional merit. MLA style sheet; footnotes may be incorporated in the text or be included on the page where the citation is made. Report within 1 month.

Payment: 6 copies of the issue; reprints may be ordered.

Copyright by NCTE.

COLLEGE ENGLISH, Richard Ohmann, Editor, Department of English, Wesleyan University, Middleton, Connecticut 06457. $10; monthly, excluding summer. Founded 1928; sponsored by the National Council of Teachers of English.

Major fields of interest: Articles of general professional importance in the following areas: (1) The working concepts of criticism: struc-

ture, genre, influence, period, myth, rhetoric, etc. (2) The nature o
critical and scholarly reasoning; implicit standards of evidence an
inference; the nature of critical explanation. (3) The structure of ou
field; implications of the way we segment it; consequences of specia
izing the usual ways; the place of rhetoric and composition. (4) Th
relevance of current thinking and research in other fields (e.g., ph
losophy, history, art history, psychology, linguistics) to the stud
and teaching of English. (5) Curriculum, pedagogy, and educationa
theory. (6) Practical affairs in the profession. (7) Scholarly book
textbooks, and journals in the field.

Long reviews and review articles on books of general interest t
the profession are assigned by the editor.

Note: No longer publishes critical articles or explications, excep
for those mainly calculated to have an impact on critical theor
curricular thinking, pedagogy, etc.

Manuscript information: Articles should usually be no more tha
40 pages. Comments on published articles and reviews should no
mally be limited to 6 pages. Revised MLA style sheet; avoid footnote
when possible, including documentation in text. Report within
months.

Payment: Copies of the issue.

Copyright by NCTE.

THE COLORADO QUARTERLY, Hellems 134, University of Colo
rado, Boulder, Colorado 80302. $4; quarterly. Founded 1952; spon
sored by The University of Colorado.

Major fields of interest: General, non-technical articles written fo
general readers by specialists in the sciences, politics, social studie
and the humanities, in a style free of academic or technical jargon
Fiction and poetry included in every issue.

Manuscript information: Articles of 4000-6000 words preferred. Un
versity of Chicago style manual followed rather closely. Footnote
are permissible when the material cannot be incorporated in th
text. Report usually within 2-3 weeks.

Payment: Reprints at cost.

Copyright: Permission to reprint is freely given, provided prope
acknowledgment is made; a fee is required of commercial public
tions.

COMITATUS, Center for Medieval and Renaissance Studies, University of California, Los Angeles, CA 90024. $4 (libraries), $2.50 (individuals); annual. Founded 1970; sponsored by Center for Medieval and Renaissance Studies.

Major fields of interest: Medieval and Renaissance literature (or any area of Medieval and Renaissance studies which has some bearing on literature, e.g. iconography). No book reviews.

Manuscript information: Articles less than 30 printed pages. MLA style sheet. Original copy only needed. Prefer footnotes typed separately at end of article. Report within 3 months during academic year.

Payment: None. Offprints may be ordered at nominal rates.

Copyright policy: Copyrighted for the author's protection.

COMMENTARY, 165 East 56th Street, New York, New York 10022. $12; monthly. Founded 1945; sponsored by American Jewish Committee.

Major fields of interest: Jewish affairs, contemporary world politics, American political, social, and cultural scene. Literary criticism. Recent titles: "Black Progress and Liberal Rhetoric," "Rewriting History," and "Poetry and Public Experience." Fiction used, but no poetry.

Manuscript information: No length restrictions. Footnotes should be placed at the bottom of each page. Report within 3-4 weeks.

Payment: About $3\frac{1}{2}$c a word; 2 copies and about 15 tearsheets.

Copyright held by American Jewish Committee.

COMMONWEAL, 232 Madison Avenue, New York, N.Y. 10016. $14; weekly. Founded 1924; edited by Catholic laymen.

Major fields of interest: Contemporary public affairs, religion, literature, arts. Interest is in timely critical and analytical approach to American and world problems. Recent titles: "Psychiatry and Belief," "Deschoolizing and Education," "The Philippines: Another Vietnam?" Creative non-scholarly material also used.

Manuscript information: 1200-3000 words preferred. Report within 2 or 3 weeks.

Payment: 2c a word on acceptance.

COMPARATIVE DRAMA, Department of English, Western Michigan University, Kalamazoo, Michigan 49001. $3.50 for individuals, $5 for libraries and institutions; quarterly. Founded 1967.

Major fields of interest: Drama of all nations and all periods. Critical studies which are international in spirit and interdisciplinary in scope especially desired.

Manuscript information: Articles of 2000-5000 words. 2 copies of the Ms. MLA style sheet; footnotes should be typed on separate pages at the end of the article; they should be kept to a minimum and whenever possible incorporated into the text. Report usually in 2-4 weeks.

Payment: None; 2 copies of the issue and 20-40 offprints.

Copyright by the editors.

COMPARATIVE LITERATURE, University of Oregon, Eugene, Oregon. $4.50; quarterly. Founded 1949; sponsored by the University of Oregon; it is the official journal of the American Comparative Literature Association.

Major fields of interest: Studies of literature from an international point of view, including studies of the manifold interrelations of literatures, theory of literature, movements, genres, periods, and authors. Longer studies on comprehensive topics and on problems of literary criticism especially welcomed.

Manuscript information: No limitations or special preference regarding length, but short notes on minor topics are seldom published. MLA style sheet; Chicago style book on matters not covered by MLA. Footnotes should be typed on separate sheets at the end of the article. Report within about 3 months.

Payment: 5 copies of the issue; offprints at cost with minimum order of 100.

Copyrighted; request for permission to reprint should be made to the editor.

COMPARATIVE LITERATURE STUDIES, Room No. 2054, Foreign Languages Building, University of Illinois, Urbana, Illinois 61801. $7.50 (foreign, add 50 cents postage); quarterly. Founded 1963; sponsored by the Program in Comparative Literature, University of Illinois.

Major fields of interest: Comparative literature, literary history, and the history of ideas, stressing North and South American relations with Europe.

Manuscript information: Articles of 2500-6000 words. MLA style sheet; notes at end of article. Report in approximately 3 months.

Copyright by the journal.

COMPUTER STUDIES IN THE HUMANITIES AND VERBAL BEHAVIOR, Floyd Horowitz, Department of English, University of Kansas, Lawrence, Kansas 66044 (for Mss. and general correspondence); Mouton & Co., P.O. Box 1132, The Hague, The Netherlands (for subscriptions). $12; quarterly. Founded 1967; sponsored by University of Kansas; published by Mouton & Co.

Major fields of interest: All areas of the Humanities, including linguistics, anthropology, library science, sociology, social psychology. Research must have used and/or describe use of the computer. Articles on research results and computer program development preferred.

Manuscript information: Medium-length articles, but can be long. Notes accepted. Style sheet optional though generally of scientific form; 2 copies of Ms. needed. Report in 2 months.

Payment: None; 5 offprints.

Copyright retained by journal if not otherwise specified.

COMPUTERS AND THE HUMANITIES, Queens College, Flushing, New York 11367. $9.50 individual, $20 institutional; 5 times yearly. Founded 1966; sponsored by Queens College.

Major fields of interest: Computer applications to humanistic studies.

Manuscript information: Articles of 5000 words; MLA style sheet. Report in 2-3 months.

Payment: None; 50 offprints.

Copyright by the journal; reprint rights available to authors.

CONCERNING POETRY, English Department, Western Washington State College, Bellingham, Washington 98225. $3; 2 issues a year. Founded 1968; sposnored by the English Department, Western Washington State College.

Major fields of interest: Critical and *explication de texte* on particular poems and poets. Also publishes poetry.

Manuscript information: MLA style sheet. Articles of 10-12 typewritten pages preferred. Report in 1-2 months.

Payment: Copies of the journal.

Copyright by journal; released to author on request.

CONRAD ANNUAL, McMurry College, Abilene, Texas 79605. $20; once yearly (September). Founded 1973; sponsored by the Joseph Conrad Society.

Major fields of interest: Miscellany of ephemera concerning all aspects of the life and work of Joseph Conrad. The annual is intended to be a compendium of all the materials which cannot find space in the tri-quarterly journal CONRADIANA or the JOSEPH CONRAD SOCIETY BULLETIN. There is little interest in original criticism, which should be published elsewhere and then noted in the annual. The idea is to note in the annual everything of interest in the world of Conrad studies which took place during the previous year: work in progress, exhibits of Conrad materials, papers read at conferences, meetings, symposia, colloquia, translations, inclusions in anthologies, masters' theses, doctoral dissertations, book reviews, bibliographies, photographs, etc. Abstracts of theses and dissertations accepted during the year. The annual is intended to be a digest, not an outlet for new work, so contributions of offprints, newspaper clippings, reviews, notices, etc., will be welcomed and credit given to the first contributor of each item included in the yearly compilation.

Manuscript information: Report within 30 days. Self-addressed stamped envelope plus notice of return required should accompany each item submitted.

Payment: 10% discount on the annual for each item by a contributor used in that issue, i.e., the contributor of ten items gets the $20 volume free.

Copyright: THE CONRAD ANNUAL will be copyrighted, but reprint rights will be more than just liberal in cases where due credit is given the publisher.

CONRADIANA, Department of English, Texas Tech University, Lubbock, Texas 79401. $4; 3 times a year. Founded 1968; sponsored by Department of English, Texas Tech University.

Major fields of interest: All aspects and phases of the life and work of Joseph Conrad. All work must be in some way related to the English novelist. Controversy, satires, parodies, etc., especially invited; poetry also published. Work from abroad especially solicited; editors in 2 dozen countries and eventually hope to cover entire world wherever Joseph Conrad lived, worked, travelled, or is published and studied on any serious level.

Manuscript information: MLA style sheet; footnotes printed after the text. 2 copies of the manuscript needed. 300 word abstract and short biographical sketch should be included. Manuscripts should be typed, double spaced, with margins of 1¼" at sides and 1½" at top and bottom. Report in 1½ to 2 months.

Coyyright by Institute for Textual Studies, Texas Tech University.

CONTEMPORA, Box 673, Atlanta, Georgia 30301. $4.50; quarterly. Founded 1969.

Major fields of interest: Creative writing. Publishes fiction, poetry, non-fiction of cultural orientation, cinema essays.

Manuscript information: Prefer articles of 6-10 pages. No style sheet preference. Report in approximately 2 weeks or less.

Payment: "Each item is purchased but the payment depends upon the item"; 2 copies, more on request.

Copyrighted.

CONTEMPORARY LITERATURE (formerly WISCONSIN STUDIES IN CONTEMPORARY LITERATURE), Helen C. White Hall, 600 N. Park St., Madison, Wisconsin 35706. $10, $16 institutional; 4 issues a year. Founded 1960; sponsored by the University of Wisconsin.

Major fields of interest: Critical and/or scholarly articles about all aspects of the "modern" in literature, chiefly since 1940.

Manuscript information: MLA style sheet; full documentation preferred, footnotes at the end of the article. Articles should be no shorter than 3000 words and may be up to 15,000. Report in 3 months.

Payment: 25 reprints and 2 copies of the magazine.

Copyrighted.

CONTEMPORARY POETRY, Fairleigh Dickinson University, Teaneck, New Jersey 07666. $5 (libraries and institutions), $4 (individuals); quarterly. Founded 1973.

Major fields of interest: Contemporary poetry, especially that written between 1950 and the present. Critical, explicatory essays. Also publishes creative non-scholarly material.

Manuscript information: Essays between 500-700 words. MLA style sheet. 2 copies needed by readers. Footnotes on separate page. Report within 3 months.

Payment: None at present; copies of journal only; small payment possible in future.

Copyright policy: Copyright by journal; right to reprint in scholarly publication given on condition of acknowledgment of original printing.

CONTEMPORARY REVIEW (incorporating THE FORTNIGHTLY), 37 Union St., London SE1, England. $13.50 p.a.; monthly.

Major fields of interest: English literature, politics, economics, history, foreign affairs, sociology. Generally, articles have a contemporary relevance. Representative titles: "Charles Morgan's Novels," "Joseph Conrad as I Remember Him," "Voltaire in England." Creative material also used.

CONVERGENCE, Box 250, Station F, Toronto M4Y 2L5, Ontario, Canada. $6; quarterly. Founded 1968; sponsored by The Ontario Institute for Studies in Education.

Major fields of interest: Adult education (research and practice). Articles are international-comparative, presenting educational methods for readership throughout the world.

Manuscript information: Articles of 2000-4000 words preferred. 1 Ms. copy needed. The journal is published in English, French, Spanish, and Russian; abstracts in English appear after articles in foreign language.

Permission of editor needed if article is to be reprinted.

THE CORNHILL MAGAZINE, 50 Albermarle Street, London W1X 4BD, England. 23 shillings; quarterly. Founded 1860.

Major fields of interest: Literature, short stories and poetry. Recent contributors: Kenneth Clark, William Sansom, Martin Secker, Arturo Vivante and Ruth Jhabvala.

Manuscript information: All material accepted on merit. Report in about 1 month.

Payment: By arrangement; 1 offprint.

Copyright vested in magazine unless requested to "register with author."

COSTERUS, Essays in English and American Language and Literature, c/o James L. W. West III, Department of English, Virginia Polytechnic Institute and State University, Blacksburg, Virginia 24061. Dfl. 30/US $9.50 per volume; irregular; minimum of 2 issues per year and in most years a third special issue. Founded 1972; sponsored by Editions Rodopi NV, Amsterdam.

Major fields of interest: All areas and genres of English and American language and literature. Articles should be rigorously researched, carefully documented. Bibliographical and textual work. We publish few straight critical readings.

Manuscript information: Approximately 2000-word minimum. Reviews are lengthy — frequent essay-reviews. MLA style sheet (rev. ed.) with modifications. 2 copies of Ms. needed by readers. Illustration of articles is emphasized. Report within 1 month. Mss. should be accompanied by an abstract of not more than 100 words, and by stamps sufficient for return postage. Prospective contributors should state their academic affiliations.

Payment: No monetary payment. Authors of articles receive 35-40 offprints; authors of reviews receive 20 offprints.

Copyright policy: Copyright on all material is held by the journal. Reprinting rights are freely given.

THE CRESSET, Valparaiso University, Valparaiso, Indiana 46383. $3 for 10 issues; September through June. Founded 1937; sponsored by Valparaiso University since 1951.

Major fields of interest: Reviews and criticism of literature, the arts, and especially public affairs. The magazine has a special interest in articles written from the point of view of Christian theology, and of interdisciplinary and exploratory character in the humanities.

Manuscript information: 2500-4000 words. University of Chicago style manual; footnotes at the end of the article. 2 copies of Ms. Report within 1 month.

Payment: $5 per printed page; 10 copies of the issue.

Copyright held by Valparaiso University. Approval to reprint upon request of the writer.

THE CRITIC, 180 N. Wabash, Chicago, Illinois 60601. $6 for 6 issues. Founded 1942; sponsored by The Thomas More Association, Chicago, Illinois.

Major fields of interest: Christian culture (in the broader sociological as well as the more limited cultural sense), books. Not a "scholarly publication," the magazine is intended for the educated Roman Catholic. Creative material also used.

Manuscript information: 2000-5000 words. Footnotes should be avoided if possible. Report within 2 to 3 weeks.

Payment: For articles, 4¢ per word; 3 copies of the issue.

Copyright held by the magazine.

THE CRITICAL QUARTERLY, The University, Manchester, England. $4.50; quarterly. Founded 1959; private sponsorship.

Major fields of interest: Critical articles on 20th-century literature: British, American, and European; but also articles of general interest on literature pre-1900. Literary criticism only. Original poetry also used.

Manuscript information: Up to 6000 words acceptable, and longer articles in exceptional cases. MLA style sheet preferred. No footnotes desired, but a minimum number acceptable. Report usually within 6 weeks.

Payment: 10 offprints.

Copyright not reserved on material later used in book form.

Bibliographical issue in March.

THE CRITICAL REVIEW: MELBOURNE, Department of English, The University of Melbourne, Parkville, Victoria, Australia 3052. $1 (Aust.) an issue, or $1.20 posted ($1.40 USA, posted); 1 issue a year at present. Founded 1958.

Major fields of interest: Articles in any field — literary, historical, sociological, etc. — as long as they are related to literary criticism. Source studies, dating of texts, etc., as such not published.

Manuscript information: Articles should run between 5000 and 6000 words, although both longer and shorter articles may be accepted. Commentary section for discussions (which can be of article length) more tentative in approach, or more freely ranging. Style sheet from Authors' and Printers' Dictionary (Oxford University Press) and Rules for Compositors and Readers at the Oxford University Press. Footnotes should be worked into the text. Report usually within 4 weeks.

Payment: 6 offprints.

Copyrighted; permission to reprint is normally given upon application to the Editor.

CRITICISM: A quarterly for literature and the arts, Department of English, Wayne State University, Detroit, Michigan 48202. $8, $14.50 for 2 years; quarterly (January, April, July, October). Founded 1959; sponsored by Wayne State University English Department; published by Wayne State University Press.

Major fields of interest: The study of literature and the other arts, scholarly analysis and evaluation of artists and their works in all periods and nations, either individually or in interrelationships, and critical theory regarding all arts and literatures. Formal aesthetic and the more technical studies in philology and linguistics are not within the scope of the journal.

Manuscript information: Articles of 15-20 pages in typescript preferred although longer and shorter articles, if subject matter justifies, are also acceptable. MLA style sheet. No outline or advance precis necessary. Footnotes desirable only when necessary. Report in about 3 months.

Payment: 25 free reprints.

Copyright by Wayne State University Press.

CRITIQUE: Studies in Modern Fiction, Department of English, Georgia Institute of Technology, Atlanta, Georgia 30332. $7.50 for 3 issues. Founded 1956.

Major fields of interest: Literary criticism of contemporary fiction; principal focus on writers who are alive and without great reputations; bibliographies of individual writers occasionally published.

Manuscript information: Follow MLA style sheet; footnotes should follow essay. Report within 4 to 6 months (frequently sooner).

Payment: 5 copies and 25 offprints.

Copyright held by CRITIQUE; surrendered to author on request.

CROSS CURRENTS, West Nyack, New York 10994. $6; quarterly. Founded 1950; sponsored by Cross Currents Corporation.

Major fields of interest: The implications of Christianity for our times. Emphasis is on posing of problems rather than on final answers. Much of the material is reprinted from foreign or out-of-the-way sources. Although founded by Catholic laymen, no point of view is automatically excluded, provided that it presents something fresh and valuable. A close study of a particular work, if of particular interest to readers, is acceptable, as well as studies in the history of ideas, relations of philosophical and religious ideas to works of art. In general the magazine prints essays by established writers of religious commitment.

Manuscript information: 3000-8000 words preferred. MLA style sheet; footnotes at bottom of page. Postcard acknowledgment of receipt; report in 3-5 weeks.

Payment: Approximately ⅓¢ per word; 50 reprints; more available at cost.

Author may retain copyright, but should acknowledge first publication when reprinting.

CUADERNOS AMERICANOS (La Revista Del Nuevo Mundo), Avenida Coyoacán 1035, México 12, D.F. 13.50 Dls.; bi-monthly. Founded 1942.

Major fields of interest: General culture; emphasis on the culture of the American continents. Articles in Spanish.

Manuscript information: Articles should range from 10 to 25 pages in length.

THE D. H. LAWRENCE REVIEW, Box 1799, University of Arkansas, Fayetteville, Arkansas 72701. $5 in USA, Canada, Mexico, $6 all other countries; 3 times annually. Founded 1968.

Major fields of interest: D. H. Lawrence and his circle — criticism, historical scholarship, reviews, notes, bibliography, and news of studies on Lawrence and other figures related to or influenced by him. Articles must be literate; they may be critical, biographical, explicatory, scholarly, etc. Creative material rarely published; it must be related to Lawrence.

Manuscript information: Articles of any length, though few very short notes or very long monographs published. MLA style sheet; incorporate as many references as possible into text; footnotes on separate sheet at end. 2 copies of Ms. will expedite reading; include return postage and self-addressed envelope. Report in about 3 months.

Payment: None; 20-25 offprints and 2 copies of issue.

Copyrighted.

Bibliography in Spring issue.

DAEDALUS, 7 Linden Street, Harvard University, Cambridge, Massachusetts 02138. $10; quarterly. Founded (in new form) 1957; sponsored by the American Academy of Arts and Sciences. Unsolicited Mss. very rarely accepted; most articles are commisioned.

Major fields of interest: Current topics of major interest on a high level, so as to create a forum for opinion and policy-making for the intelligent citizen as well as the academic specialist. Each issue is devoted to a single topic, such as higher education, and is about 2-3 years in preparation. Creative material almost never used.

Manuscript information: Articles of 5000-10,000 words preferred. The DAEDALUS style sheet is based on the Chicago style manual and Webster's DICTIONARY. Footnotes should be kept to a minimum and numbered consecutively throughout the article; footnotes, annotations, and bibliographies are placed at the end of the article. 2 Ms. copies. Include a biographical statement of about 100 words. Mss. are read immediately though publication may be deferred because of the organization of each issue around a central theme.

Payment: Honorarium plus 10 free copies.

Copyrighted.

THE DALHOUSIE REVIEW, Dalhousie University, Halifax, Nova Scotia, Canada. $4, $10 for 3 years; quarterly. Founded 1921; sponsored by Dalhousie University and the Review Publishing Company.

Major fields of interest: The humanities, including literature (in English), philosophy, history, politics, art, and music, "by specialists but not for specialists." Critical and explication de texte articles are acceptable only if the subject is of more than limited specialist interest. THE DALHOUSIE REVIEW is not one of the specialist scholarly journals, although it welcomes some of the types of articles that appear in such journals. It is interested in articles on major literary figures and movements: e.g., Dickens, but not Shenstone. Creative material occasionally used, and some verse.

Manuscript information: Articles of about 5000 words preferred; articles should not be less than 3000 words or more than 7000. MLA style sheet is satisfactory but the standard form is SCHOLARLY REPORTING IN THE HUMANITIES (Humanities Research Council of Canada). Footnotes should be placed at the end of the article; footnotes are required for scholarly articles but are optional for more general articles. About 3 months for report.

Payment: $1 per page for articles; 25 free offprints; more at cost if ordered in advance.

Copyrighted.

DECEMBER, Box 274, Western Springs, Illinois 60558. $2; irregularly. Founded in 1958, published by Curt Johnson.

Major fields of interest: Fiction, poetry, artwork, movie criticism, and contemporary commentary.

Manuscript information: No restrictions; decision within 8 weeks.

Copyright by C. L. Johnson; reverts to author on request.

DeKALB LITERARY ARTS JOURNAL, Mel McKeen, Editor, DeKalb College, Clarkston, Georgia 30021. $5; quarterly. Founded 1966; sponsored by DeKalb College.

Major fields of interest: Not specified. A few critical and biographical articles taken. Creative work published.

Manuscript information: MLA style sheet; footnotes at end of article. Report in about 3 months.

Payment: In copies.

Copyrighted.

DELTA, 12 Hardwick Street, Cambridge, England CB3 9JA. $4 for 3 issues, including surface mail; 3 times yearly. Founded 1953.

Major fields of interest: The arts, especially literature. Creative work used. Also literary criticism and reviews, academic criticism.

Manuscript information: MLA style sheet; footnotes allowed "but not sought after." Articles may be up to 8000 words. Report within 3 months.

Payment: 5 offprints (further if requested).

Copyright by the Editors, but permission for reprinting always given.

THE DENVER QUARTERLY, University of Denver, Denver, Colorado 80210. $4; quarterly. Founded 1966; sponsored by University of Denver.

Major fields of interest: Modern (20th century) literature and culture. Articles of criticism and history of ideas preferred. Original poetry and fiction published.

Manuscript information: Articles of 4000-8000 words. MLA style sheet; "dislike footnotes; most are unnecessary, or can be incorporated in text." Report in 2 months. All entries must be accompanied by self-addressed stamped envelope.

Payment: $5 per printed page of prose, $10 per page for poetry; offprints variable, by arrangement.

Copyright by the journal; First North American Serial rights only; rights revert to author on request.

DESCANT, English Department, Texas Christian University, Fort Worth, Texas 76129. $2 for 4 issues. Founded 1956; a publication of the Texas Christian University Press.

Major fields of interest: Short stories, poems, critical articles. DESCANT is chiefly literary in nature, although articles approaching the study of literature through philosophical, religious or other methods of analysis (excluding political and social) would be acceptable.

Manuscript information: Articles of 5-10 printed pages (about 2500-5000 words) are preferred. MLA style sheet. About 6 weeks for report.

Payment: 5 copies of the issue.

Copyright by Texas Christian University.

DEUTSCHE VIERTELJAHRSSCHRIFT FÜR LITERATURWIS-
SENSCHAFT UND GEISTESGESCHICHTE, Professor Dr. Richard
Brinkmann, 74 Tübingen, Im Rotbad 30, Germany and Professor Dr.
Hugo Kuhn, 8 München 23, Veterinärstr. 2, Germany. DM 70; quar-
terly. Founded 1923.
  Major fields of interest: German and foreign languages and litera-
tures, history of arts, history of ideas, etc.
  Copyright by J. B. Metzlersche Verlagsbuchhandlung 7, Stuttgart
1, Kernerstrasse 43, Germany.

DIACRITICS, Department of Romance Studies, 278 Goldwin Smith,
Cornell University, Ithaca, New York 14850. $6 yearly (2 years, $10.50;
3 years, $15); 4 times yearly. Founded 1971; sponsored by Depart-
ment of Romance Studies, Cornell University.
  Major fields of interest: Critical.
  Manuscript information: MLA style sheet. 15 typewritten pages.
Footnotes on separate page.
  Payment: None. 2 copies of journal given to contributor. Reprints
ordered separately.
  Bibliographical issue in Winter.

DICKENS STUDIES ANNUAL, English Department, Southern Illinois University, Carbondale, lllinois 62901. Subscription price to be
announced; annually. Founded 1969; sponsored by Southern Illinois
University.
  Major fields of interest: Dickens, his age, and his work. All types of
articles considered.
  Manuscript information: Articles of 15-60 type-written pages preferred. MLA style sheet. Ms. should be double spaced througout
including footnotes and quotations. Footnotes should be placed at
end of Ms. Report in 3 months.
  Copyright by Southern Illinois University Press.

THE DICKENS STUDIES NEWSLETTER, Department of English,
Duke University, Durham, North Carolina 27706, Professor Lionel
Stevenson, Editor. $5 (free to members of The Dickens Society);
quarterly. Founded 1970; sponsored by The Dickens Society.

Major fields of interest: Critical articles about Dickens. Scholarly book reviews. Checklist of recent publications on Dickens.

Manuscript information: No more than 10 typed pages for articles, 4 pages for reviews. MLA style sheet. Footnotes at end of manuscript.

Payment: None.

Copyright retained by contributor.

THE DICKENSIAN, Dickens House, 48 Doughty Street, London W.C. 1N 2LF, England. Overseas subscription rate on application. 3 issues a year. Founded 1905; sponsored by The Dickens Fellowship.

Major fields of interest: The life and work of Charles Dickens.

Manuscript information: Preferred length: 2000-3000 words. Style sheet available on request.

No payment.

THE DILIMAN REVIEW, c/o Department of Philosophy, 3025 Faculty Center, UP Diliman Quezon City D-505, Philippine Islands. 3 pesos per no. (12 pesos a year); quarterly. Founded 1953; sponsored by UP College of Arts and Sciences.

Major fields of interest: "Arts, Letters, and Discussion." All types of articles considered. Creative material used.

Manuscript information: No policy on length. 2 copies of Ms. Report in 1 week.

Payment: 100 reprints; payment of 25 pesos per contribution projected.

Rights not reserved.

DRAMA & THEATRE (successor to FIRST STAGE), Department of English, State University College, Fredonia, New York 14063. $4.50; tri-annually. Newly established 1968; sponsored by the State University of New York.

Major fields of interest: New, original drama and new drama in translation. Articles and interviews on the theatre, book reviews.

Manuscript information: Articles and interviews should be about 3000 words in length. Report within 3-4 months.

Payment: 10 copies of the magazine.

Copyright: Every play must be copyrighted before it is accepted.

THE DRAMA REVIEW (TDR), 32 Washington Pl., Rm. 73, New York, New York 10003. $7.50, $9.50 foreign, $6.50 student; quarterly. Founded 1955; sponsored by New York University School of the Arts.

Major fields of interest: Performance, all periods and all countries, in theatre, happenings, film, music, with emphasis on the contemporary and experimental. Theoretical articles, interviews, documents and descriptive material on productions desired. Creative work and photos published.

Manuscript information: No maximum or minimum length; "quality determines acceptance." See previous issues of the journal for style; full citation for necessary footnotes. Report in less than 1 month.

Payment: 2¢ per printed word for author, 1¢ per translated word for translator; 2 copies of the issue plus unlimited reprints at cost of reprinting and shipping.

Copyright by the journal unless author requests otherwise; "if other sources request permission to reprint TDR articles, fee is set, and fee split between TDR and author, 50% each."

Bibliography in each volume of 4 issues.

DRAMATICS, College Hill Station, Box E, Cincinnati, Ohio 45224. $5 for 8 issues (October through May). Founded 1929; sponsored by The International Thespian Society.

Major fields of interest: Articles containing information about both educational and professional theatre; original plays. Articles should be directed toward secondary school teachers and students.

Manuscript information: Articles should be 2000 words in length with 2 photographs preferred. Footnotes not desired. Report in 3 months.

Payment: From $15 to $25 per Ms.; 2 copies of the issue.

Copyright by The International Thespian Society.

DREISER NEWSLETTER, English Department, Indiana State University, Terre Haute, Indiana 47809. $2.50/4 issues. 2 issues a year (Spring and Fall). Founded 1970; sponsored by English Department, Indiana State University.

Major fields of interest: Dreiser studies with priority given to material of a bibliographical nature.

Manuscript information: 1500-2000 words. MLA style sheet. Footnotes at end of article. Report within 2 weeks.

Payment: 2 copies of Newsletter.

Copyright policy: Copyright held by DN.

Annual bibliography in Fall issue.

THE DUBLIN MAGAZINE (Editor: John Ryan), Elstow, Knapton Road, Dun Laoire Co., Dublin, Ireland. $4; quarterly. Founded 1961.

Major fields of interest: Articles by Irish writers on any subject connected with literature and allied arts, or articles by non-Irish writers on the same subject but showing a relationship of the subject to Ireland and Irish interests. Poetry and short stories of 2500-5000 words in length, with footnotes used at the writer's discretion. Report in 1-3 months.

Payment: 6 copies.

Copyright by the writer.

DURHAM UNIVERSITY JOURNAL, 43 North Bailey, Durham, England. £1.5/-; 3 issues yearly (December, March, and June). Founded 1876; sponsored by University of Durham.

Major fields of interest: Literature, history, philosophy, and theology, but articles on science, sociology, and political thought are also included. Scholarly articles preferred. Creative materials only occasionally and "exceptionally" used.

Manuscript information: Articles of 4000-6000 words preferred. Footnotes should be placed after text. 2 Ms. copies needed. Report in approximately 3 months.

Payment: 25 offprints.

Permission normally granted authors to reprint articles published.

DUTCH QUARTERLY REVIEW, Dr. M. Buning, PB 7339 Amsterdam, Holland. £22.50; 4 times a year. Founded 1971; sponsored by Dutch Modern Language Association, British Council, Cultural Department American Embassy.

Major fields of interest: The whole field of Anglo-American Letters (including Linguistics). Critical emphasis throughout; scholarship as ancillary discipline, not final.

Manuscript information: Maximum 15 pages, average 11 pages. MLA style sheet. Minimal number of footnotes. 2 copies needed for readers. Report within 3 months.

Payment: None. 2 offprints.

EARLY AMERICAN LITERATURE, Bartlett Hall, University of Massachusetts, Amherst, Massachusetts 01002. $5; 3 times yearly. Founded 1966; sponsored by MLA Early American Literature Group.

Major fields of interest: American literature through the early national period. Literary and intellectual studies and editions preferred.

Manuscript information: No length preference. MLA style sheet; footnotes typed at end of article. Report in 3 months at most.

Payment: None; 10 copies of the article.

Copyrighted.

EDDA: Nordisk Tidsskrift for Litteraturforskning, Universitetsforlaget, Blindern, Oslo 3, Norway. $6; bi-monthly. Founded 1914.

Major fields of interest: Scandinavian and Western literature. Articles in Norwegian, Danish, Swedish, occasionally English, and perhaps once a year an article in German or French. Recent titles: "The Criticism of Ronald S. Crane," "Ibsen's Portrayal of the Artist."

Manuscript information: Report in 2-3 weeks, except during summer.

EDUCATIONAL THEATRE JOURNAL, c/o American Theatre Association, 1317 F. Street, N.W., Washington, D.C. 20004. Journal distributed without charge to members of the University and College Theatre Association. Membership $20. Individual subscriptions for ATA members not in the University and College Theatre Association $9 per year. Library subscriptions $12.50 per year, $23.50 for two years. $31.50 for three years. Single copies $2.50 to ATA members, $3.50 to non-members. Quarterly (March, May, October, December). Founded 1949; sponsored by the American Theatre Association. Editor: Anthony Graham-White, Theatre Department, Southern Methodist University, Dallas, Texas 75275.

Major fields of interest: Scholarship and criticism in the theater arts. All methodologies welcomed. Book and theater reviews.

Manuscript information: Articles may be of varying lengths, from 3000 to 12,000 words. MLA style sheet; footnotes on separate pages. Submit 2 copies (original and Xerox copy satisfactory). Editor acknowledges receipt immediately; report in 8 weeks.

Payment: 5 copies of the issue.

Copyright by the Association (ATA).

EIGHTEENTH-CENTURY STUDIES: AN INTERDISCIPLINARY JOURNAL, Department of English, University of California, Davis, California 95616. $9 for individuals, $12 for institutions; quarterly. Founded 1967; sponsored by the American Society for Eighteenth-Century Studies; published by University of California Press for the University of California, Davis, and the University of Southern California.

Major fields of interest: Eighteenth-century studies. Prefer scholarly essays of any kind that make an original contribution to eighteenth century studies and that are of general interest to specialists in different disciplines.

Manuscript information: Articles limited to 6500 words. MLA style sheet. Report within 4 months.

Payment: 1 copy of issue; 25 gratis offprints; additional offprints available for purchase if ordered before publication.

Copyright by University of California Press.

ÉIRE-IRELAND (a journal of Irish studies), Box 5026, College of St. Thomas, St. Paul, Minnesota 55105. $10; quarterly. Founded 1965; sponsored by the Irish American Cultural Institute. Unsolicited Mss. published, but a query beforehand is helpful.

Major fields of interest: The whole range of Irish civilization: history, literature, archaeology, folklore, music, etc. Expository and critical articles preferred.

Manuscript information: 1000-8000 words, 2500 preferable. MLA style sheet. Report in 5-7 weeks.

Payment: 6 or more complete journals.

Copyright by the journal; permission freely given.

Bibliography occasionally.

ELH, The Johns Hopkins University, Baltimore, Maryland 21218. $12 (institutions), $8 (individuals); quarterly (March, June, September, December). Founded 1933.

Major fields of interest: Critical contributions in English and American literature. Critical articles preferred; explication, source, etc., are suitable insofar as they contribute to critical understanding of major texts.

Manuscript information: No length restrictions within reason. MLA style sheet. One copy needed by readers; report within 30 days.

Payment: 10 offprints, with option to purchase more.

Copyright policy: The JHU press retains copyright.

EMILY DICKINSON BULLETIN, 4508 38th Street, Brentwood, Maryland 20722. $5, $10 if invoiced; semi-annually (June, December). Founded 1968; sponsored by Frederick L. Morey, editor-publisher and national board of eight ED scholars.

Major fields of interest: Dickinson's poetry, research, explication, and her period; Emerson, Higginson, etc. Critical and bibliographical articles, explication of 3 or more poems for comparative study preferred.

Manuscript information: Articles of up to 3000 words, or multiples thereof for instalments. MLA style sheet; footnotes at bottom of page or end of article. Report in 2 weeks.

Payment: 1 copy of the issue, plus any proofs or tearsheets available.

Copyright retained by author.

ENGLISH JOURNAL, P.O. Box 112, East Lansing, Michigan 48823. $12; monthly (except June, July, August). Founded 1911; sponsored by the National Council of Teachers of English.

Major fields of interest: Any aspect of the teaching of English in junior and senior high school or on general topics in the field of English of interest to secondary school teachers. Poems about school, students, teachers, and the teaching of English.

Manuscript information: Manuscripts should be typed double-spaced, not more than 15 typewritten pages. Footnotes should be kept to a minimum; prefer documentation incorporated in text. Include with manuscript a self-addressed envelope with sufficient postage to insure its return. Report within 1 to 3 months.

Payment: None; 6 copies of issue for articles, 4 copies for poems. Offprints may be purchased from printer.

Copyright by NCTE.

ENGLISH LANGUAGE NOTES, Hellems Bldg., University of Colorado, Boulder, Colorado 80302. $7 personal; $12 institution (includes Supplement, *Romantic Movement Bibliography*); quarterly. Founded 1963; sponsored by University of Colorado.

Major fields of interest: All areas in English and American literature and language study. Scholarly rather than critical articles preferred; criticism and explication accepted only when they arise out of historical, biographical, or bibliographical facts.

Manuscript information: No long articles; maximum length 10 double-spaced typewritten pages, minimum less than 1 page. MLA style sheet; footnotes on separate page for setting at bottom of page, or when appropriate in parentheses in text. Report in 1-6 months.

Payment: 2 copies of the issue; offprints by arrangement.

Copyright by ELN.

ENGLISH LITERARY RENAISSANCE, Department of English, University of Massachusetts, Amherst, Massachusetts 01002. $10 (individuals), $15 (libraries); 3 times a year (Spring, Autumn, Winter). Founded 1971; sponsored by Provost of the University of Massachusetts/Amherst.

Major fields of interest: Scholarly essays and studies, and rare texts and Mss. of Tudor and early Stuart England and its literary accomplishment (1485-1668). The journal likes varied approaches to literature and gives equally serious attention to all of them.

Manuscript information: Texts should retain old-spelling, with introduction, tables of variants, and necessary glosses. Essays on rare texts should treat provenance. Ribbon copies of works only (no Xeroxes, no carbons). 10-50 pages in typescript. MLA style sheet. Footnotes on separate pages at the end. One copy needed for readers, but 2 speed up readings. Report usually within 8 weeks, except during the summer and holidays.

Payment: None; 2 complimentary copies of the entire issue (offprints may be bought at cost, however).

Copyright policy: In name of ENGLISH LITERARY RENAISSANCE; we contract for first rights and make arrangements with author for subsequent publications in whole or part.

Bibliographies in each issue. Index and Abstracts published separately and annually.

ENGLISH LITERATURE IN TRANSITION (formerly ENGLISH FICTION IN TRANSITION), Department of English, Arizona State University, Tempe, Arizona 85281. $3 in U.S. (single nos. $1 each), $4 foreign mailing (single nos. $1.50 each); 4 issues yearly. Founded 1957; mainly self-supporting, partially sponsored by English Department, Northern Illinois University.

Major fields of interest: English literature, 1880-1920, articles of all kinds, bibliographies of abstracts of writings about some 100 authors, bibliographies of primary works, manuscript location lists, reviews. Explication de texte generally not used. Inquire about annotated bibliographies on major authors like Conrad, Hardy, and Lawrence, and many minor authors. Articles and bibliographies on dramatists and poets are now especially in demand.

Manuscript information: No special limitations on length of articles. Contributors should consult a copy of ELT for style. Give complete bibliographical data in footnotes; list footnotes at end of article; run quotations of fewer than 10 lines in the text. 2 Ms. copies preferred. Report within 6-8 weeks.

Payment: 2 copies of the issue, offprints of the article at modest fee.

Copyright by the journal; authors are freely granted permission to reprint with usual credit line.

One issue a year has Bibliography, News, and Notes section.

ENGLISH MISCELLANY, Editor Professor Mario Praz, Via Zanardelli 1, 00186 Rome, Italy. Assistant Editor Professor Giorgio Melchiori, Via Capodistria 9, 00198 Rome. Business address: Edizioni di Storia e Litteratura, Via Lanullotti 18, 00186 Rome.

Major fields of interest: English literature, history, art, and music, studied specifically or from an international point of view; the relations between England and the Continent, both of individuals and movements of ideas, are the principal subjects of contributions. Contributions may be either in English, Italian, French, German, or Spanish; English contributors are expected to deal with international aspects and not to write merely critical appraisals of the works of their countrymen. Explications not desired.

Manuscript information: Articles generally do not exceed 20-30 pages (9000-10,000 words), but longer contributions (up to 60 pages) are accepted. Footnotes are printed on the pages to which they belong, with separate numeration for each page; authors of books quoted in small capitals. Report in 1 month.

Articles published in this journal should not appear in book form until two years after initial publication.

THE ENGLISH QUARTERLY, Department of English, University of Waterloo, Waterloo, Ontario, Canada. $10; quarterly by 1971 (1 issue in 1968, 2 in 1969, 3 in 1970). Founded 1968; sponsored by the Canadian Council of Teachers of English.

Major fields of interest: Teaching of English at all levels, kindergarten to Ph.D.; also scholarly articles on literature. Critical or pedogogical articles preferred. Some creative work also published; so far only humorous prose.

Manuscript information: Not more than 4000 words; shorter articles (1200-1500 words) on classroom practices are welcome. MLA style sheet; footnotes as endnotes. 2 copies of Ms. Report in 2-3 months.

Payment: None.

Copyright remains with author.

THE ENGLISH RECORD; Daniel J. Casey, Editor, Department of English, State University of New York, Oneonta, New York 13820. $10 annual subscription, $2 individual copies; issued quarterly. Official publication New York State English Council.

Major interests: Literary criticism, articles on language, communication, rhetoric, and film directed to teachers of English, as well as poetry and fiction.

Manuscript information: Articles run from 1000 to 4000 words, documentation included. No duplicated manuscripts; no simultaneous submissions. Acknowledge immediately; report on rejections within 6 weeks.

Payment: None; 2 complimentary copies of issue in which contribution appears.

ENGLISH STUDIES, c/o Professor Dr. R. Derolez, Rozier 44, 9000 Ghent, Belgium. Dutch guilders 47.50 for 6 issues yearly. Founded 1919; published by Swets & Zeitlinger, B.V., Keizersgracht, 471 & 487, Amsterdam, The Netherlands.

Major fields of interest: The whole field of English language and literature, including American English and American literature. Articles should be well-written, readable, and as concise as possible.

Manuscript information: Articles should be typewritten and conform to the style sheet in Vol. 52 (1971), p. 103 f. (copies may be obtained from the editor). They should not be longer than 8000 words (perferably 3000-6000). Footnotes should be typed on separate sheets. Report within 8 weeks.

Payment: 20 offprints; more at cost.

Requests for permission to reprint should be addressed to the publishers.

ENGLISH STUDIES IN AFRICA: A JOURNAL OF THE HUMANITIES, Witwatersrand University Press, Jan Smuts Avenue, Johannesburg, South Africa. R3.00 for 2 issues per year (March and September). Founded 1957; sponsored by the Universities of South Africa; conducted by an Editorial Board of University teachers of English.

Major fields of interest: English and American language and literature, literary criticism, articles in the humanities of a non-technical nature. Commissioned book reviews and readers' discussions of points arising from previous articles.

Manuscript information: Articles generally should not exceed 5000 words. Manuscripts should be typed on A4 sheets; 2 copies to reach the Publications Officer by 15 May or 15 October of each year. Footnotes should be numbered consecutively and placed at the bottom of each page.

Copyright by Witwatersrand University Press.

Bibliographical issue in the second number of each year.

ENGLISH SYMPOSIUM PAPERS, Douglas H. Shepard, State University College, Fredonia, New York 14063. Free; annual. Founded 1970; sponsored by Department of English, SUC Fredonia.

Major fields of interest: Topic of previous Symposium. Papers included are chosen from those delivered at the English Department's Annual Symposium. No unsolicited Mss.

Manuscript information: Turabian style sheet. Report within 1 month.

Payment: None.

Copyright policy: Secured by editor, released to author on request.

ENLIGHTENMENT ESSAYS, 1126 W. Granville Avenue, Chicago, Illinois 60660. $7.50; quarterly. Founded 1969; sponsored by Private Foundations.

Major fields of interest: Interdisciplinary 18th century ["Enlightenment"].

Manuscript information: 12-30 pages typed. MLA style sheet, 2 copies needed by readers. Report within 60 days maximum (rejection within 30 days). Footnotes discouraged.

Payment: Reviews, $10; articles, none. Offprints: 5 copies.

Copyright policy: Held by *EE*, but given freely to author for reprint.

EPOCH, 245 Goldwin Smith Hall, Cornell University, Ithaca, New York 14850. $3 a volume; 3 times a year. Founded 1947; sponsored by the English Department, Cornell University.

Major fields of interest: Original fiction and poetry, book reviews, notes and speculations. Report within 3 months.

No payment.

Copyright assigned to author on request.

ERASMUS IN ENGLISH, Collected Works of Erasmus, University of Toronto Press, Toronto, Ontario M5S 1A6, Canada. Free; annual, at least, and more often if available material and interest warrant. Founded 1970; sponsored by University of Toronto Press, with assistance of the Killam Awards Programme of the Canada Council.

Major fields of interest: The aim of the ERASMUS IN ENGLISH is to serve as a clearing-house for information about Erasmian studies, especially in the English-speaking world, and to publish papers, reviews, and the like that are of related interest. Articles related to Erasmus and his time.

Manuscript information: Articles of shorter or medium length. MLA style sheet or Chicago Manual of Style; 2 copies needed by readers. Report within a few weeks.

Payment: 6 complimentary copies of the issue in which article appears.

Copyright by University of Toronto Press.

Bibliographical section in each issue.

ESQ, A Journal of the American Renaissance, English Department, Washington State University, Pullman, Washington 99163. $10 for 4 issues. Founded 1955 by The Emerson Society.

Major fields of interest: American 19th-century literature; general Romanticism, and American Transcendentalism. All types of articles within the field are printed.

Manuscript information: Articles may be of any length; MLA style sheet. Documentation important. 2 copies needed. Report within 2-4 months.

ESSAYS IN CRITICISM, c/o Stephen Wall, Keble College, Oxford, England. $9 or £3; quarterly. Founded 1951.

Major fields of interest: Literary criticism with basis in scholarship; emphasis is on English and continental literatures rather than on American. Preference is given to articles arising from earlier discussions in journal. Long "Critical Forum" (letters to editor) in each issue.

Manuscript information: Articles of 4000-5000 words preferred; no objection to MLA style. Most footnotes are to be incorporated in the text. Report in 2-3 weeks.

Payment: Payment for commissioned articles; 12 offprints provided without payment; more may be specially ordered.

ESSAYS IN LITERATURE, Department of English, Western Illinois University, Macomb, Illinois 61455. $3 yearly, $8 for three years; $4 for institutions; semi-annually. Founded 1973; sponsored by Departnent of English and Department of Foreign Languages and Literatures, Western Illinois University.

Major fields of interest: Literature in the British and American traditions and the modern European languages. The Editors welcome studies concerning any literary period, figure, genre, or work. Book reviews are not published.

Manuscript information: All contributions must be written in English, and all material quoted in a foreign language must be accompanied by a translation in the text of the paper. 2000 to 8000 words (five to twenty printed pages) preferred. MLA style sheet with footnotes at end of text. Report generally in 2 to 3 months.

Payment: 3 copies of journal (offprints may be ordered).

All articles copyrighted by journal.

ESSAYS IN LITERATURE, University of Denver, Denver, Colorado 80210. $5; quarterly. Founded 1972; sponsored by Graduate Student Association, University of Denver.

Major fields of interest: Critical studies of English and American literature. Journal designed for graduate students, edited exclusively by graduate students, and distributed to over 35 countries.

Manuscript information: 10-20 pages, but flexible. MLA style sheet. Report within from 2 weeks to 2 months.

Payment: 3 copies of journal.

Not copyrighted.

ESSEX INSTITUTE HISTORICAL COLLECTIONS, 132 Essex Street, Salem, Massachusetts 01970. $10; quarterly. Founded 1859; sponsored by the Essex Institute.

Major fields of interest: Colonial history; all aspects of history pertaining to Essex County, Massachusetts. Prefer biographical articles and source studies.

Manuscript information: MLA style sheet. Report time variable, depending on readers.

Payment: None; 20 offprints, 5 copies of the journal.

Copyright by the journal; author always consulted for permission to reprint.

ETC.: A REVIEW OF GENERAL SEMANTICS, International Societ
for General Semantics, P.O. Box 2469, San Francisco, California 9412(
$6; quarterly. Founded 1943.

Major fields of interest: Semantics; general semantics; the rela
tion of language and thought to human behavior. Because of its sub
ject matter, ETC. is interdisciplinary. Its literary articles assum
acquaintance with (or at least sympathy with) the social sciences
its social articles are concerned with humanistic implications. A
kinds of articles are welcome: practical, theoretical, reports of scien
tific experiment, essays, satire, verse, book reviews, and discussion:

Manuscript information: Short contributions and long article
are used. An entire issue (40,000 words) would be devoted to a sing!
monograph if a suitable one turned up. Style according to the Amer
can Psychological Association Publications Manual. 2 copies of th
Ms. are preferred, but not mandatory. Use as few footnotes as po
sible. Report in 1 to 3 months.

Payment: 10 complimentary copies.

Contents copyrighted by the International Society for General S
mantics, solely for protection of contributor, who may on reque:
use the material again in any way he pleases without charge.

ÉTUDES ANGLAISES, L. Bonnerot, Professor à la Sorbonne, 12
avenue du G^R de Gaulle 92170, Vanves, France. 50 fr.; quarterl

Major fields of interest: English and American literature; som
comparative studies. Articles in either English or French.

Manuscript information: Length of articles varies, but general!
12-15 printed pages is typical. Shorter pieces used in the Notes an
Documents section. Report within 2 months. Mss. not accepted a
not returned.

ÉTUDES LITTÉRAIRES, Presses de L'Université Laval, C.P. 244
Québec 2, Canada G1K 7R4. $6; 3 issues yearly. Founded 1968; spo
sored by Faculté des Lettres, Université Laval.

Major fields of interest: Mainly French literature and its relatio
ship with other literatures; literary criticism and esthetics (eac
issue devoted to one major subject). Critical articles, and occasio
ally articles dealing with literary history, preferred. Journal contai
3 sections: articles, documents, and book reviews.

Manuscript information: About 15 pages. See the journal's "proto-cole de rédaction" for style. Report in 1-2 months.
Payment: $2 per page or 50 offprints.

EVELYN WAUGH NEWSLETTER, c/o English Department, Nassau Community College, State University of New York, Garden City, New York 11530. $2.50; 3 times yearly (Spring, Autumn, and Winter). Founded 1967; sponsored by Dr. Paul A. Doyle.

Major fields of interest: Any material related to any aspect of the life and literary works of Evelyn Waugh, influences, associations, etc. Creative work accepted, if related to Waugh's life or work.

Manuscript information: 200-800 words. MLA style sheet; footnotes incorporated in text. Report in 2 weeks.

Payment: None; 3 offprints.

No copyright.

Bibliography in Spring number.

EVERGREEN REVIEW, 53 E. 11 Street, New York, New York 10003. $5; quarterly. Founded 1957; sponsored by Grove Press, Inc.

Major fields of interest: No restrictions. Creative non-scholarly material a major interest.

Manuscript information: Length of article varies; no preference about style sheet. Footnotes may be placed at the bottom of each page or at the end of the article. Length of time for report varies.

Payment: $20 per printed page.

Copyright by Grove Press, Inc.

EXERCISE EXCHANGE: A Journal for Teachers of English in High Schools and Colleges, c/o Department of English, University of Vermont, Burlington, Vermont 05401. Published twice a year.

Major field of interest: The exchange of classroom ideas among teachers of English. Actual examples of teaching exercises used. In addition to language, literature, and writing, acceptable topics include film and other non-print media, creative drama, and inter-disciplinary approaches. Explications *per se* are not desired. Contributors should indicate the class level and courses for which their methods are most appropriate: high school, junior college, and college.

Manuscript information: Articles may range in length from 1 to 15 pages; Illustrations may be used. MLA style sheet; eliminate foot- notes. Report usually within 4 to 6 weeks.

Payment: 2 copies of the issue on publication.

THE EXPLICATOR, Virginia Commonwealth University, Richmond, Virginia 23220. $3.00 USA, $3.50 foreign; monthly (September through June). Founded 1942; partially sponsored by Virginia Commonwealth University.

Major field of interest: Exclusively explication de texte.

Manuscript information: Maximum of 100 typed lines (average of 70 characters to the typed line); shorter articles preferred. No foot- notes — incorporate in the body of the article. Report in 6-8 months.

Payment: 10 copies; additional copies to contributors at special rates of 15¢ each.

Copyright by the magazine.

Bibliographical issue in June.

EXTRAPOLATION: A Journal of Science Fiction and Fantasy, The College of Wooster, Box N3186, Wooster, Ohio 44691. $3, $7.50 for 3 years; twice yearly (December and May). Founded 1959; sponsored by MLA Conference on Science Fiction and the Science Fiction Re- search Association, Inc.

Major fields of interest: Any kind of study relating to fantasy or science fiction: bibliographical, historical, critical, world literature; problems and achievements in teaching the subject.

Manuscript information: 1000-5000 words. MLA style sheet; foot- notes printed at end of article if they occur with frequency, simple pagination of a text noted in body of article. 2 copies of Ms. prefer- able. Report in 4-6 weeks.

Payment: None; 2-6 offprints.

Copyright by journal; no charge for reprint rights.

THE FALCON, Mansfield State College, Mansfield, Pennsylvania 16937. $2; twice yearly (Spring and Winter). Founded 1970; spon- sored by Mansfield State College.

Major fields of interest: Contemporary poetry and fiction. Inter- views, book reviews; creative non-scholarly material also published.

Manuscript information: 1500-3000 words; report within 30-60 days.
Payment: 3 copies.
Copyright policy: All issues copyrighted.

FAR-WESTERN FORUM, A Review of Ancient and Modern Letters, Professor Elie R. Vidal, 20 Poppy Lane, Berkeley, California 94708. $6 per year, $2.25 per issue; 3 times a year (Feb., June, Nov.). Founded 1973; sponsored by an independent group of academicians.

Major fields of interest: Literary criticism about all literatures and genres; scholarship. Book reviews (solicited and on request — decision by Editor). Literature, literature and philosophy, literature and art, literature and religion, literature and etc. — no restrictions so long as the study deals with literature. Critical articles, explication de texte, interpretation, literary criticism, review-articles preferred. Comparative studies in literature. Also publishes some creative non-scholarly material, but to a lesser extent.

Manuscript information: MLA style sheet. Text in English or foreign languages. 12 to 35 typewritten pages (double spacing); 2 copies needed by readers. Least possible footnotes. Report in 25-30 days.

Payment: Some payment; 15 offprints.

Copyright policy: At the convenience of authors and FWF, and by agreement between authors and FWF.

FAULKNER CONCORDANCE NEWSLETTER, R. H. Moore, Editor, English Department, University of Maryland, College Park, MD 20742. Free; occasional publication. Founded 1972; sponsored by Department of English Language and Literature, University of Maryland.

Major fields of interest: Faulkner studies. Do not desire unsolicited manuscripts.

FEMINIST STUDIES, 417 Riverside Drive, New York, New York 10025. $10 (institutions), $6 (individuals); 3 times a year. Founded 1972; no sponsor: "independent of any group or institution."

Major fields of interest: Interdisciplinary — "The journal was founded to encourage analytic responses to feminist issues and analyses that open new areas of feminist research and critique." Prefer critical articles: original essays, studies, book reviews, notes, exchanges/responses to articles previously published. Occasionally publishes creative non-scholarly work also.

Manuscript information: Chicago style sheet; 2 copies needed by readers. Report within 3-4 weeks.

Payment: None.

Copyright held by FEMINIST STUDIES.

FIELD, Rice Hall, Oberlin College, Oberlin, Ohio 44074. $3; twice yearly. Founded 1969; sponsored by Oberlin College.

Major fields of interest: Contemporary poetry and poetics only. Critical articles preferred.

Manuscript information: Articles may be from 12-20 pages. MLA style sheet. Report in 4 weeks.

Payment: $10 per printed page; 2 offprints.

Copyrighted.

FILM CRITIC, 333 Avenue of the Americas, New York, New York 10014. $5; bi-monthly. Founded 1972 (previous title — since 1965 — FILM SOCIETY REVIEW); sponsored by American Federation of Film Societies.

Major fields of interest: Social, political and media (film and TV) criticism. Emphasis on substantive issues and ideas. Prefer social-context film criticism. Also publishes creative non-scholarly work.

Manuscript information: 500-5000 words. Standard style sheet. Report immediately.

Payment: Penny-a-word *minimum*. Offprints: "Authors' copies."

Copyright policy: All rights remain with the author.

"For efficient submission, contributors should be familiar with FILM CRITIC and its predecessor, FILM SOCIETY REVIEW, preferably from the beginning of the 1970's."

FILM HERITAGE, College of Liberal Arts, Wright State University, Dayton, Ohio 45431. $2; quarterly. Founded 1965; sponsored by Wright State University and donors.

Major fields of interest: Film. Critical articles preferred — no reviews. An occasional poem or drawing is used.

Manuscript information: Articles of about 10 pages preferred. Length of time for editorial decision: 6-8 weeks.

Payment: Copies for unsolicited Mss.

FILM HERITAGE generally reserves rights.

FILM QUARTERLY, University of California Press, Berkeley, California 94720. $5; quarterly. Founded 1945. Unsolicited Mss. desired, but queries are welcome.

Major fields of interest: Film criticism, history, theory; gossip and personality material not accepted. Type of material preferred: retrospective articles on directors, survey articles on film trends and new developments, and articles on artistic issues posed by films. Desire material in any field from scholars "who have something to say about film; however, . . . standards are such that familiarity with film literature is important for aspiring contributors."

Manuscript information: Articles should be "as long as needed, but as short as possible." No preferred style sheet; spelling follows Webster III. Footnotes at foot of page if sparse, otherwise at end of article. Report in 1-10 weeks.

Payment: About 1.5¢ per word, upon publication; 2 copies of the issue.

Copyright by publisher; no subsidiary use permitted without author's consent.

FILMS IN REVIEW, 210 East 68th Street, New York, New York 10021. $7; monthly (bi-monthly in June-July and August-September). Founded 1950; sponsored by the National Board of Review of Motion Pictures, Inc.

Major fields of interest: *All* aspects of the motion picture, including its television ones. Factual, critical, historical, esthetic, philosophical articles accepted. Creative work also published.

Manuscript information: Articles from 2500-10,000 words; *only* footnotes which amplify a point in the text used, *not* bibliographical ones. Report in 2-3 weeks.

Payment: None; "a reasonable number of copies of the issue will be given."

Copyright retained by the author.

FITZGERALD/HEMINGWAY ANNUAL, c/o M. J. Bruccoli, Department of English, University of South Carolina, Columbia, South Carolina 29208. Articles on Hemingway may be sent to the Associate Editor: C. E. F. Clark, Jr., 1490 Sodon Lake Dr., Bloomfield Hills, Michigan. $15; annually. Founded 1969; published by Microcard Editions.

Major fields of interest: F. Scott Fitzgerald, Ernest Hemingway, and circle.

Manuscript information: No length restrictions. MLA style sheet; footnotes should be placed at end of article. Report within 2 weeks.

Payment: 50 offprints.

Copyright is negotiable.

THE FLANNERY O'CONNOR BULLETIN, Box 608, Georgia College, Milledgeville, Georgia 31061. $2; yearly. Founded 1972; sponsored by Georgia College.

Major fields of interest: Thought and fiction and essays of Flannery O'Connor. Prefer critical, biographical, explication de texte, source studies, etc.

Manuscript information: 8-15 pages. Chicago style sheet. Report within brief period of time.

Payment: None. Offprints: 10 copies.

Copyright policy: "Will return to writer for his own needs."

THE FLORIDA QUARTERLY, 336 Reitz Union, University of Florida, Gainesville, Florida 32601. $3, $8 for 3 years; 3 times yearly. Founded 1966; sponsored by English Department and Alumni Association, University of Florida.

Major fields of interest: Original contemporary poetry, fiction, art and reviews preferred; emphasis is on non-critical contemporary work. This is a magazine of the creative arts rather than a scholarly review, although some critical Mss. are published.

Manuscript information: Not more than 40 typewritten pages. Report in 4 weeks.

Payment: None; journal rates reduced to 75¢ per author copy.

Copyright by the journal; permission necessary for any kind of reproduction.

FOCUS ON ROBERT GRAVES, University of Colorado Library, Boulder, Colorado 80302. Free; once or twice a year. Founded 1972; sponsored by University of Colorado Library.

Major fields of interest: Critical, bibliographical, biographical information relating to Robert Graves.

Manuscript information: Any standard style sheet. Report within 1 month.

Payment: 20 offprints.

Copyright policy: Copyright by University of Colorado Library.

FOLKLORE, University College, Gower Street, London W.C.1, England. £3.15; quarterly. Founded 1890; published by The Folklore Society.

Major fields of interest: Folklore in all its aspects, both records of actual customs and beliefs and theories concerning the root causes of these; folklore from all over the world.

Manuscript information: Articles of 1000-8000 words preferred. Typed and numbered pages, either quarto or foolscap; footnotes should be numbered consecutively. Report usually in 2-3 weeks.

Payment: 20 offprints.

Bibliographical works are published separately, as required, by the Society.

FOLKLORE FORUM, 504 N. Fess, Bloomington, Indiana 47401. $4; 4 issues yearly (Bibliographic and Special Series). Founded 1968; sponsored by graduate students at Indiana University Folklore Institute.

Major fields of interest: Folklore, popular culture and related aspects of anthropology, ethnology, sociology, literature, etc. Longer articles should deal with folklore theory and methodology; short articles (under 1800 words), notes, or queries may deal with any subject in the field. Book, film, and record reviews also published; unsolicited reviews *will* be considered, but query first.

Manuscript information: Articles of 1000 to 5000 words. MLA style sheet. Report in 3-6 weeks.

Payment: None; 3 copies of the issue.

No copyright at present.

Bibliographic issues appear irregularly as selected numbers of the Special Series.

FORUM, University of Houston, 3801 Cullen Boulevard, Houston, Texas 77004. $1 per issue; 3 times yearly. Founded 1956; sponsored by the University of Houston.

Major fields of interest: The humanities, the fine arts, and the sciences. "We also welcome articles bearing on business and technology." Customarily an art section in the magazine is devoted to photographs, variously, of paintings.

Manuscript information: Articles should be from 12 to 20 typewritten pages. University of Chicago style manual. Report usually within a month.

Payment: Up to 50 reprints; more if there is a special need.

Copyright assigned to the writer as desired.

FORUM ITALICUM (Quarterly of Italian Studies), 221 Crosby Hall, State University of New York at Buffalo, Buffalo, New York 14214. $4; quarterly (March, June, September, December). Founded 1967; sponsored by the Faculty of Arts & Letters, State University of New York at Buffalo.

Major fields of interest: Italian literature and literatures connected with Italian. Critical, structural comparative linguistics articles preferred. Poetry, fiction, and translations also published.

Manuscript information: Prefer short articles. MLA style sheet. Report in less than 1 month generally.

Payment: None. 5 copies of the journal.

Copyrighted.

Four Quarters, La Salle College, Philadelphia, Pennsylvania 19141. $3; quarterly. Founded 1951; sponsored by La Salle College faculty.

Major fields of interest: Short story, familiar essay, poetry, literary criticism.

Manuscript information: Articles of 2000-5000 words preferred. MLA style sheet; 6 weeks for report.

Payment: $25 on publication for stories and articles; $5.00 for poems.

THE FREDERIC HERALD, Editor, Thomas F. O'Donnell, English Department, SUC, Brockport, New York 14420. Free; 3 times yearly (April, September, January). Founded 1967.

Major fields of interest: Harold Frederic: biographical, critical, & bibliographical articles.

Manuscript information. No minimum length, maximum 500 words. See copies of the journal for style; footnote material handled according to the editor's judgment. Report almost immediately.

Payment: 5 or more copies on request.

FREE LANCE, A Magazine of Poetry and Prose, 6005 Grand Avenue, Cleveland, Ohio 44104. $1; semi-annually. Founded 1952; sponsored by Free Lance Poets, Prose Workshop.

Major fields of interest: Music, art (articles only), poetry, short stories, literary studies; theory (technical mechanics explained) of the above fields. Critical and psychological articles preferred.

Manuscript information: Articles may be up to 5000 words. No style sheet; each issue strives for different effect. Footnotes should be placed immediately below the line referred to. Reports are slow, usually within 4 months; query if longer.

Payment: 2 copies.

Copyright optional.

FRENCH STUDIES, Taylor Institution, Oxford OX1 3NA, England. Since January 1961 the organ of the Society for French Studies; subscription for members £3.50; for non-members £4.50 (or $10.80); quarterly.

Major fields of interest: French, chiefly literature and language, but not excluding occasional articles dealing with history, art, or other manifestations of French culture. Comparative studies sometimes used. Articles must be written in either French or English.

Manuscript information: 10 to 12 printed pages. Footnotes should be grouped at the end of the article. Report time varies.

Payment: 30 copies of each article; 12 copies of each review.

Permission to reproduce is required, whether in whole or in part.

FRESHMAN ENGLISH NEWS, Professor Gary Tate, Department of English, Texas Christian University, Fort Worth, Texas 76109. $2; 3 times a year. Founded 1972.

Major fields of interest: News and articles about freshman English in both 2-year and 4-year colleges. Book reviews and review articles. Interested in the teaching of freshman English, programs, writing labs, advanced placement, experimental courses and methods, etc.

Manuscript information: News items no more than 8 double-spaced typed pages. No articles normally accepted. Footnotes on separate page. Report within 1 month.

Payment: 5 copies of issue.

No copyright.

FURMAN STUDIES, Furman University, Greenville, South Carolina 29613. Free on request; published twice a year as part of the quarterly THE BULLETIN OF FURMAN UNIVERSITY. Certain issues now given over to THE SOUTH CAROLINA REVIEW. Founded 1928; sponsored by Furman University. Contributors normally members of the faculty, former members of faculty, or alumni; guest contributors only rarely.

Major fields of interest: Interdisciplinary; publishes articles in all fields of English and American literature, as well as in all fields in all other disciplines.

Manuscript information: Articles should not be over 15 typewritten pages. Chicago style manual for English studies; styles normally acceptable in other disciplines.

Each author may copyright his own article if he wishes.

[See also THE SOUTH CAROLINA REVIEW.]

GENERAL LINGUISTICS, published by the Pennsylvania State University Press, University Park, Pennslyvania 16802. $12.50; quarterly. Founded 1955.

Major fields of interest: linguistics, sociolinguistics, anthropological linguistics.

Manuscript information: Articles, notes, and review articles considered. LSA style sheet. Footnotes kept to a minimum and placed at the end of the article. Time for report usually 6 months maximum.

Payment: 25 offprints free.

Y GENHINEN, J.D.Lewis and Sons Ltd., Gomerian Press, Llandyssul, Cards., Wales. 11/4; quarterly. Founded 1950; sponsored by the publishers. Unsolicited Mss. not desired.

Major fields of interest: Critical and biographical articles on Welsh literature in any period. Also creative material used.

Manuscript information: Articles should be about 2000-3000 words in length. Footnotes should be placed at the end of the article. Report in about 3 months.

Author may copyright.

GENRE, Department of English, SUNY, Plattsburgh, N.Y. 12901. $5 (individuals, USA and Canada), $6 (libraries), $7 (foreign — all subscriptions); quarterly. Founded 1968; sponsored by the University of Illinois at Chicago Circle.

Major fields of interest: All works of literature. Critical articles from a genre point of view and theoretical articles defining genres preferred.

Manuscript information: Length is not important; no notes published. MLA style sheet; footnotes at the end of the article. 2 copies of Ms. Report in 2 months.

Payment: None; 8 copies of the issue.

Copyright: Must request reprint rights from the editors.

THE GEORGIA REVIEW, University of Georgia, Athens, Georgia 30602. $3; quarterly; sponsored by the University of Georgia.

Major fields of interest: 19th and 20th century literature; literary criticism; history of ideas. Prefers articles appealing to the intelligent general reader, which are not too specialized. Stories, poems and book reviews are also used.

Manuscript information: Articles of not more than 8000 words preferred. MLA style sheet. Footnotes avoided. Report in 3 to 4 weeks.

Payment: 1¢ a word for prose; 50¢ a line for poetry.

Permission to reprint must be obtained from the magazine.

GERMANIC REVIEW, 319 Hamilton Hall, Columbia University, New York, New York 10027. $7.50; quarterly. Founded 1926; sponsored by Columbia University.

Major fields of interest: German literature, linguistics, criticism. Literature of other Germanic languages except English. Does not publish translations or original literature or studies of German society.

Manuscript information: Articles of 5000-7000 words preferred, but not strictly adhered to. MLA style sheet. Footnotes are at the foot of the page, numbered consecutively in the Journal, but Ms. should have footnotes on separate sheets. Report in 4-8 weeks.

Payment: 10 free copies; offprints at cost.

Copyright remains with magazine.

THE GISSING NEWSLETTER, 10 rue Gày-Lussac, 59110 La Madeleine, France. £1 for individuals, £1.50 for libraries; quarterly. Founded 1965.

Major fields of interest: George Gissing, his life and works. Interested in critical, biographical, bibliographical, topographical articles concerning Gissing.

Manuscript information: Prefer articles of 1000 to 5000 words. MLA style; footnotes should be kept to a minimum and will be printed at the end of the article. Report in 2 weeks.

Not copyrighted.

Note: All correspondence concerning subscriptions, back numbers, etc., should be sent to C. C. Kohler, 141 High Street, Dorking, Surrey, RH4 1AQ, England.

GLOSSA — AN INTERNATIONAL JOURNAL OF LINGUISTICS, Simon Fraser University, Burnaby 2, B.C., Canada. $6; 2 issues a year. Founded 1967; sponsored by the Glossa Society.

Major field of interest: Contemporary linguistics. GLOSSA is the major international publication in Canada for scholarly contributions to general linguistics, linguistic theory, interdisciplinary relationships such as psycholinguistics, sociolinguistics, mathematical linguistics, anthropological linguistics, language description.

Manuscript information: No restrictions on length. LSA style sheet; footnotes on separate sheet in Ms., abstract required. Report in 1-3 months maximum.

Payment: 25 offprints of articles, notes, reviews.

Copyrighted.

GREEN RIVER REVIEW, Box 812, Owensboro, Kentucky 42301. $2.50; semi-annually. Founded 1968.

Major fields of interest: Short stories, poems, essays. Scholarly footnoted articles are not published.

Manuscript information: Stories of 3000-4000 words. Report in 2 months.

Copyright by publisher.

THE GYPSY SCHOLAR, A Graduate Forum for Literary Criticism, Department of English, Michigan State University, East Lansing, Michigan 48823. $5, 1 year; $8, 2 years; 3 times a year. Founded 1973.

Major fields of interest: Speculative, venturesome, inquiring, and controversial approaches to literature, language and pedagogy. Contributions limited to graduate students.

Manuscript information: 2500-4000 words. MLA style sheet preferred. 2 copies needed by readers. Report within 4 weeks. Endnotes, but sparingly.

Payment: None; 2 copies of entire issue.

Copyright policy: Each issue copyrighted. Rights revert to author.

HARPER'S MAGAZINE, 2 Park Ave., New York, N.Y. 10016. $8.50; monthly. Founded 1850; owned by the Minneapolis Star and Tribune Company.

Major fields of interest; Broad range of interests — politics, art, foreign affairs, literature, youth, social change, personal opinion, etc. Articles, fiction, verse, photos.

Manuscript information: Articles vary in length from 2000 to 5000 words. Report within 3 weeks, but longer time required if editors are really interested. Welcomes queries about proposed articles.

Payment: Rates vary; average piece about $400.

Copyrighted: North American Serial rights; will transfer copyright to author upon request.

HARTFORD STUDIES IN LITERATURE, University of Hartford, West Hartford, Connecticut 06117. $4.50 to individuals, $6 to institutions, 10% additional for foreign; 3 times yearly. Founded 1968; sponsored by the University of Hartford.

Major fields of interest: Literary criticism as informed by any other discipline: e.g. depth psychology, social science, natural science, philosophy.

Manuscript information: 5-10 printed pages. MLA style sheet; footnotes at the end of the article, may be printed at foot of page. 3 copies of Ms. Report in at least 90 days.

Payment: None; offprints at cost.

Copyright by University of Hartford.

HARVARD LIBRARY BULLETIN, 505 Lamont Library, Cambridge, Massachusetts 02138. $15; quarterly. Founded 1947; sponsored by Harvard University Library.

Major fields of interest: "Articles related to collections of the Harvard University Library or based, at least in part, on research in its collections, which cover essentially all fields of knowledge."

Manuscript information: Articles of 10-30 typewritten pages preferred. MLA style; footnotes should be typed on separate sheets at end of Ms. Report in 2-3 weeks.

Payment: 50 offprints.

Copyright by University; permission to reprint given when authorized or requested by author.

HARVARD THEOLOGICAL REVIEW, Harvard Divinity School, Cambridge, Massachusetts 02138. $8; quarterly (January, April, July, October). Founded 1907; sponsored by Harvard Divinity School.

Major fields of interest: Theology, church history, Bibical studies, ethics, philosophy of religion, and cognate subjects. Recent titles: "The Universal Perspective and Moral Development" and "Acrostics and Metrics in Hebrew Poetry."

Manuscript information: No restrictions on length — short notes to long articles; monographs published as supplements. Footnotes should be placed at the end of article. Report within 8-12 weeks.

Payment: 50 offprints.

Copyright by the President and Fellows of Harvard University; permission to reprint usually given upon request.

HAWTHORNE JOURNAL, Editor, Matthew J. Bruccoli, Department of English, University of South Carolina, Columbia, South Carolina 29208. Approx. $15; yearly. Founded 1971.

Major fields of interest: Nathaniel Hawthorne.

Manuscript information: Contact editor for further information.

THE HEBREW UNIVERSITY STUDIES IN LITERATURE, Dr. A. Serper, Editor, The Institute of Languages and Literatures, The Hebrew University, Jerusalem, Israel. $5; 2 times a year. Founded 1972; sponsored by The Hebrew University.

Major fields of interest: Literature of all nations and periods, either individually or as they are related. Comparative literature and literary theory. Articles in English and French. Book reviews.

Manuscript information: MLA style sheet. Footnotes at end of manuscript. Report in 2 months.

Payment: None.

Copyright by The Hebrew University.

HEMINGWAY NOTES, Dickinson College, Carlisle, Pennsylvania 17013. $3/year; $5/2 years; twice a year (Spring and Fall). Founded 1971; sponsored by Department of English, Dickinson College.

Major fields of interest: Works and life of Ernest Hemingway. Critical, biographical, *explication de texte*, source study, etc.

Manuscript information: MLA style sheet. Report within 3 months. Footnotes at end of article.

Payment: None. 3 offprints.

Copyright policy: HEMINGWAY NOTES retains copyright, but will re-assign on author's request.

Current bibliography on Hemingway every issue.

HERMATHENA, A Dublin University Review, Trinity College, Dublin 2, Ireland. Annual subscription £3 ($7.50); twice yearly (spring and autumn). Founded 1873; published by Hodges, Figgis (Dublin), The Academic Press (London). Publication of articles and reviews restricted to members, including graduates, of Dublin University.

Major fields of interest: The humanities, including the history and philosophy of science.

Manuscript information: Report within 6-9 months.

Payment: 25 offprints and 1 copy of the journal.

HIGGINSON JOURNAL OF POETRY, 4508 38th St., Brentwood, Maryland 20722. $5 if cash, $10 if invoiced; semi-annual. Founded 1971; sponsored by Higginson Press Enterprises, Frederick Morey, editor-publisher.

Major fields of interest: Interests of Col. T. W. Higginson: women poets, esp. Emily Dickinson, social reform, black studies, prosody, contemporary poets, feminism. Popular level of Emily Dickinson; anything pertaining to Col. Higginson and his circle. Also publishes creative non-scholarly material.

Manuscript information: 1000 to 4000 words (3-10 pages). MLA style sheet with endnotes. Report within 2 weeks average; no acknowledgement of receipt.

Payment: None; 1 copy to contributor.

Copyright policy: Usually not copyrighted, unless there is a major scholarly article.

HISPANIC REVIEW, Williams Hall, University of Pennsylvania, Philadelphia, Pennsylvania 19104. $9.50; quarterly. Founded 1933; sponsored by the Department of Romance Languages, University of Pennsylvania.

Major fields of interest: Spanish. Articles on Spanish influences in English and American Literature occasionally published. Articles which are chapters of a forthcoming book are not used.

Manuscript information: Articles of 15-25 pages preferred; MLA style sheet; footnotes should be placed on a separate sheet after the article and double-spaced. Report in 1-4 weeks.

Payment: 15 offprints for articles; 10 for reviews.

THE HOLLINS CRITIC, Box 9538, Hollins College, Virginia 24020. $2; 5 issues yearly. Founded 1964; sponsored by Hollins College. All essays contracted for in advance.

Major fields of interest: Critical essays, written by contributing editors, on current writers and poets.

HOPKINS RESEARCH BULLETIN, 114 Mount St., London, England W1Y 6AH. £2 or $6; annually. Founded 1969-70.

Major fields of interest: G. M. Hopkins and his circle (Bridges, Dixon, Patmore). Unpublished Hopkins material; bibliographical entries; information on new studies; details of 'research in progress'; items of interest. No unsolicited manuscripts. Hopkins Society Publications are restricted to members only. Members receive annually 3 publications: annual lecture, annual sermon, HOPKINS RESEARCH BULLETIN.

Manuscript information: MLA style sheet. Report within 3 months.
Copyright policy: Copyright belongs to the editor.
Each issue contains an annual bibliography.

HORIZON: A Magazine of the Arts, 1221 Ave. of the Americas, New York, New York 10020. $20 for 4 issues. Founded 1958. Published by American Heritage Publishing Co., Inc. A Subsidiary of McGraw-Hill, Inc.

Major fields of interest: Social and cultural history, the arts. Articles should be written for the general intelligent reader.

Manuscript information: Articles of 2000-5000 words. No official style sheet; MLA style could be used. Footnotes are not used. Report in a month.

Payment: $300-$700; no offprints.

Copyright will be reassigned if the author wishes it.

THE HUDSON REVIEW, 65 East 55th Street, New York, New York 10022. $8; quarterly (April, July, October, January). Founded 1948.

Major fields of interest: Broadly the area called the humanities. The material published includes poetry, fiction, and essays (by eminent contemporaries as well as young writers); literary criticism; reviews of music, art, theater, film, and dance; reports from foreign countries; book reviews.

Manuscript information: Articles of 5000-10,000 words preferred. University of Chicago style manual. Excessively footnoted material is discouraged. Report in 1-2 months.

Payment: 2½¢ per word for prose. Offprints must be paid for by the author.

Copyright by The Hudson Review, Inc.

HUMANITIES ASSOCIATION REVIEW, c/o P. W. Rogers, John Watson Hall, Queen's University, Kingston, Ontario, Canada. $3; quarterly. Founded 1950; sponsored by the Humanities Association of Canada.

Major fields of interest: Articles of broad interest in all branches of the humanities. Some creative non-scholarly material also published.

Manuscript information: MLA style sheet; footnotes should be collected at the end of the article.

Payment: 25 offprints.

THE HUNTINGTON LIBRARY QUARTERLY, Henry E. Huntington Library and Art Gallery, San Marino, California 91108. $7.50 for 4 issues. Founded 1937; sponsored by the Huntington Library.

Major fields of interest: History and interpretation of English and American civilization, i.e., history and literature, with special attention to the research fields of Huntington Library collections. The main collections of the Library, spanning the twelfth to the twentieth centuries, are concerned with the literature and political, economic, and social history of Great Britain and North America. Illustrated.

Manuscript information: Articles should be under 35 pages. MLA style sheet. Footnotes should be numbered consecutively throughout article, double-spaced on separate sheets at the end of the article. Report within 6 weeks.

Payment: 1 copy of the issue and 25 complimentary offprints.

Copyright by The Huntington Library.

ILLINOIS ENGLISH BULLETIN, c/o Donald Nemanich, 100 English Building, Urbana, Illinois 61801. $5; monthly (October through May). Founded 1907; sponsored by the Illinois Association of Teachers of English.

Major fields of interest: Materials on the teaching of English, with specific reference to the secondary level. Articles with particular appeal for Illinois teachers are favored.

Manuscript information: Articles should range from 2500-4000 words in length. Footnotes should be held to a minimum and should be brief. Report within 6 weeks.

Payment: 5 offprints; more if requested in advance.

Ordinarily no copyright.

ILLINOIS QUARTERLY, Illinois State University, Normal, Illinois 61761. Free; quarterly (Sept., Dec., Feb., April). Founded 1938; sponsored by Illinois State University.

Major fields of interest: Broad disciplinary approach, literature, social sciences, education, humanities, etc. Some poetry. Scholarly studies but sufficiently broad to be interesting and valuable to nonspecialists in the field; material written basically for the specialist generally is rejected as too narrow.

Manuscript information: Articles should be under 20 pages, double spaced, including footnotes; 10-12 pages best. MLA style sheet; 2 copies needed by readers. Report within 8 weeks. Footnotes at end of article.

Payment: 8-10 copies of issue for articles, 5 for poetry.

Copyright policy: Copyright held by Illinois State University; reprint rights given with permission of author.

THE INDEPENDENT SHAVIAN, Journal of New York Shavians, Incorporated, 14 Washington Place, Apt. 5E, New York, N.Y. 10003. Mrs. Vera Scriabine, Editor; Joseph M. Ricciardi, Assistant Editor. Dues: $10 for persons living within 50 miles of Manhattan; $5 for others in U.S.A. and $3.50 for persons outside U.S.A.; library subscriptions: $3 for U.S.A., $3.10 for Canada and Mexico, and $3.50 elsewhere; for individuals subscription included with membership; 3 issues a year.

Major fields of interest: Critical and biographical studies of Bernard Shaw, his circle, and related materials, including book and theater reviews.

Manuscript information: Maximum length 2000 words. MLA style sheet. Report in 3 weeks.

Payment: 6 copies of the issue.

Copyright by the journal.

INDIAN JOURNAL OF AMERICAN STUDIES, American Studies Research Centre, Hyderabad 500007, India. $4 (includes the Journal semi-annually and the book review supplement, *IJAS REVIEWS*); quarterly. Founded 1969; sponsored by American Studies Research Centre.

Major fields of interest: American Studies, with particular reference to literature, history, and political institutions.

Manuscript information: 5000 word maximum for articles and 200 word maximum for accompanying abstracts. MLA style sheet; place footnotes at the end of the article. 2 Ms. copies needed. At least 3 months before report.

Payment: 25 offprints.

Copyright rests with the American Studies Research Centre.

INDIAN WRITING TODAY, c/o Popular Book Depot, Dr. Bhad-kamkar Road, Bombay 7, India. $8; quarterly. Founded 1967; sponsored by Centre for Indian Writers, Poona.

Major fields of interest: Reviews of books of significance in Indian languages and analytical articles tracing trends and developments in Indian writing. Also draws attention to important books on philosophy, history, the arts, linguistics, and social and natural sciences published in India.

Manuscript information: Articles may be 8000 to 10,000 words. 2 copies of Ms. needed.

Payment: 25 offprints in addition to payment.

INDIANA NAMES, Department of English, Indiana State University, Terre Haute, Indiana 47809. $2; twice yearly. Founded 1970; sponsored by Department of English, Indiana State University.

Major fields of interest: Indiana names, onomastic theory and methodology. Linguistic or folkloristic analysis of names.

Manuscript information: 15-20 pages. MLA style sheet; 2 copies needed by readers. Report within 3 weeks. Notes at end of article.

Payment: 10 copies of the journal.

Copyright policy: Copyright held by journal.

INDIANA FOLKLORE, Dr. Linda Dégh, 504 North Fess, Bloomington, Indiana 47401. $7 (institutions), $5 (individuals), $3.50 (students); twice yearly. Founded 1968; sponsored by Hoosier Folklore Society.

Major fields of interest: Folklore and Folklife, rural and urban, including local legends, ballads, folk medicine, folk belief concepts, traditional crafts, immigrant folklore, folk religion. American folklore (including all states and regions, and immigrant folklore). Source study; collections with context and analysis.

Manuscript information: 20 to 30 pages (varies). Chicago style sheet. Report in about 2 months.

Payment: 2 offprints.

Copyright policy not yet established.

INSULA, Revista Bibliográfica de Ciencias y Letras, Benito Gutiérrez, 26, Madrid 8, Spain. $11; monthly. Founded 1946; Editor, Enrique Canito; sponsored by Insula Bookshop.

Major fields of interest: General literary or scientific studies; subject only to Spanish government restrictions. Articles in Spanish. Recent special issue devoted to Américo Castro. Creative material also used.

Manuscript information: Articles should be from 700-1000 words in length. No footnotes. No correspondence about unsolicited articles. No payment.

Copyright by the author.

Each issue contains 4 bibliographical pages.

INTER-AMERICAN REVIEW OF BIBLIOGRAPHY / REVISTA INTER-AMERICANA DE BIBLIOGRAFIA, Division of Philosophy and Letters, General Secretariat, Organization of American States, Washington, D.C. 20006. $3; quarterly. Founded 1951; sponsored by the Division of Philosophy and Letters of the General Secretariat, Organization of American States.

Major fields of interest: Studies of the Americas. Bio-bibliographic or critical articles in humanistic bibliography, history, literature of the Western Hemisphere. All issues are partly bibliographic. Book reviews and notes are published. Contributions are published in any one of the following 4 languages: English, Spanish, French, and Portuguese.

Manuscript information: Chicago manual of style. Footnotes should be placed at the bottom of the corresponding page and should be double-spaced.

Payment: $50-$75 per solicited article.

INTERNATIONAL JOURNAL OF AMERICAN LINGUISTICS, Department of Anthropology, Indiana University, Bloomington, Indiana 47401. $8; quarterly. Founded 1917; sponsored by AAA, LSA, ACLS, and Indiana University.

Major fields of interest: American Indian languages. Interested in special problems on technical parts of grammars. Whole grammars are published in parts. Abstracts and Translations section publishes anthropological linguistics not restricted to American Indian, and Notes and Reviews emphasis is concerned with languages of the world.

Manuscript information: Articles should be about 20 pages long; glosses in italics; footnotes are typed on separate sheet, numbered consecutively; no terminal bibliography. Report in 6 months.

Payment: 100 offprints for articles; 25 for reviews or notes.

INTERNATIONAL JOURNAL OF PSYCHOLINGUISTICS, Editor-in-chief, Professor T. Slama-Cazacu; Rahovei 108 or University of Bucharest, Laboratory of Psycholinguistics, Pitar Mos 7-13, Bucharest. 18 Dutch Guilders per issue, 22 D. guilders single issue; twice a year. Founded 1972; sponsored by Mouton Publishers, The Hague, P.O. Box 1132.

Major fields of interest: Psycholinguistics (general and applied — to foreign language learning, etc.). Research, mostly experimental. Theoretical-methodological. Orientative in the field. Each issue contains book reviews.

Manuscript information: 20 pages plus 1 page abstract; 2 copies needed by readers. Articles are published about 1 year from postal reception of manuscript; unpublished Mss. are not returned.

Payment: 25 (up to 50 if desired) offprints free of charge.

Copyright policy: Mouton Publishers. For translation and reproduction also ask editor's permission.

INTERNATIONAL REVIEW OF APPLIED LINGUISTICS IN LANGUAGE TEACHING ("IRAL"), Institut für Linguistik: Anglistik Universität, 7000 Stuttgart-1, Germany. DM 56; quarterly. Founded 1963.

Major fields of interest: Linguistics and its application to language teaching. Prefer project reports and articles of general interest.

Manuscript information: 10-15 pages.

Payment: None; 50 offprints.

Copyright by Julius Groos Verlag.

INTERPRETATION: A JOURNAL OF BIBLE AND THEOLOGY, 3401 Brook Road, Richmond, Virginia 23227. $7 (1 year), $18 (3 years); quarterly. Founded 1947; sponsored by Union Theological Seminary.

Major fields of interest: Historical and contemporary interpretation of the Bible and its use in theology. Critical, biographical, *explication de texte,* source study, etc. Also publishes creative non-scholarly material.

Manuscript information: 6600-8250 words. 70 space line, double spaced. Report usually within 2 months. Footnotes double spaced at end of manuscript.

Payment: $35 for freelance material used. No offprints — may be ordered from printer.

Copyright policy: Quoted material and reprinted articles by permission only.

THE IOWA ENGLISH BULLETIN: YEARBOOK, Department of English, Iowa State University, Ames, Iowa 50010. $1.50, $7.50 for 5 years; annually. Founded 1956; sponsored by Iowa Council of Teachers of English.

Major fields of interest: English and American language and literature; the teaching of English in elementary school, high school, and college. Critical and scholarly — but not narrowly specialist — articles desired, preferably on important writers, works, or genres.

Manuscript information: Articles of 2000-4000 words preferred. Original copy (no carbons); minimal use of footnotes. Report generally within 2 months; rarely more than 3.

Payment: 2 copies of the issue and normally 10 offprints.

THE IOWA REVIEW, EPB 453, The University of Iowa, Iowa City, Iowa 52240. $6; quarterly. Founded 1969; sponsored by the School of Letters, University of Iowa.

Major fields of interest: Modern and contemporary literature. Critical articles preferred. Creative work also used.

Manuscript information: 10-25 pages, average length. MLA style sheet; "footnotes not encouraged." Report in 6-8 weeks.

Payment: $10 per page for criticism, $15 per page for fiction, $1 per line for poetry.

Copyright by The School of Letters, The University of Iowa.

IRISH UNIVERSITY REVIEW, Department of English, University College, Dublin 4, Ireland. $3.30 per copy postpaid; twice yearly (Spring and Fall). Founded 1970.

Major fields of interest: Irish studies. The subject-matter is mainly literary historical, but occasionally touches on archaeology, art history, political theory, etc. Also publishes creative non-scholarly material.

Manuscript information: 4000-8000 words (flexible). MLA style sheet. Report within 1 month, often less. Footnotes grouped as a unit concluding the article.

Payment: 10 offprints.

Copyright policy: Normally held by IUR, but for legal reasons purely.

ITALICA, c/o Prof. Olga Ragusa, Editor, Columbia University, New York, New York 10027. $8; quarterly. Founded 1924; sponsored by American Association of Teachers of Italian.

Major fields of interest: Restricted to articles and reviews on Italian literature and language, including pedagogy. Recent titles: "More on Fenoglio: An Unpublished Novel in English and an Enlish Source," "John Florio's Contribution to Italian-English Lexography."

Manuscript information: Articles may be up to 25 printed pages. MLA style sheet; footnotes are grouped at the end of the study. Report within 1 month.

Payment: No free offprints, but contributor can order any desired number for set reprint rates.

No copyright.

Bibliography in each issue.

JACK LONDON NEWSLETTER, Hensley C. Woodbridge, Editor and Publisher, Southern Illinois University Library, Carbondale, Illinois 62901. $5; 3 times yearly. Founded 1967.

Major fields of interest: Biographical and critical material on Jack London and Jesse Stuart, reviews of reprints of their books, and reviews of works about them.

Manuscript information: Articles up to 5000 words. MLA style sheet; footnotes at bottom of page. Report immediately.

Payment: None; copies of the journal available at reduced price.

No copyright.

Bibliographical data in each issue.

JAHRBUCH FÜR AMERIKASTUDIEN, (a) Amerika-Institut der

Universität, D-6000 Frankfurt, Kettenhofweg 130 (Professor Christadler [articles]), (b) Seminar für Englische Philologie der Universität, D-6500 Mainz, Jakob-Welder-Weg 18 (Professor Lubbers [reviews and review articles]), Germany. 32.-DM, 22.-DM for members of Deutsche Gesellschaft für Amerikastudien; annually. Founded 1956; sponsored by Deutsche Gesellschaft für Amerikastudien (German Society for American Studies).

Major fields of interest: Any field of American Studies. Each volume includes reviews.

Manuscript information: Articles of about 25 pages. See an issue of the journal for style; footnotes attached at end of article. Report in around 2 months.

Payment: 2.50 DM per printed page; 20 offprints.

Copyright in accordance with Berne Convention.

Bibliography in each volume; index volume (covering vols. I-X) published in 1966.

JAMES JOYCE QUARTERLY, c/o Thomas F. Staley, Dept. of English, University of Tulsa, Tulsa, Oklahoma 74104. $5; quarterly. Founded 1963; sponsored by University of Tulsa.

Major fields of interest: All aspects of James Joyce and his milieu. Comparative studies, bibliographical and biographical articles, and collectors notes are also desired. Poems dealing with Joyce or his work occasionally published.

Manuscript information: Articles of less than 25 pages preferred. MLA style sheet, but see the journal for exceptions concerning Joyce's work. Footnotes, except for references to Joyce's work, which are cited in the text, should be placed at the end of the article. Notification of receipt within 10 days; report in 6 to 12 weeks.

Payment: 2 copies of the issue, reprints at cost.

Copyrighted, but material released to the author for use in book form.

Bibliographical section in each volume.

JAPAN QUARTERLY, c/o Asahi Shimun Publishing Company, Yurakucho, Chiyodaku, Tokyo, Japan. $5.50; quarterly. Sponsored by Asahi Shimbun.

Major fields on interest: Whole field of Japanese history, literature, art, and culture. Critical and biographical articles of general interest to the reader seeking information on Japan rather than articles of exclusively scholarly interest. Articles in English. Representative titles: "Fenollosa and the American Dream," "Western Drama in Japan." Creative material with a Japanese slant also published.

Manuscript information: Articles usually range from 2000-6000 words. 2 copies of the Ms. needed. Report in 1 month.

Payment: Uusally $20 to $25 per 1000 words; 1 copy of the issue. Offprints by arrangement.

Copyright by the editor.

JOHNSONIAN NEWS LETTER, 610 Philosophy Hall, Columbia University, New York, New York 10027. $3, $3.50 foreign; quarterly. Founded 1940.

Major fields of interest: Restoration and 18th-century English literature; scholarly news and queries.

Manuscript information: Articles must be short, about a page at most. Footnotes not desired. Report within 2-3 months.

No payment.

JOSEPH CONRAD SOCIETY BULLETIN, McMurry College, Abilene, Texas 79605. $4 to nonmembers; 4 times yearly. Founded 1973; sponsored by The Joseph Conrad Society.

Major fields of interest: The BULLETIN is intended to be a newsletter for the current information of members of the Society. The object of the BULLETIN will be to offer information on the events of the immediate past and notice of events in the immediate future. There will be no room for original studies of any length, so contributions will necessarily have to be write-ups in brief of plans re Conrad of interest to members. A special feature will be queries to the group about matters concerning in-depth Conrad studies. Bibliographic items of immediate interest will be noted, but there will be no systematic bibliography published.

Manuscript information: Report within 30 days of receipt.

Payment: None.

The BULLETIN will be copyrighted once the Society has been incorporated in the State of Texas.

THE JOURNAL OF AESTHETIC EDUCATION, Editor, Ralph A. Smith, 288B Education, University of Illinois, Urbana, Illinois 61801. $7.50, $8 foreign; quarterly (October, January, April, July). Founded 1968; sponsored by the University of Illinois Press. Unsolicited Mss. accepted, but prior correspondence with editor is advisable.

Major fields of interest: Concerned with aesthetic education in its most extensive meaning. "It features articles devoted to an understanding of problem areas critical to education in the arts and the humanities; articles dealing with the aesthetic aspects of the art and craft of teaching in general; articles concerned with the aesthetic character of other disciplines; . . . and articles treating the aesthetic import of the new communications media and environmental arts in their various forms."

Manuscript information: Articles are generally 4000-5000 words but may be shorter or longer. 2 copies of Ms. Report "within 1 or 2 months." Footnotes should be placed on separate page at end of article.

Payment: None.

Copyright by University of Illinois Press.

THE JOURNAL OF AESTHETICS AND ART CRITICISM, John Fisher, Editor, Department of Philosophy, Temple University, Philadelphia, Pennsylvania 19122. $15, $16 foreign; quarterly. Founded 1941; sponsored by The American Society for Aesthetics.

Major fields of interest: Aesthetics: "The term 'aesthetics,' in this connection, is understood to include all studies of the arts and related types of experience from a philosophic, scientific, or other theoretical standpoint, including those of psychology, sociology, anthropology, cultural history, art criticism, and education. 'The arts' include the visual arts, literature, music, and theater arts." Articles should take the theoretical, critical, or historical approach.

Manuscript information: Articles of 3000-7000 words preferred. A Manual of Style, University of Chicago; footnotes should be listed numerically at the end of the Ms.

Payment: 50 offprints.

Copyright by The American Society for Aesthetics.

Bibliographical issue in June.

JOURNAL OF AMERICAN FOLKLORE, c/o Barre Toelken, editor, Department of English, University of Oregon, Eugene, Oregon 97403; Elizabeth Powers, managing editor, University of Texas Press, Box 7819, Austin, Texas 78712. Articles for the JOURNAL should be sent to the editor; address all other correspondence to the managing editor. $10 individual membership in the American Folklore Society; $12 institutional subscriptions; $2 per copy; quarterly. Founded 1888; official organ of the American Folklore Society.

Major fields of interest: Critical and interpretive articles (not simply collections of texts) on folklore. Includes book and record reviews.

Manuscript information: No restriction on length, but preference is given to articles shorter than 10,000 words. MLA style sheet, with minor exceptions explained in the JOURNAL's own style sheet.

Payment: 25 offprints without covers.

JOURNAL OF AMERICAN STUDIES, Department of American Studies, University of Manchester, Manchester M13 9PL, England. £6; 3 times yearly (April, August, December). Founded 1967; sponsored by Cambridge University Press and British Association for American Studies.

Major fields of interest: History, literature, government, etc., of the United States (any period from 1620). Critical studies or historical documents preferred.

Manuscript information: 5000 words. MLA style sheet; footnotes printed at foot of page in JOURNAL. 2 copies of Ms. appreciated. Report in 8 weeks on the average.

Payment: None; 25 offprints, others may be purchased.

Copyright held by Cambridge University Press under conditions that allow author maximum rights.

THE JOURNAL OF COMMONWEALTH LITERATURE, School of English, University of Leeds, Leeds, LS2 9JT, England; publisher and business address (including advertising and subscriptions), Oxford University Press, Press Road, Neasden, London, N.W.10, England. £2.50; twice yearly. Founded 1965; sponsored by the University of Leeds.

Major fields of interest: Literature in English from British Commonwealth and former British Commonwealth countries, including comparative studies of Commonwealth and American writers. All kinds of articles considered, but less interested in purely biographical material.

Manuscript information: About 4500 words, but each Ms. considered on its merits. Oxford Press conventions of style; footnotes on separate sheet. 2 copies of Ms. Report time varies.

Payment: £4 per 1000 words; 1 copy of the issue.

Copyright by the publisher.

Bibliography in second issue of the year (December), the even-numbered issue.

JOURNAL OF COMMUNICATION, Daniel E. Costello, Editor, 304 Communication Center, University of Iowa, Iowa City, Iowa 52242. $10 for individuals, $15 for libraries; quarterly with occasional supplements. Published since 1951 by the International Communication Association (formerly the National Society for the Study of Communication).

Major fields of interest: Multidisciplinary studies of communication theories, processes, and skills as they obtain in (1) Information systems, (2) Interpersonal communication, (3) Mass communication, and (4) Organizational communication.

Manuscript information: Style sheet available upon request. All manuscripts must be submitted in duplicate, with a 100-250 word abstract and a 50-150 word biography of the author. Footnotes should be placed on a separate page.

No payment.

Copyright by International Communication Association.

JOURNAL OF ENGLISH AND GERMANIC PHILOLOGY, 100 English Building, University of Illinois, Urbana, Illinois 61801. $7.50; quarterly. Founded 1897; sponsored by the Graduate College of the University of Illinois.

Major fields of interest: English, German, and Scandanavian languages and literatures in all phases of scholarly investigation.

Manuscript information: Articles of over 10 pages preferred. MLA style sheet; place footnotes at the end of the Ms.

Payment: 6 free copies of issue; further offprints may be purchased.

Copyrighted.

JOURNAL OF ENGLISH LINGUISTICS, Western Washington State College, Bellingham, Washington 98225. $3; annually (March). Founded 1966.

Major fields of interest: The English language. Subject matter includes the modern and historical periods of the language, all dialects and world varieties of English. Research findings are preferred.

Manuscript information: No length specifications. MLA or LSA style sheet; footnotes typed separately at end of Ms. Writer should retain copy of Ms. Report in 6-8 weeks.

Payment: None.

Copyright by the journal.

JOURNAL OF ENGLISH TEACHING TECHNIQUES, American Language Skills Program and Literature and American Language Program, Southwest Minnesota State College, Marshall, Minnesota 56258. $3; quarterly. Founded 1968.

Major fields of interest: Proven classroom teaching techniques in any area of English. Research studies also welcomed.

Manuscript information: No set length. MLA style sheet; endnotes preferred. 2 copies of Ms. Include biographical information. Report in not less than 6 weeks.

Payment: None; 5 copies of the issue.

Copyright by the journal.

JOURNAL OF ETHNIC STUDIES, College of Ethnic Studies, Western Washington State College, Bellingham, Washington 98225. $8; quarterly. Founded 1972; sponsored by Western Washington State College.

Major fields of interest: Inter-ethnic and multi-disciplinary, the JES will be devoted to the history, literature, art, social, and cultural institutions of major non-white (Asian American, Black, Spanish-speaking, and American Indian) and white ethnic groups in the Western Hemisphere. Prefer essays; scholarly, discursive, and theoretical. "As a rule, we will not consider articles that are limited to reporting empirical findings."

Manuscript information: MLA style sheet; 2 copies needed by readers. Report in 6 to 8 weeks.

Payment: None. Offprints at author's expense.

All issues copyrighted.

JOURNAL OF EUROPEAN STUDIES, Seminar Press, 74-78 Oral Road, London NW1, England. £5.20 (overseas); quarterly. Founded 1971.

Major fields of interest: Interdisciplinary studies relating to literature, history and thought of Europe. Critical articles, *explication de texte*, source study, etc.

Manuscript information: 2 copies needed by readers; report in 3 to 4 months.

Payment: None; 25 offprints.

Copyright belongs to Seminar Press.

JOURNAL OF THE FOLKLORE INSTITUTE, 714 East 8th St., Bloomington, Indiana 47401. Business address: Co-Libri, P.O. Box 482, The Hague 2076, The Netherlands. Dglds. 27; 3 times a year. Founded 1964.

Major fields of interest: International folklore research and scholarship.

Manuscript information: MLA style sheet. Report in 2 weeks to 3 months.

JOURNAL OF THE GYPSY LORE SOCIETY, c/o D. E. Yates, Editor, The University Library, Liverpool, England. £3; quarterly or double numbers bi-annually. Founded 1888; sponsored by the members of the Society. Most contributors are subscribers, but occasional unsolicited Mss. used if dealing with "Gypsy" material.

Major fields of interest: Gypsy lore, exclusive of religious or political matter. Interest is on linguistic, ethnological, musical, or artistic matters. Occasional use of non-scholarly creative matter.

Manuscript information: About 5000 words preferred. Original photographs or drawings may be included. Footnotes should be kept to a minimum. Report within a month.

Payment: 6 copies of the issue.

Copyright belongs to the writer of the article.

JOURNAL OF THE HISTORY OF IDEAS, The City University of New York/Graduate Center, 33 West 42nd St., New York, N.Y. 10036. $10; quarterly. Founded 1940; sponsored by The City College of New York with the initial aid of the American Philosophical Society and the American Council of Learned Societies.

Major fields of interest: Cultural and intellectual history; studies should emphasize the inter-relations of several fields of historical study — the history of philosophy, of literature and the arts, of the natural and social sciences, of religion, and of political and social movements.

Manuscript information: Articles and notes up to approximately 25 pages. Footnotes to be numbered serially; consult issues of the magazine for form. Report within 3 months.

Payment: 50 offprints and honoraria to authors.

Copyright by The Board of Directors of the magazine; permission to reprint materials must be requested.

THE JOURNAL OF IRISH LITERATURE, P.O. Box 361, Newark, Delaware 19711. $7; three times a year. Founded 1972; sponsored by Proscenium Press.

Major fields of interest: Anglo-Irish literature. Also publishes creative non-scholarly material.

Manuscript information: Prefer short articles, but will publish long or very long articles if they warrant it; will read unsolicited Mss., and have accepted some. Prefer that documentation be kept to a minimum. Report usually within a month.

Payment: In copies of the magazine.

Copyright retained by the magazine, except often in the case of creative material.

JOURNAL OF LITERARY SEMANTICS, Trevor Eaton, 18 Highfield Rd., Willesborough, Ashfort, Kent, England TN 24 0JJ. 18 D. Glds., single issue 22 D. Glds.; no fixed interval between issues, each number appearing as soon as sufficient good material has accrued. Founded 1972; sponsored by Mouton & Co., The Hague.

Major fields of interest: All aspects of literary semantics; philosophical articles attempting to relate the study of literature to other disciplines, such as linguistics, mathematics, psychology, neurophysiology, history; articles dealing with the educational problems inherent in the study of literature. Prefer articles whose emphasis is theoretical.

Manuscript information: Any length articles; report in about 1 month. Style will change according to own standards; footnotes at the end of the Ms.

Payment: 25 offprints.

Copyright belongs to Mouton & Co., The Hague.

JOURNAL OF MEDIEVAL AND RENAISSANCE STUDIES, Duke Station 4666, Durham, N.C. 27706. $10; twice yearly. Founded 1971; sponsored by Duke University Press.

Major fields of interest: Medieval and Renaissance studies, transition from Medieval to Renaissance period. Prefer cross-disciplinary articles.

Manuscript information: Prefer longer articles. MLA style sheet. Report in 6 to 8 weeks.

Payment: 25 offprints.

JOURNAL OF MODERN LITERATURE, Temple University, Philadelphia, Pennsylvania 19122. $8; 5 issues a year. Founded 1970; sponsored by Temple University.

Major fields of interest: Literature of the past hundred years — fiction, drama, poetry, cinema, critical theory. Prefer research-oriented scholarship and criticism.

Manuscript information: No length restrictions. MLA style sheet; footnotes should be typed separately. Report in 4-6 weeks.

Payment: "An honorarium of undetermined amount will be paid for articles." Number of offprints given varies.

Copyright by journal; fees for reprint permission will be shared with author.

Annual bibliographic supplement appears during summer.

THE JOURNAL OF NARRATIVE TECHNIQUE, English Department, Eastern Michigan University, Ypsilanti, Michigan 48197. $3; tri-annually. Founded 1970; sponsored by Department of English, Eastern Michigan University.

Major fields of interest: Critical studies of technique in narrative literature in English prose and verse: short stories, novels, narrative poems, drama.

Manuscript information: Emphasis is on substantial articles, although short notices will be published. MLA style sheet; footnotes should be kept to a minimum and incorporated into the text when possible.

Payment: 10 copies of the relevant issue.

Copyright by Eastern Michigan University Press.

JOURNAL OF POPULAR CULTURE, U Hall, Bowling Green University, Bowling Green, Ohio 43403. $5 for students, $10 other; quarterly. Founded 1967; sponsored by Center for Study of Popular Culture.

Major fields of interest: "Popular culture" in its broadest interpretation.

Manuscript information: Prefer articles of 10 pages, but much longer ones accepted. MLA style sheet; only bibliographical footnotes are used, and they are placed at end of article. Report in 2 months.

Payment: 50 offprints.

Copyright by the editor of the journal.

THE JOURNAL OF POPULAR FILM, 101 University Hall, Bowling Green State University, Bowling Green, Ohio 43403. $4; quarterly. Founded 1972; sponsored by Bowling Green University Popular Press.

Major fields of interest: Popular Film in the broadest sense of that term. Articles on film theory and criticism are invited as well as interviews, filmographies, bibliographies, and book reviews. Concentration is upon the commercial cinema: stars, directors, individual films, genres. Also publishes poetry dealing with popular films.

Manuscript information: 10-15 typewritten pages. MLA style sheet; 2 copies needed by readers. Footnotes at end. Report in 1 month.

Payment: between 25 and 50 offprints.

Copyright owned by three editors.

JOURNAL OF THE RUTGERS UNIVERSITY LIBRARY, Rutgers University, New Brunswick, New Jersey 08901. Free to the Friends of Rutgers University Library (membership open; dues not less than $2 annually); two issues a year (June and December). Founded 1937; sponsored by Associated Friends of the Rutgers University

Library. Unsolicited Mss. considered if based on material in the Rutgers University Library.

Major fields of interest: Articles in any scholarly discipline as long as they are based to some degree on material in the Rutgers University Library.

Manuscript information: Less than 3500 words. MLA style sheet; footnotes at the end, double-spaced, on separate sheet. Report within a month.

Payment: 10 copies of the issue; offprints to be paid for.

No copyright.

JOURNAL OF THE WARBURG AND COURTAULD INSTITUTES, Warburg Institute, Woburn Square, London WC1H 0AB, England. £6 plus postage and packing; annually. Founded 1937; sponsored by The University of London.

Major fields of interest: Historical articles on the survival of the classical tradition in any field — philosophy, religion, magic, and science, festivals, literature, education, art, history, etc.

Manuscript information: Articles may be up to 15,000 words in length. Footnotes should be confined mainly to bibliographical references, numbered consecutively, and typed on separate pages at the end of the article. Notes for contributors are published in each volume.

Payment: 15 offprints.

Copyrighted; the Editors will normally grant permission to an author for his contribution to be reprinted after its appearance in the Journal.

THE JOURNAL OF THE WILLIAM MORRIS SOCIETY, William Morris Society, 25 Lawn Crescent, Kew, Surrey, England. For members only 50p.; annually. Founded 1961; sponsored by the Society. Articles from non-members welcomed.

Major fields of interest: William Morris, his life, work, associates, and times; and ideas about Morris and his relevance to current problems.

Manuscript information: Articles of about 2000 words are preferred.

JUNCTION, 237C La Guardia Hall, Brooklyn College, Brooklyn, New York 11210. $3; twice yearly. Founded 1972; sponsored by Brooklyn College Graduate English Student Association.

Major fields of interest: Anything of literary interest both critical and creative.

Manuscript information: approximately 3500 words maximum. MLA style sheet. Self-addressed envelope; biography if accepted. Report in 2 months or less.

Payment: 3 copies of journal.

Copyright policy: First serial rights to *Junction;* permission to reprint is given in return for acknowledgment of first publication.

KALKI: STUDIES IN JAMES BRANCH CABELL, Department of English, University of Cincinnati, Cincinnati, Ohio 45221; subscriptions to Paul Spencer, Secretary, James Branch Cabell Society, 665 Lotus Avenue, Oradell, New Jersey 07649. $5; quarterly. Founded 1967; sponsored by The James Branch Cabell Society.

Major fields of interest: Cabell's work or milieu. All types of articles considered; desire variety. At present, publishing out-of-print book-length studies of Cabell; will consider original material of similar length. Creative work accepted, if relevant to Cabell.

Manuscript information: Any length, from brief notes to book-length material which is published serially (if possible). MLA style sheet; footnotes on separate sheets following the text, but references should be worked into the text whenever possible. 2 copies of Ms. needed. Report within 30 days.

Payment: 2 copies of the issue (or issues).

Copyright by The James Branch Cabell Society; author may request to hold copyright on his own work in exceptional cases.

KANSAS QUARTERLY (formerly KANSAS MAGAZINE), edited at English Department, Kansas State University, Manhattan, Kansas 66506. $7.50; quarterly. Published by KQ Associates.

Major fields of interest: 2 numbers entirely creative — short stories, poems, an occasional play. Each of the other numbers is mostly given over to special subjects in (I) literary criticism, (II) art, & (III) history-sociology-economics. These latter numbers contain some poetry and other creative work.

Manuscript information: No specified length. Report usually within 2 months for poetry, 3 for stories and articles. Announced special numbers allow writers to arrange to make contributions on special topics.

Payment: 2 copies of the issue.

KARAMU, English Department, Eastern Illinois University, Charleston, Ill. 61920. $3 for 4 issues; once yearly. Founded 1967; sponsored by Karamu Association.

Major fields of interest: Short stories, poems, contemporary literature. Prefer critical articles.

Manuscript information: 10,000-20,000 words. Report in 5-6 months. Footnotes after text.

Payment: in copies only. 2 offprints.

Copyright policy: first North American rights.

KEATS-SHELLEY JOURNAL, c/o Rae Ann Nager, Houghton Library, Harvard University, Cambridge, Massachusetts 02138. $7.50 (subscription is by membership in the Keats-Shelley Association, only); annually. Founded 1951; sponsored by Keats-Shelley Association of America, Inc.

Major fields of interest: Keats, Shelley, Byron, Hunt, Hazlitt, and their circles.

Manuscript information: Articles are from 5000-8000 words; shorter contributions are published as Notes in News and Notes section. MLA style sheet, using University of Chicago manual of style for reference in complicated cases; footnotes double-spaced on separate pages, items numbered on line with text of note, number followed by period. Extra Ms. copies speeds reading, but not necessary; report time varies, averages 6 months.

Payment: 2 copies of Journal.

Copyrighted.

KEATS-SHELLEY MEMORIAL BULLETIN, c/o Dorothy Hewlett, Longfield Cottage, Longfield Drive, London S.W., England. £1.25; annually. Founded 1906; sponsored by Keats-Shelley Memorial Association.

Major fields of interest: The English Romantic period "impinging on Keats, Shelley, Byron, and Leigh Hunt." Factual articles preferred.

Manuscript information: 2000-3000 words preferred.

Payment: 1 copy and 10 offprints.

KENTUCKY FOLKLORE RECORD, Box 169 Western Kentucky University, Bowling Green, Kentucky 42101. $3; quarterly. Founded in 1955; sponsored by Kentucky Folklore Society.

Major fields of interest: Kentucky folklore, folklore in literature, folklore in education. Critical studies and collections.

Manuscript information: Short articles (5000 words or less) preferred. Fillers accepted. MLA style sheet; footnotes at end. Report within 30 days.

Copyright in name of Kentucky Folklore Society; reprinting granted on request.

THE KIPLING JOURNAL, c/o The Kipling Society, 18 Northumberland Avenue, London WC2N 5BJ, England. USA membership: $5 individuals, $6 libraries; quarterly. Founded 1927; sponsored by The Kipling Society. Mss. desired from members or by request.

Major fields of interest: Rudyard Kipling: his life and works.

Manuscript information: Articles of 1000-2000 words preferred. Use footnotes sparingly.

No payment.

Copyright retained by author.

LA MONDA LINGVO-PROBLEMO, Nieuwe Binnenweg 176, Rotterdam-3002, Netherlands. Hfl. 25.-; 3 issues yearly. Sponsored by the Centre for Research and Documentation on the Language Problem. Subscriptions should be sent to Mouton, P.O. 482, The Hague-2076, Netherlands.

Major fields of interest: The journal is "devoted to the general study of the language problem. Its aim is to gather under a single cover a wide variety of research and discussion of fundamental concern to all those linguists, educators, legislators, administrators, and others with an interest in language planning, i.e. in the selection and implementation of specific policies with regard to the use of languages. To this end the language problem is approached from the viewpoints of sociology, linguistics, law, psychology, economics and political science." Publishes "original papers in various languages, with summaries in Esperanto, plus occasional reviews and notes." Sample titles: "The Language Problem in Diplomacy," "The Changing Status of Melanesian Pidgin," "Langues et ethnies en Belgique," "Sprachenfrage und soziale Unruhe in Pakistan."

LANDFALL, The Caxton Press, P.O. Box 25-088, Christchurch, New Zealand. $4; quarterly. Founded 1947.

Major fields of interest: New Zealand writers; primarily devoted to imaginative writing in prose and verse, but critical studies on subjects of all kinds and commentaries on the arts also printed.

LANGUAGE, c/o William Bright, Department of Linguistics, University of California, Los Angeles, California 90024. $16; quarterly. Founded 1925; sponsored by the Linguistic Society of America.

Major fields of interest: Technical papers in linguistic science in all its aspects. Articles must be addressed to professional linguists.

Manuscript information: Average articles run 8-10 printed pages. Special style sheet for this journal. Complete scholarly documentation preferred. Report averages 6 weeks.

Payment: 100 offprints.

Copyright by Linguistic Society of America.

LANGUAGE AND SPEECH, c/o Professor D. B. Fry, Department of Phonetics and Linguistics, University College, Gower Street, London WC1E 6BT, England. £10 or $27; quarterly. Founded 1958.

Major fields of interest: Fundamental research in the field of language and speech. The journal attempts to deal with all aspects of this field, including language structure, psychology of language and speech, transmisssion and reception of speech, mechanical translation, mechanical speech recognition and synthesis, language statistics and abnormalities of language and speech. Reports of experimental work and theoretical and speculative articles are acceptable.

Manuscript information: No length restrictions. Summary of the article must be included for publication at the beginning of the paper.

Appropriate sub-headings should be inserted in the body of the paper. A complete list of sources referred to in the paper should be provided on separate sheets in the following form:

SCRIPTURE, E. W. (1904). *The Elements of Experimental Phonetics* (New York).

FLETCHER, J., WEGEL, R. S. (1922). The frequency-sensitivity of normal ears. *Phys. Rev.,* 19, 553. In the text of the paper, references should be shown by giving in brackets the author's surname only and the publication year thus: (Scripture, 1904). Phonetic symbols should be restricted to those used by the International Phonetic Association and their occurrence in the text should be marked by the insertion of oblique strokes thus: /p, t, k/. Figures should be large line drawings in India ink. All figure legends should be typed together on a separate sheet and numbered. The approximate position of figures and tables should be indicated in the text. Footnotes should be typed on a separate sheet. Report in about 3 months.

Payment: 50 offprints; each additional 50 at cost.

LANGUAGE AND STYLE: An International Journal, c/o Department of English, Southern Illinois University, Carbondale, Illinois 62901. $7.50; quarterly. Founded 1968; sponsored by Southern Illinois University.

Major fields of interest: Studies of style in every art.

Manuscript information: 1000-10,000 words preferred, but not limited to these lengths. MLA style sheet; footnotes and tables on separate sheet. Report in 3 weeks.

Payment: None; 6 offprints.

Copyright by Southern Illinois University, but released to authors.

LANGUAGE IN SOCIETY, 3812 Walnut St., Philadelphia, Pennsylvania 19104. $12; twice yearly. Founded 1972; sponsored by Cambridge University Press.

Major fields of interest: Sociolinguistics, anthropology, linguistics, sociology. Speech and language as aspects of social life. Analysis of data.

Manuscript information: 2 copies needed by reader.

Payment: None; 2 offprints.

LANGUAGE LEARNING, North University Building, University of Michigan, Ann Arbor, Michigan 48104. $3 per volume for individuals, $5 for libraries; 1 volume of 2 double issues per year. Supplements to individual volumes published, i.e., Selected Articles and Special Issues. Founded 1948; sponsored by the Research Club in Language Learning.

Major fields of interest: Analyses of languages, linguistic theory applied to pedagogy, descriptive analyses useful in classroom situations, English as a second language or as a foreign language, second language learning, translation.

Manuscript information: Articles may range in length from 2000-6000 words. Linguistic Society of America *Style Sheet* or *Publication Manual* of the American Philological Association; Footnotes should be placed at the end of the article. Report within 2 to 4 months.

Payment: 50 offprints.

Copyright by the Research Club in Language Learning.

THE LANGUAGE OF POEMS, Richard Gunter, Department of English, University of South Carolina, Columbia, S.C. 29208. Free; published irregularly, two or three times per year. Founded January 1972; sponsored by Richard Gunter.

Major fields of interest: The linguistic aspects of poems, especially difficult syntax and kindred matters such as ungrammaticality, invention, innovation and the like.

Manuscript information: All major articles are assigned; but shorter notes and criticisms of articles that have already appeared in The LOP are welcome. Whoever wishes to send in such notes should consult the description of such notes in Volume I-1-3 and II-1.

LATIN AMERICAN LITERARY REVIEW, Modern Languages, Baker Hall, Carnegie-Mellon University, Pittsburgh, Pennsylvania 15213. $7; biannual. Founded 1972; sponsored by Carnegie-Mellon University.

Major fields of interest: Latin American Literature; critical articles.

Manuscript information: 10 to 30 page articles. MLA style sheet. 2 copies needed by readers. Report within 2 months.

Payment: 20 offprints.

Copyright policy: reprints allowed with our permission.

THE LEAFLET, c/o Mr. Lee E. Allen, Editor, Needham High School, 609 Webster Street, Needham, Massachusetts 02194. $6 for membership and 4 issues during the school year. Founded 1901; sponsored by The New England Association of Teachers of English.

Major fields of interest: The teaching of English in all levels from elementary school through college and related subjects. Articles descriptive of teaching methods, courses of study, experiments; photographs, poems, short stories and reviews are desired.

Manuscript information: Articles of 1800-2000 words preferred. No payment.

Copyrighted.

IL LETTERATO, Via Roma, 74, Consenza, Italy. Lire 5000; monthly. Founded 1952. Directed and founded by Prof. Luigi Pellegrini.

Major fields of interest: Modern literature, essays and reviews on the film, etc. Critical articles, biographical articles, and interviews with major contemporary writers desired. Creative material also desired. Articles in Italian.

THE LIBRARY: Transactions of the Bibliographical Society, c/o P. H. Davison, Department of English, St. David's University College, Lampeter, South Wales. Free to members of the Bibliographical Society (annual dues: £5.25); 65p. an issue to the public; quarterly. Founded 1893; sponsored by the Bibliographical Society; published by Oxford University Press.

Major fields of interest: All aspects of bibliographical studies.

Manuscript information: Articles and bibliographical notes are welcomed. Scholarly documentation required; footnotes should be placed at the bottom of the page. Report normally in 4-6 weeks.

Payment: 25 offprints of articles; 12 offprints of shorter notes; 6 offprints of reviews to reviewer, 2 to publisher.

Copyright by the Society and the contributor; articles may be reprinted elsewhere after a reasonable time.

THE LIBRARY CHRONICLE, University of Pennsylvania Library, Philadelphia, Pennsylvania 19174. $5 for members of Friends of the Library, $6 for non-members, bi-annually (December and May). Founded 1933; sponsored by Friends of the University of Pennsylvania Library.

Major fields of interest: Articles and notes of bibliographical or bibliophile interest. Articles are preferred which have some connection with books and manuscripts in the University of Pennsylvania Library collections; exceptions, however, are frequently made. "Broadly speakng, articles dealing with the humanities are welcome. Specifically, articles of bibliographical interest, descriptions of manuscripts, or articles dealing with printing, binding, or any of the phases of book making."

Manuscript information: 20 printed pages the preferred length. MLA style sheet; footnotes should appear at the end of the article. Mss. must be submitted 3 months before publication (December and May).

Payment: 25 offprints.

THE LIBRARY CHRONICLE OF THE UNIVERSITY OF TEXAS AT AUSTIN, P.O. Box 7219, Austin, Texas 78712. Published three times yearly; subscription through Friends of the Library. Unsolicited Mss. not desired.

Major fields of interest: focuses mainly on special collections at The University of Texas at Austin; contributions outside this area occasionally accepted.

Copyright by the Humanities Research Center, The University of Texas at Austin.

LINGUA, International Review of General Linguistics, c/o A. Reichling, Amsteldijk 86111, Amsterdam -Z-, The Netherlands. $15 per volume; 2-3 volumes yearly. Founded 1947.

Major fields of interest: General linguistics. Studies should be in English, French, or German.

Manuscript information: See "Instructions to authors" printed in each issue.

Payment: 50 offprints.

Publication elsewhere permitted only with the permission of the editors.

LINGUA E STILE, Instituto di Glottologia, Universita, Via Zamboni, 38, Bologna, Italy 40126. L. 6,000; three times a year. Founded 1966.
Major fields of interest: Linguistics and literary criticism.

Manuscript information: Double spaced. 2 copies needed by

readers. Footnotes at the end of essay. Report in 3-5 months. Payment: 30 offprints.

THE LINGUISTIC REPORTER, Center for Applied Linguistics, 1611 North Kent Street, Arlington, Virginia 22209. $2.50; $4.50 airmail; 10 times a year.

Note: The Center for Applied Linguistics serves as "a clearing-house and informal coordinating body in the application of linguistics to practical language problems." THE LINGUISTIC REPORTER reflects the interests and activities of the Center.

LINGUISTICS: AN INTERNATIONAL REVIEW, Mouton & Co. N.V., P.O. Box 1132, The Hague, The Netherlands. $3 per issue; ir-regularly. Founded 1963.

Major fields of interest: Theoretical and applied linguistics. Ana-lytical, critical articles preferred.

Manuscript information: No length preference. Style will change according to own standards; footnotes at the end of the Ms. Report in 6-12 months.

Payment: $3 per page; 20 offprints. Extra reprints: 10 Dutch cents per page. Minimum order: Hfl 35.

Copyright by the publishers.

THE LISTENER, Broadcasting House, London WIA 1AA, England $16; weekly. Founded 1929; sponsored by the British Broadcasting Corporation. Unsolicited Mss. not desired except for poetry.

Major fields of interest: Reprints a selection of talks broadcast in the BBC's services as well as book reviews, articles, criticism of sound and television programs and art, music, and literature.

Payment: Two pounds a hundred words, or by arrangement.

First British serial rights belong to the publication; copyright remains with the author.

LISTENING, Journal of Religion and Culture, 7200 W. Division St. River Forest, Illinois 60305. $5; 3 times yearly. Founded 1965; inde-pendent, a non-profit journal incorporated in the State of Illinois.

Major fields of interest: Philosophy, theology, social science, in-terrelation of the foregoing with the arts. Critical studies preferred, "new and unusual approaches and even subject matter welcome." Creative material used. Books reviewed and Books received dept.

Manuscript information: Articles up to 3500 words. Footnotes at the end of the Ms. 2 copies of Ms. Report in 3 months, longer in summer. (Footnotes to be double-spaced).

Payment: None except for commissioned articles.

Copyright by the journal.

Index published once a year at end of volume.

THE LITERARY CRITERION, Professors' Quarters, Mysore-9, India. $1.25 (7sh. 6d.); twice yearly. Founded 1952; sponsored by C. D. Narasimhaiah.

Major fields of interest: English, American and Commonwealth literatures, including Indian writing in English. Critical articles preferred.

Manuscript information: Articles of about 3000 words. MLA style sheet; footnotes should be kept to a minimum and included in body of text, not appended to the Ms. 2 copies of Ms. desirable. Report in 4 months to 1 year.

Payment: 10 offprints.

Copyright held by the author.

Bibliography at indefinite intervals.

THE LITERARY HALF-YEARLY, 52 Professors' Quarters, Mysore-9, India. $4; twice yearly. Founded 1960; sponsored by the Department of English, University of Mysore.

Major fields of interest: General literature. Critical articles and creative material preferred

Manuscript information: 3000 words for prose articles, 30 lines for verse. MLA style sheet. Report in 2 months.

Payment: None; 10 offprints.

Copyrighted.

Bibliography published occasionally.

LITERARY MONOGRAPHS, Department of English, University of Wisconsin, Madison, Wisconsin 53706. Volume price varies; publication variable: roughly annual. Founded 1967; sponsored by Department of English, University of Wisconsin.

Major fields of interest: English and American literature and language. Monographs making significant contributions to knowledge; the quality of the paper and the importance of the subject both considered. Monographs on single works must be on works of considerable stature. ("We have found, after considerable experience, that unrevised dissertations, or portions thereof, are extremely unlikely to be publishable — they should not be sent with the expectation of receiving free professional advice.")

Manuscript information: 75-100 pages; monographs must be 15,000 to 35,000 words if they are to be considered for publication. MLA style sheet, but see "Notes on Submissions" included in the prefatory material of each volume. Report time variable. Ms. must be accompanied by self-addressed envelope and sufficient postage for return of Ms.; otherwise Ms. will not be returned. Material integral with argument in footnotes; other material in endnotes.

Payment: None. No offprints; copies of volume in which monograph appears sent to authors included in volume.

Copyright UW Press.

THE LITERARY REVIEW, Fairleigh Dickinson University, Rutherford, New Jersey 07070. $7; quarterly. Founded 1957; sponsored by Fairleigh Dickinson University.

Major fields of interest: Literature in the United States and abroad. Although essays of an analytical or explicatory nature are sometimes published, the magazine stresses creative rather than critical writing. Titles typical of articles which have been published in the past are: "Prose Fiction of Waldo Frank," "Yeats, AE, James Stephens . . . ," "Poetic Mask of E. E. Cummings," "The Humiliation of Emma Woodhouse," "Joseph Conrad."

Manuscript information: Desired length depends on substance of the article. Report in about 10 weeks.

Payment: Copies of the issue.

Copyright held by the magazine.

LITERATUR IN WISSENSCHAFT UND UNTERRICHT, Department of English, University of Kiel, Kiel, Germany. $4; quarterly. Founded 1968; sponsored by Ministry of Education, Kiel.

Major fields of interest: Criticism and teaching of English, American, German, and French literatures. Critical articles, with "a heavy emphasis on explication de texte," preferred.

Manuscript information: 4000-7500 words. MLA style sheet; footnotes unrestricted and unlimited. Report in 4-6 months.

Payment: None at the moment; 20 offprints.

Copyright arranged individually.

LITERATURE AND PSYCHOLOGY, c/o Department of English, Fairleigh Dickinson University, Teaneck, New Jersey 07666. $5 to individual subscribers, $18 to libraries and institutions; quarterly. Founded 1951; sponsored by Discussion Group General Topics 10 of MLA.

Major fields of interest: Literary criticism as informed by the various schools of depth psychology and psychoanalysis. Critical articles and explications may cover literature in any modern language or in the classics. Bibliographical contributions may be used, but the editors should be queried first to avoid duplications.

Manuscript information: About 10 pages of double-spaced typescript preferred, although the length may vary in either direction. MLA style sheet; footnotes at bottom of page or source-notes at end, or both. Extra copies of Ms. shortens reading time Report usually within 3 months.

Payment: 12 copies of the issue; extra copies at cost.

Copyright arranged with individual contributor.

Annotated bibliography in 4th issue of year.

LITERATURE EAST & WEST, c/o Dr. Roy Teele, Box 8107, University Station, Austin, Texas 78712. $8; quarterly. Founded Spring, 1954; sponsored by Oriental-Western Literary Relations Group of MLA.

Major fields of interest: Literatures of the Near and Far East, India and Southeast Asia, and Africa: translations, criticism, explication. Creative non-scholarly material related to those areas also published.

Manuscript information: Articles of less than 20 pages preferred. MLA style sheet. Immediate report.

Payment: 25 offprints.

Copyright by the editor; permission granted author on application.

LITERATURE/FILM QUARTERLY, Salisbury State College, Salisbury, Maryland 21801. $5 individuals, $4 students, $6 libraries; 4 times a year. Founded 1973; sponsored by Salisbury State College.

Major fields of interest: The relationship between literature and film; cinematic adaptation(s) of a single work; a director's style of adaptation; theories of film adaptation; "cinematic" qualities in literary works; reciprocal influences between literature and film. Critical articles; also interviews with directors, screen writers, literary figures; reviews of current "literary" films. Poems about film also published. No regular bibliographical issue, but filmographies welcomed.

Manuscript information: Ordinarily less than 3000 words; 1500 for book and movie reviews. MLA style sheet. 2 copies needed by readers. Report in no more than 2 months. Footnotes at end of essay, kept to a minimum.

Payment: 3 offprints.

Copyright Salisbury State College.

LITTERAIR PASPOORT, c/o Meulenhoff & Co. N.V., Beulingstraat 2-4, Amsterdam-C, Holland. ffl. 27,50 for 10 issues (monthly except summer). Founded 1945; sponsored by Meulenhoff & Co. N.V., Book Importers.

Major fields of interest: Contemporary literature with the exception of Dutch literature. Main accent is on English, American, French, and German literature. Multilingual. Articles should be geared to the general reader who takes an intelligent interest in foreign literature (novels, poetry, and essays). Specialized or highly scholarly articles unacceptable. Subscribers include many writers, booksellers and publishers.

Manuscript information: Articles of over 2000 words are acceptable only where important recent books or well-known authors of wide interest are concerned. Footnotes should be eliminated if possible. Quick report.

Payment: Payment varies. Copies of the issue available free or at moderate terms.

Copyright remains with contributor, but no articles may be published in other magazines or journals.

THE LITTLE REVIEW, P.O. Box 2321, Huntington, W. Virginia 25724. $2.50; twice yearly. Founded in 1968; sponsored by The Little Review Press.

Major fields of interest: Contemporary poetry in English and translations in English of foreign writers who merit attention. The only kind of articles we publish are critical book reviews and satirical lampoons. Creative non-scholarly material also published.

Payment: 3 offprints.

Copyright by Editor, John McKernan.

LOCK HAVEN REVIEW, Raub Hall 222, Lock Haven State College, Lock Haven, Pennsylvania 17745. Free; annual. Founded 1957; sponsored by faculty of Lock Haven State College.

Major fields of interest: Art, literature, music, philosophy, history, (literature: analysis, critique, prose, poetry). Scientific articles are solicited if in acceptable English prose. Creative non-scholarly material also published.

Manuscript information: 6000 to 7000 words. MLA style sheet. One copy for readers (must be original). Report in three weeks. Footnotes on one sheet for end of article insertion. Deadline for receipt of material: October 1.

Payment: 3 copies of the Review; offprints at author's expense.

Copyright policy: Permission usually granted on request.

Bibliographical issue every 10 years; first one to be in 1974.

THE LONDON MAGAZINE, 30 Thurloe Place, London S.W.7, England. £5 or $14; monthly. Founded 1954; sponsored by private individuals.

Major fields of interest: Literature in general; critical articles, reminiscences, poetry, short stories.

Manuscript information: 3000-5000 words preferred. Report in U.K. within 1 or 2 weeks; abroad depends on postage rates/air mail/surface.

Payment by arrangement.

LONG ROOM: Bulletin of the Friends of the Library of T.C.D., Trinity College Library, Dublin 2, Ireland. £2 (ordinary members), £3 (institutional members); twice a year in spring and autumn. Founded 1970; sponsored by Friends of the Library, T.C.D.

Major fields of interest: Bibliographies and checklists of Irish authors; material relating to Anglo-Irish studies and to Irish printing, particularly of the 18th century. More widely, studies based on the collections in Irish libraries.

Manuscript information: Unsolicited Mss. desired, but prior correspondence preferred. 2000-5000 words. MLA style sheet acceptable. One copy needed by readers. Report without delay. Glossy prints with scale for illustration. Footnotes typed double-spaced at end of article; at foot of page in journal.

Payment: 10 offprints.

Copyright of all articles vested in Friends but permission to reprint always given to contributors.

THE MALAHAT REVIEW, University of Victoria, P.O. Box 1700, Victoria, B.C., Canada. $5; quarterly. Founded 1967; sponsored by the University of Victoria.

Major fields of interest: Contemporary poetry, fiction, art, criticism, letters. Prints nothing that has previously appeared in English.

Manuscript information: Articles under 5000 words preferred. Report in approximately 6 weeks.

Payment: Upon acceptance, $25 per 1000 words of prose and $10 per page of poetry; 2 copies of magazine; offprints at cost.

Copyright: First world serial rights only.

MANKATO STUDIES IN ENGLISH, Mankato State College, Mankato, Minnesota 56001. Annually. Founded 1965; sponsored by the Department of English. Unsolicited Mss. not desired.

MANUSCRIPTS, c/o Paul V. Lutz, 1023 Amherst Dr., Tyler, Texas 75701. Dues: $10 for individuals, $20 for institutions; quarterly. Founded 1948; sponsored by The Manuscript Society.

Major fields of interest: The magazine is the organ of The Manuscript Society and all articles should be of interest to members and should "encourage the meeting of autograph collectors and stimulate and aid them in their various collecting specialties . . . to facilitate the exchange of information and knowledge among collectors and scholars." Approximately 30% of the articles are devoted to literary studies.

Manuscript information: Articles should not be over 4500 words, but shorter articles are quite acceptable. Report in 3-4 weeks.

Payment: 5 copies of the issue.

Copyrighted; permission to quote if requested.

MARK TWAIN JOURNAL, Kirkwood, Missouri 63122. $3; semi-annually. Founded 1936; sponsored by the Mark Twain Society.

Major fields of interest: Critical and biographical articles on Mark Twain and American, English, and foreign authors. Special consideration given to personal recollections of authors and biographical accounts giving new material on authors. Each issue contains some original poems.

Manuscript information: No preference as to length of article. Any style sheet; footnotes are placed on a separate sheet at the end of the article. Report within 2 weeks.

Payment: Usually pay in subscription and extra copies, but if an author can submit only on cash basis, the journal will pay.

Copyright retained by author.

THE MARKHAM REVIEW, Horrmann Library, Wagner College, Staten Island, New York 10301. Free, at present; 3 issues a year. Founded 1968; sponsored by the Markham Archives.

Major fields of interest: Edwin Markham and authors of the period 1865-1940, including the general literary scene during that period in American literature.

Manuscript information: Maximum length is 7500 words. MLA style sheet; footnotes should be placed at end of article. Report in 3 weeks.

Payment: 24 copies of journal; more on request.

Copyrighted.

MARY WOLLSTONECRAFT NEWSLETTER, Department of English, J. M. Todd, University of Puerto Rico, Mayaguer, Puerto Rico 00708. $4 first year, $2 afterwards; publication erratic, 2 issues to a volume. Founded 1972.

Major fields of interest: Eighteenth- and nineteenth-century topics concerning women writers, women in literature. Historical, critical, biographical articles — very flexible.

Manuscript information: Contributors must be subscribers. 3000 to 5000 words. 1 copy needed. Report in 1 month.

Payment: None. Up to 6 offprints on request.

Copyright owned by newsletter.

THE MASSACHUSETTS REVIEW, University of Massachusetts, Amherst, Massachusetts 01002. $7; quarterly. Founded 1959.

Major fields of interest: Literature, arts, public affairs. Broad, wide-ranging interests, predominantly literary and creative; each 200 page issue contains 40-60 pages of poetry and fiction, special art inserts, book reviews, creative non-academic articles.

Manuscript information: Report within 6 weeks.

Payment: Honorarium.

Copyrighted.

MASSACHUSETTS STUDIES IN ENGLISH, Department of English, University of Massachusetts, Amherst, Massachusetts 01002. $2; twice yearly. Founded 1967; sponsored by University of Massachusetts Graduate English Program.

Major fields of interest: English and American literature and language. All *original* critical approaches are welcome.

Manuscript information: Less than 5000 words. MLA style sheet. 1 copy needed. Footnotes double-spaced at the end of article. Report in 2 months.

Payment: 5 offprints.

Copyright held by MSE.

MEANJIN QUARTERLY, University of Melbourne, Parkville 3052, Victoria, Australia. $10; quarterly. Founded 1940; sponsored by University of Melbourne and the Literature Board of the Australian Council for the Arts. MEANJIN is unable to publish much material from non-Australian contributors; it does, however, commission articles and essays from leading writers and critics overseas. The editor would welcome suggestions from intending contributors.

Major fields of interest: Imaginative writing, literary and art criticism, history of ideas. The magazine is not a learned journal, though most of its contributors are senior members of Australian university departments (mainly the humanities) and leading Australian and foreign writers. Intention is to provide a serious and responsible forum for the specialist in the various disciplines of the humanities to communicate with an intelligent reading public.

Manuscript information: Articles are generally from 2000-5000 words, but some essays are 10,000 words. Footnotes should follow Oxford University Press style. Report in 1-3 months.

Payment: No payment to foreign contributors because of dollar restrictions; 12-24 offprints, or free copies of journal.

Copyright is reserved for contributors.

MEDIAEVAL STUDIES, Department of Publications, 59 Queen's Park, Toronto, Ontario, Canada M5S 2C4. $12; annually. Founded 1939; sponsored by Pontifical Institute of Mediaeval Studies.

Major fields of interest: A journal of the thought, life, letters, and culture of the Middle Ages.

Payment: 50 offprints.

Copyrighted.

MEDIEVALIA ET HUMANISTICA: STUDIES IN MEDIEVAL AND RENAISSANCE CULTURE, P.O. Box 13348, North Texas State University, Denton, Texas 76203. $9.95; annually cloth-bound illustrated edition; individual, institutions and libraries may receive a full 10% discount by placing a standing order. Founded 1943; sponsored by the Medieval Interdepartmental Section of the Modern Language Association of America; publication in the series is open to contributions from all sources.

Major fields of interest: All aspects of Medieval and Renaissance culture, including literature, art, architecture, law, history, science, philosophy, music, social and economic institutions. MEDIEVALIA ET HUMANISTICA encourages the individual scholar to examine the relationship of his discipline to other disciplines and to relate his study in a theoretical or practical way to its cultural and historical context. Review articles examine significant recent publications, and contributing editors report on the progress of Medieval and Renaissance studies in the United States and Canada. The editorial board welcomes interdisciplinary, critical, and historical studies by young

121

or established scholars and urges contributors to communicate in an attractive, clear, and concise style the larger implications in addition to the precise material of their research, with documentation held to a minimum.

Manuscript information: The length of the article, of course, depends upon the material, but in general it should average from 15-20 typed pages. Brief notes or overlong papers are not invited. Texts, maps, illustrations and diagrams will be considered when they are of particular importance and essential to the argument of the article. Quotations and references should be carefully checked and fully identified before submission. Footnotes should conform to the second edition of the MLA style sheet or the style of SPECULUM and should be numbered consecutively, double-spaced, and placed on a separate page at the end of the article. The original copy of the completed article should be submitted in the final state intended and in a form ready for publication and should be accompanied by a stamped, self-addressed manuscript envelope. Report within 2 months. A 1-paragraph abstract in English should be sent.

Payment: 25 free offprints and 40% discount to the author on the volume in which his article appears.

Copyright by The Medieval and Neo-Latin Society.

THE MEDITERRANEAN REVIEW, Orient, New York 11957. $8; quarterly. Founded 1970; privately owned and published.

Major fields of interest: Mediterranean area and general new literature. Critical articles. Creative non-scholarly material also published.

Manuscript information: 2000-4000 words. One copy needed. Report in 30 days.

Payment in copies. No offprints given.

Copyright by Mediterranean Review.

MEDIUM AEVUM, c/o Professor J. A. W. Bennett, Magdalene College, Cambridge, England. 50/-; 3 times a year. Founded 1932; sponsored by Society for the Study of Mediaeval Languages and Literature.

Major fields of interest: Mediaeval languages and literature.

Manuscript information. All contributions must be submitted in a state ready for publication.

"Italics will be written for words and phrases not in the language in which the article is written, for titles of books and periodical publications. These should be marked with a single underline. The meaning of a word will be marked by single inverted commas ....

"Short quotations in prose will be marked by single quotation marks, quotations within quotations by double quotation marks. Poetical and longer prose quotations will be printed in small roman as separate paragraphs.

"Footnotes should be placed continuously at the end of the article.

"The order of bibliographical reference should be normally as follows:

(1) Author's name, with initials preceding.

(2) Title of work. At the first reference, titles should be given without verbal abbreviations; in succeeding references, any conventional or easily recognizable abbreviation may be used.

(3) Place and date of publication   )

(4) Size, where desirable   ) within round brackets

(5) Numerical reference.   )

"When the numerical reference consists of page and/or column only, arabic numerals are used with a preceding p./col. When the reference includes volume, book, part, chapter, page, etc. p./col. is omitted (except when the page number is roman). Volume will be indicated by large roman numerals (marked with a triple underline), book, part, act, canto, by small roman capitals (marked with a double underline), chapter, scene, stanza by lower case roman. Folios of Mss. are designated by f. (plural ff.) and the verso indicated by v. For special reasons titles of Mss. may be put in italics and the recto indicated by ʳ. In the citation of periodicals it is preferable to give both volume and year, the year (in round brackets) immediately following the volume number. Titles of articles in periodicals will be in roman type within inverted commas, and followed immediately without punctuation by the title of the periodical in italics."

Payment: None; 12 offprints for articles, 6 for reviews.

META, Journal des traducteurs/Translators' Journal, Ecole de traduction, Université de Montréal, Montréal 101, Canada. $7; four issues a year. Founded 1955; sponsored by Université de Montréal.

Major fields of interest: Translation, terminology, linguistics applied to translation problems. Critical articles and source study. Some creative non-scholarly material also published, if of interest to translators.

Manuscript information: No length restrictions. One copy needed. Report in 3 months.

Payment: 10 complete numbers of the review.

Copyright policy: permission on request.

THE MICHIGAN ACADEMICIAN, Tuomy House, 2117 Washtenaw Ave., Ann Arbor, Michigan 48104. $15 per year, $4 a copy (members of the Academy receive a year's subscription with membership fee); quarterly (Summer, Fall, Winter, Spring). Sponsored by The Michigan Academy of Science, Arts and Letters.

Major fields of interest: Papers read by members at the Annual meetings are eligible to be considered for publication. Membership in the Academy is open to all. Unsolicited manuscripts are not accepted, and will be returned only when accompanied by self-addressed envelopes or international postal orders. No responsibility assumed for injury or loss.

THE MICHIGAN QUARTERLY REVIEW, 3032 Rackham Building, University of Michigan, Ann Arbor, Michigan 48104. $6, $11 for 2 years, $15 for 3 years; quarterly (January, April, July, October). Founded 1934 as MICHIGAN ALUMNUS QUARTERLY REVIEW, reorganized with current name 1962; sponsored by the University of Michigan.

Major fields of interest: Primarily a literary magazine, but all fields of general interest in humanities, social sciences, and sciences, particularly cross disciplinary views and ideas.

Manuscript information: Articles of 3000-4000 words preferred. MLA style sheet; footnotes should be kept to a minimum and incorporated in the text when possible. Report within 2 weeks.

Payment: Honoraria for unsolicited articles. 2¢ a word for stories, 50¢ a line for poems.

Copyright by the University of Michigan, but assigned to the author on request, and on execution of legal form.

THE MIDWEST QUARTERLY, Kansas State College of Pittsburg, Pittsburg, Kansas 66762. $2.50; quarterly (January, April, June, October). Founded 1959; sponsored by Kansas State College of Pittsburg.

Major fields of interest: Scholarly articles on a broad range of general subjects of contemporary significance. The journal seeks discussions of an analytical and speculative nature rather than heavily documented research studies.

Manuscript information: Articles should not exceed 5000 words in length.

Copyright held by the college.

MILL NEWS LETTER, c/o Professor John M. Robson, Principal, Victoria College, Toronto, Ontario, Canada M5S IK7. Free; semi-annually (Spring and Fall). Founded 1956; sponsored by Victoria College and the University of Toronto Press.

Major fields of interest: Materials relating to John Stuart Mill and his circle (and, to a lesser extent, his times), and James Mill.

Manuscript information: Prefer articles of 1000-2000 words, or shorter, longer articles occasionally used. MLA style sheet. Report within 1 month.

Payment: 6 offprints (possibly more on request).

Not copyrighted.

Bibliography of writings on Mill in every issue, as well as "Recent Works."

MILTON QUARTERLY (formerly THE MILTON NEWSLETTER), Ellis Hall, Ohio University, Athens, Ohio 45701. $4; quarterly (March, May, October, December). Founded 1967; sponsored by Milton Society of America.

Major fields of interest: Milton and the seventeenth century.

Manuscript information: 3-15 typewritten pages. MLA style sheet; footnotes at end of article. Report within 4-6 weeks.

Payment: 5 copies of the issue (except for solicited Mss.); 5 offprints.

Copyright by the editor.

MILTON STUDIES, English Department, University of Pittsburgh, Pittsburgh, Pennsylvania 15213. $9.95; annually. Founded 1969. Subscriptions should be sent to Sales and Promotion Manager, University of Pittsburgh Press, Pittsburgh, Pennsylvania 15213.

Major fields of interest: Milton.

Manuscript information: Articles over 3000 words preferred. MLA style sheet; footnotes are printed at the end of each essay. Report in 3-4 months.

Payment: 1 free copy; others may be purchased at 40% discount.

Copyright by the University of Pittsburgh Press.

THE MISSISSIPPI QUARTERLY: THE JOURNAL OF SOUTHERN CULTURE, Editorial, Box 5272, Business, Box 23, Mississippi State, Mississippi 39762. $6, $7 foreign; quarterly. Founded 1947; sponsored by Mississippi State University.

Major fields of interest: Southern culture (the U. S. South); interdisciplinary articles preferred in the humanities and the social sciences, and notes, queries, documents (including letters of critical or historical interest). Each summer issue since 1964 has been devoted to William Faulkner.

Manuscript information: Articles up to 4000 words preferred. MLA style sheet. Report in 8-12 weeks.

Payment: 15 reprints; 1 copy of the issue.

Copyright by Mississippi State University.

Beginning in 1969, the spring issue publishes "the annual annotated checklist (articles and books) of scholarship, prepared by the bibliography committee of the Society for the Study of Southern Literature."

THE MISSISSIPPI VALLEY REVIEW OF CREATIVE WRITING, Western Illinois University, Macomb, Illinois 61455. $1.50; 2 issues a year (Fall or Winter and Spring). Founded 1971; sponsored by College of Arts and Sciences, Western Illinois University.

Major fields of interest: American literature since Whitman, contemporary poetry and poetry in translation. "Most of what we print is creative writing."

Manuscript information: Poems: 112 lines max., stories: any length; criticism: 2500 words or less. MLA style sheet. One copy needed. Report in 6 to 8 weeks. Minimal documentation. Prefer use of parenthetic information in text. Include self-addressed stamped envelope. All Mss. double-spaced.

Payment: Payment in copies, depends on amount of material.

Copyright policy: Consent to publish only.

MLN, Johns Hopkins University Press, Baltimore, Maryland 21218. $18 institutions, $15 individuals; 6 issues a year. Founded 1886; sponsored by Johns Hopkins University.

Major fields of interest: Romance, German literature. No restrictions as to periods. Will consider any article with a significant bearing on literatnre.

Manuscript information: MLA style sheet. Prompt report.

Payment: 10 reprints.

Copyrighted; request for re-use must be addressed to Johns Hopkins University Press.

MODERN DRAMA. Graduate Centre for Study of Drama, University of Toronto, Toronto, Ontario M5S 2E1, Canada. $5; quarterly. Founded 1958; editor, Professor Frederick J. Marker.

Major fields of interest: The drama since Ibsen.

Manuscript information: Articles should normally not exceed 4000 words. Book reviews limited to 500 words. MLA style sheet. Report in 4-5 weeks.

Payment: 15 offprints.

Copyrighted; permission to reprint if credit is given.

Bibliographical issue and special issue published at regular intervals.

MODERN FICTION STUDIES, Department of English, Purdue University, Lafayette, Indiana 47907. $4 domestic, $5 domestic institutions and all foreign; quarterly. Founded 1955; sponsored by the Purdue Department of English.

Major fields of interest: Criticism, scholarship, and bibliography of American, English, and European fiction of the past 100 years. Articles may make use of any legitimate approach that illuminates a work of fiction, a writer, or a problem in fictional technique. The journal also welcomes studies of an author's total work, and of the forms, techniques, styles, and uses of fiction; it encourages comparative studies in fiction and studies which interrelate various other disciplines with the study of fiction. Two issues each year are often devoted to individual writers, groups of writers, or specific topics. Future special numbers are listed on the inside back cover of each issue. Book reviews are all assigned.

Manuscript information: Articles may be from 2500-7500 words; shorter articles are included in "Notes and Discussion" section. MLA style sheet. Report within 2-4 months.

Payment: 2 copies; 40 clippings of contributions.

Copyright by Purdue Research Foundation.

THE MODERN LANGUAGE JOURNAL, University of Colorado, Boulder, Colorado 80302. $6; 16 times a year. Founded 1916; sponsored by NFMLTA.

Major fields of interest: Teaching modern foreign languages. Creative materials also used.

Manuscript information: MLJ stylesheet (January 1969 issue). Report time varies, approximately 3 months.

Payment: Two copies of journal, gratis.

Copyrighted.

MODERN LANGUAGE QUARTERLY, University of Washington, Seattle, Washington 98195. $6; quarterly. Founded 1940; sponsored by the University of Washington.

Major fields of interest: American, English, Germanic, and Romance languages and literature. Articles must be of a critical nature.

Manuscript information: Articles of 4500-5000 words preferred. MLA style sheet; report as soon as possible.

No payment; offprints may be purchased.

MODERN LANGUAGE REVIEW, c/o Professor C. B. Brand, David Hume Tower, George Square, Edinburgh. £3 ($7.50) to members of MHRA; quarterly. Founded 1905; sponsored and published by the Modern Humanities Research Association and is the official journal of the association.

Major fields of interest: Research and criticism on English, Romance, Germanic, and Slavonic language and literature, also hitherto unprinted texts and documents, and reviews of books in these fields.

Manuscript information: Articles in English. MHRA Style Book; footnotes at end are acceptable. Reports as soon as possible.

Payment: 20 offprints; 10 offprints for reviews; more available at cost.

Copyright remains with the editor.

MODERN PHILOLOGY, University of Chicago, 1050 East 59th Street, Chicago, Illinois 60637. Institutions, USA: $12; individuals, USA: $8; other countries add $1; quarterly. Founded 1903; sponsored by Division of the Humanities, University of Chicago.

Major fields of interest: By its own definition, the publication is "a journal devoted to research in medieval and modern literature." The journal is interested in all significant developments in the fields of literary study. Short notes are used only when of exceptional importance.

Manuscript information: No limitations on length, but all articles must justify their space. Minor deviations from MLA style sheet; 1-3 months for report.

Payment: 50 offprints for articles.

Copyright by the University of Chicago.

MODERN POETRY STUDIES, 147 Capen Blvd., Buffalo, New York 14226. $6; three times a year. Founded 1970; privately sponsored.

Major fields of interest: Contemporary poetry, criticism of neglected modern poets and of poets who have made their reputations after World War II, and reviews of current books of poetry. "We are a literary magazine and are not interested in religious, political, or psychological ideas except as these ideas relate to works of art." Critical studies based upon thematic or aesthetic concerns, restricted to the corpus of a single writer preferred. No *explication de texte*, biographical or source studies *per se*. Creative non-scholarly material also published.

Manuscript information: "We prefer articles to run at least 5000 to 10,000 words although we have accepted shorter items." MLA style sheet acceptable. One copy needed. Notes should be kept at a minimum; they go at the end of the article. Report one to eight weeks, or longer.

Payment: 3 copies of issue.

MODERNA SPRAK, Box 41, Saltsjö-Duvnäs, Sweden. 55 Swedish crowns; quarterly. Founded 1907; sponsored by The Swedish Modern Language Teachers' Association.

Major fields of interest: German, English, and French languages, and literatures. Articles are in German, English, and French. Creative material also used.

Manuscript information: Articles of 16 pages preferred.

Payment: 50 offprints.

MODERNIST STUDIES: LITERATURE AND CULTURE 1920-1940, Department of English, University of Alberta, Edmonton, Alberta, Canada T6G 2E1. $6 ($10 institutions); 3 times yearly. Founded 1974.

Major fields of interest: Restricted to studies of the "twenties" and "thirties." Any study which furthers the aim of a better understanding of literature and culture in the years 1920 to 1940.

Manuscript information: 5000 to 10,000 word articles preferred. MLA style sheet. One copy needed by readers. Report within 3 months.

Payment: 25 offprints.

Bibliographical issue will be published.

MONATSHEFTE FÜR DEUTSCHEN UNTERRICHT, DEUTSCHE SPRACHE UND LITERATUR, Department of German, Van Hise Hall, University of Wisconsin, Madison, Wisconsin 53706. $7.50 (individuals); $15 (institutions); quarterly. Founded 1899; sponsored by the German Department, University of Wisconsin and published by the University of Wisconsin Press.

Major fields of interest: Serves the professional interests of German teachers, primarily at the college level. Publishes articles of general interest dealing with the language and literature of the German-speaking countries, and with cultural matters which have linguistic, literary, or pedagogical significance. Articles may be in English or German, though the former are given preference.

Manuscript information: Articles of 10-20 typewritten pages preferred. MLA style sheet; footnotes should be kept to a minimum;

all brief references should be incorporated into the body of the text. Report within 2 months.

Payment: 10 copies; reprints at commercial rates.

THE MONTH, 114 Mount Street, London W1Y 6AH, England. $10; monthly. Founded 1864; sponsored by Society of Jesus (Eng. Prov.).

Major fields of interest: The magazine is a general cultural and Catholic review with interest in historical, philosophical, social questions; literature; current political problems. Interested in non-technical articles based on original research and presented in a form that will be understood by the non-specialist. Creative material rarely used.

Manuscript information: Articles of 3000-4000 words. No responsibility taken for loss of typescript. Footnotes should be kept to a minimum. Report within 1 month.

Payment: On publication.

Copyright reserved to editors; in case of reproduction by another magazine, half of fee is given to author.

MOREANA, B.P. 858, 49005 Angers, France. $8.50 for individuals, $15 for libraries; quarterly. Founded 1963; sponsored by The Amici Thomae Mori.

Major fields of interest: Thomas More and his universe; Erasmus, Henry VIII, humanism, Reformation, especially in England, political economy; all aspects of More's personality or significance: religious, political, cultural, legal, artistic, and philological. Variety and debate are encouraged. Creative non-scholarly material is not excluded.

Manuscript information: 30 pages is the maximum length. Report within 3 months.

Payment: 20 offprints.

Not copyrighted.

MOREHEAD STATE UNIVERSITY BULLETIN APPLIED LINGUISTICS, Box 681, Morehead State University, Morehead, Kentucky 40351. $2.50; weekly, mailed bi-weekly (36 issues per academic year). Founded 1963; sponsored by Morehead State University.

Major fields of interest: Applied linguistics: original applications desired.

Manuscript information: Articles of 1000-1500 words. MLA style sheet. 2 copies of Ms. Report in 2-3 weeks.

Payment: None; 10 copies of the journal.

MOSAIC: A Journal for the Comparative Study of Literature and Ideas (University of Manitoba, 208 Tier Building, Winnipeg, Canada. R3T 2N2). Quarterly; $8 p.a. Founded 1966. Unsolicited articles required, English and French.

Fields of interest: Criticism, world literature, with a minor modern and comparative basis. Material restricted in special Theme Issues announced well in advance; at least two issues per year which are general in content. Critical articles preferred, some explication and comparisons also accepted. Creative work generally not accepted. Book reviews and review articles by invitation.

Hard-cover editions of special issues available; also the MOSAIC Essay Series, collected articles on the Novel, History and Literature, and the Theatre.

Manuscript information: Articles average 5000 words. MLA style sheet (old version); footnotes at end of article. Report usually within 3 months.

Payment: By commission only; 25 offprints, others at 25 for $5.

Copyright by the sponsor: The University of Manitoba Press.

MUNDUS ARTIUM: A JOURNAL OF INTERNATIONAL LITERATURE AND THE ARTS, Ellis Hall, Ohio University, Athens, Ohio 45701. $6; 2 issues a year. Founded 1967; sponsored by International Poetry Forum in Pittsburgh.

Major fields of interest: International Literature and the Arts. Publishes fiction, short stories, American poetry, foreign poetry in bilingual form, essays, photographic reproductions of art works and interdisciplinary essays.

Manuscript information: No specific rules on length. Prefer non-academic articles.

Payment: 2 copies of journal for contributors. Also payment.

Copyright by Editor.

THE MYSTERY AND DETECTION ANNUAL, 152 South Clark Drive, Beverly Hills, California 90211. $15; annual hardbound. Founded 1972; sponsored by Donald K. Adams (editor and publisher).

Major fields of interest: History, literary analysis and bibliography of the genre of mystery, Gothic, detective, crime, supernatural and espionage literature. Critical articles, biographical, *explication de texte*, source study, plus authorial reminiscence and comment, and short informal articles and notes on aspects of the genre. "Imaginative non-scholarly critical speculation."

Manuscript information: Any length article up to about 30 manuscript pages. MLA style sheet. 2 copies for readers would be welcome. Footnotes preferred at end of article, but acceptable in text. Report in 1 to 6 months.

Payment: Up to 12 offprints.

Copyright, unless requested by author, remains with publisher.

NAMES, c/o Conrad M. Rothrauff, Editor, Department of English, State University College, Potsdam, New York 13676. $8, $10 for libraries; quarterly. Founded 1953; sponsored by American Name Society.

Major fields of interest: American place and personal names. Literary names; linguistic aspects of all categories of names.

Manuscript information: Average length of articles, 12-15 published pages; notes are published at end of each issue. MLA style sheet. Footnotes should be typed at the end of the article but will be printed at page-bottom. Report in 2 months.

Payment: 25 offprints.

Copyrighted.

Bibliography of American Place Names and Bibliography of American Personal Names are published each year.

NASSAU REVIEW, English Department, Nassau Community College, SUNY, Garden City, New York 11530. Complimentary; once yearly in Spring. Founded 1964; sponsored by Nassau Community College, State University of New York.

Major fields of interest: English and American literature, history, philosophy, art, especially. Interested in all fields of knowledge — both humanities and science. Critical articles preferred. Also much interested in *explication de texte*. Poems, short stories and short plays.

Manuscript information: MLA style sheet with footnotes at end of article. One copy needed. Report in 4 to 5 months.

Payment: 5 offprints.

Copyrighted, but reprint rights freely given.

NATHANIEL HAWTHORNE JOURNAL, 1490 Sodon Lake Drive, Bloomfield Hills, Michigan 48013. $13; annual. Founded 1971; sponsored by Burccoli-Clark Publishers.

Major fields of interest: Material by or about Nathaniel Hawthorne, particularly biographical, bibliographical, and textual material.

Manuscript information: Short essay of 15-20 pages. MLA style sheet. One copy needed. Report in 2 weeks.

Payment: Payment for solicited articles. 25 offprints.

Copyrighted by publisher with right of anthology reprint to contributor.

THE NATION, 333 6th Avenue, New York, New York 10014. $15; weekly. Founded 1865. Carey McWilliams, Editor.

Weekly journal of independent critical opinion with a wide range of interests and concerns — social, political, economic, cultural, with a special emphasis on investigative reporting. Each issue contains editorials, articles, and a back-of-the-book section devoted to books, theater, movies, dance, graphic arts and music.

Manuscript information: an average length NATION piece is from 10 to 12 pages, double-spaced. Return postage must accompany manuscripts.

Payment: on publication.

Copyright will be reassigned on request.

NATIONAL REVIEW, 150 East 35th Street, New York, New York 10016. $16 ($10 for the 44-page issues, and $7 for the 8-page issues published on the alternate weeks); weekly. Founded 1955.

Major fields of interest: This is a conservative political journal, which includes a section on arts and books. Topical articles are desired.

Manuscript information: Articles of 1000-2000 words the preferred length. Report in 2-4 weeks.

Payment: $75 per printed page and 2 copies of the issue.

NEGRO AMERICAN LITERATURE FORUM, School of Education, Indiana State University, Terre Haute, Indiana 47809. $4; quarterly. Founded 1967; sponsored by Indiana State University.

Major fields of interest: Critical articles and creative material.

Manuscript information: No length restrictions. MLA style sheet. Report in 1 month.

Payment: None; 3 offprints, more on request.

Copyrighted; $12.50 paid to author if used by commercial source, though author can negotiate for more.

NEOHELICON, 1118 Budapest, Ménesi ut 11-13, Hungary. Hfl.60--; quarterly, or double issues twice a year. Founded 1971; sponsored by International Comparative Literature Association.

Major fields of interest: Methods of comparative literature, comparative literature studies, comparative stylistics, literary theory, history of ideas, semiotics. Comparative articles, critical-analytical, source study, *explication de texte*, review articles, book reviews. Languages are English, French, German and Russian.

Manuscript information: 20-25 pages; 3-5 pages for book review. 24-26 lines per page. Two copies needed. Please give notes as usual in PMLA or Poetics; indicate them at the end of the articles. Report in 1-2 months.

Payment: 50 offprints.

Copyright by Akadémiai Kiadó.

Distributed by Co-Libri, P.O. Box 482, The Hague, The Netherlands.

NEUE DEUTSCHE LITERATUR, Friedrichstrasse 169/170 -DDR, 108 Berlin, German Democratic Republic. 3-M a Heft; monthly. Founded 1953; sponsored by Deutscher Schriftstellen-Verband.

Major fields of interest: Modern German literature; translations of modern world literature; literary and linguistic essays and criticism. Articles in German. Original fiction and poetry also published.

Manuscript information: Articles may be up to 30 pages in length. 2 copies of the Ms. needed. Report within a month.

Payment: 2 copies of the issue.

Copyright by the author.

DIE NEUEREN SPRACHEN, Verlag Moritz Diesterweg, Frankfurt, Germany. DM 40.-; monthly. Founded 1951; sponsored by Verlag Moritz Diesterweg.

Major fields of interest: Modern literature, philological research (especially English, French, Spanish, and Italian) and problems of modern language teaching. Critical essays, explications, and articles on language teaching are desired and may be written in German, French, English, Italian, or Spanish.

Manuscript information: 8-12 pages preferred.

Payment: 20 offprints and DM 10.- per page.

neues hochland, Kösel-Verlag, München 19, Germany. $10 (including postage); 6 issues a year. Founded 1903.

Major fields of interest: All fields of science and arts. Articles in German. Creative material also published.

Manuscript information: Essays may be up to 650 typewritten lines; articles up to 150 typewritten lines.

Payment: Honorarium and 10 offprints.

NEUPHILOLOGISCHE MITTEILUNGEN, Porthania, The University, 00100 Helsinki 10, Suomi (Finland). $8; quarterly. Founded 1899.

Major fields of interest: English, Romance, and Germanic languages and literatures, excluding the Scandinavian countries. Articles accepted for publication are essentially of the same kind as those published, e.g., in MODERN LANGUAGE NOTES, THE MODERN LANGUAGE REVIEW, MODERN PHILOLOGY, and THE JOURNAL OF ENGLSH AND GERMANIC PHILOLOGY. Articles must be the results of sound first-hand personal research, never previously printed, with a high standard of scholarship. Articles dealing with the aesthetic aspects of developments in literature since about the middle of the 19th century are not normally accepted. Articles must be written in flawless English, German, French, Italian, or Spanish.

Manuscript information: 5 to 10 pages. MLA style sheet, including treatment of footnotes.

Payment: 50 offprints; 25 for reviews.

The reprinting of articles published in the journal must be authorized by the editors.

THE NEW ENGLAND QUARTERLY, Hubbard Hall, Brunswick, Maine 04011. $8; quarterly. Founded 1928; sponsored by The Colonial Society of Massachusetts.

Major fields of interest: Scholarly articles on the history and literature of New England. Articles should deal with the New England scene or with authors who have a definite association with New England.

Manuscript information: 25 double-spaced typewritten pages are the maximum length. 2 copies of the Ms. will expedite report. Footnotes in accord with standard practice except that ibid. is not used; instead use an abbreviated form after the original citation in full. Report in about 6 weeks.

Payment: 25 offprints and a year's subscription to the magazine.

Copyright held by the magazine, but "permission usually given to quote elsewhere."

March issue contains bibliography of material on New England for the preceding year.

THE NEW LEADER, 212 Fifth Avenue, New York, N.Y. 10010. $12; bi-weekly. Founded 1924; sponsored by the American Labor Conference on International Affairs, Inc.

Major fields of interest: Political and literary. Emphasis on articles with contemporary relevance, aimed at the general reader.

Manuscript information: Articles should not be less than 750 words and usually not more than 3000.

Copyright by the journal.

NEW LITERARY HISTORY, 210 Wilson Hall, University of Virginia, Charlottesville, Virginia 22903. $8; 3 times yearly (November, February, May). Founded 1969; sponsored by the University of Virginia.

Major fields of interest: Articles on theory of literature that deal with such subjects as the reasons for literary change, the definitions of periods and their uses in interpretation, the evolution of styles, conventions, genres and their relationship to each other and to the periods in which they flourish, the interconnection between national literary histories, the place of evaluation in literary history, etc.; and articles from other disciplines that help interpret or define the problems of literary history. Although all articles are published in

English, the journal welcomes articles submitted in foreign languages.

Manuscript information: 20-30 pages. MLA style sheet. Report in 2-4 months.

Payment: 25 offprints.

Copyright by *New Literary History*.

NEW ORLEANS REVIEW, Loyola University, New Orleans, Louisiana 70118. $6; quarterly. Founded 1968; sponsored by Loyola University, New Orleans.

Major fields of interest: Poetry, fiction, essays on any subject.

Manuscript information: 3000-5000 words. Any style sheet; prefer notes to be worked into text, rather than added as footnotes, when possible. Report in 4 weeks.

Payment: $75 per article. Offprints may be ordered.

Copyright by Loyola University; may be transferred to author on request.

THE NEW RAMBLER, Journal of the Johnson Society of London, The Editor, Broadmead, Eynsford Road, Farningham, Kent, England. $4; twice yearly (Spring and Autumn). Founded 1941; sponsored by The Johnson Society of London.

Major fields of interest: Eighteenth-century studies, especially Dr. Johnson and his circle. Desire critical, biographical, and research papers; also articles of interest to the general reader.

Manuscript information: 900-3000 words. MLA style sheet; documentation at end of article. 2 copies of Ms. Report in approximately 1 month.

Payment: None; journal is produced by voluntary help. 3 copies of the issue are given, additional at reduced rate.

Copyright remains with author.

THE NEW REPUBLIC, 1244 19th Street, N. W., Washington, D.C. 20036. $15; weekly. Founded 1914.

Major fields of interest: Politics, economics, literary criticism, the arts. Socio-economic articles and criticism geared to an intelligent, literate audience are desired. Creative material also published.

Manuscript information: Articles should be about 1800 words in length. Report within 3 weeks.

Payment: 8¢ per word, or $75 per printed page.

NEW STATESMAN, 10 Great Turnstile, London WC1V 7HJ, England. £8.50 ($21), $28 by air; weekly. Founded 1913.

Major fields of interest: General literature, current affairs, music, art, drama. Articles should be written for the general, intelligent reader. Creative work also published.

Manuscript information: 1500 words the preferred length.

Payment at standard rates.

Journal holds first serial rights and World Syndication unless otherwise reserved.

NEW YORK FOLKLORE QUARTERLY, Farmer's Museum, Cooperstown, New York 13326. $5; quarterly. Founded 1945, affiliated with the New York State Historical Association.

Major fields of interest: Folklore, particularly of New York and neighboring states. An attempt is made to balance popular and scholarly studies in the magazine. Interest in the many facets of American culture today; British and Dutch colonial tradition, Indian, Negro, and all immigrant strains. Folk arts and crafts with pictorial materials also desired. Other departments include folklore in schools and colleges, country lore, G.I. lore, epitaphs, proverbs, and songs. Creative material occasionally used if genuine folklore.

Manuscript information: Articles of 500-1500 words preferred, although length depends on subject. Footnoting of quoted materials essential, although not always included in published form. Report in 2-3 weeks.

Payment: 3 copies of the issue; reprints may be ordered when contributors return galley proofs.

Copyright by the New York Folklore Society, but contributors are free to use the material if permission is requested.

THE NEW YORK REVIEW OF BOOKS, 250 West 57th Street, New York, N.Y. 10019. $10; published 22 times per year, bi-weekly except in July, August, September, December and January when monthly. *New York Review* accepts no responsibility for unsolicited manuscripts.

THE NEW YORK TIMES BOOK REVIEW, 229 West 43rd Street, New York, New York 10036. $13; weekly. Sponsored by THE NEW YORK TIMES. Unsolicited Mss. will be considered.

Major fields of interest: Critical book reviews. Creative material also published.

Manuscript information: Articles of 400-1500 words preferred.

THE NEWBERRY LIBRARY BULLETIN, Newberry Library, 60 West Walton, Chicago, Illinois 60610. Published irregularly. Founded 1944; published by The Newberry Library. Editor should be queried before submission of unsolicited Mss.

Major fields of interest: Articles in the fields of interest in which the Newberry Library collections are particularly helpful to scholars.

Manuscript information: 3000-5000 words. Report in 3 months; publication may be delayed a year or more.

No payment.

Copyright by The Newberry Library.

NEWSLETTER, AMERICAN SOCIETY FOR THEATRE RESEARCH, c/o Professor Blossom Feinstein, Department of English, C.W. Post College, Greenvale, N.Y. 11548. $10 for Society Membership; twice annually. Founded 1956; sponsored by the American Society for Theatre Research. Contributors must be subscribers.

Major fields of interest: Theatre history, both national and international, in critical and comparative articles or source materials.

NEWSLETTER OF THE AMERICAN DIALECT SOCIETY, c/o Dr. A. Hood Roberts, Editor, Center for Applied Linguistics, 1611 North Kent Street, Arlington, VA. 22209. $12.50 (also includes subscription to ADS *Publications*, and *American Speech*); 3 issues per year. Founded 1969; sponsored by The American Dialect Society.

Major fields of interest: American dialects. In addition to articles, also publishes news of activities of ADS members, reports on research, and queries. Consult an issue for entire range of subjects and style.

NIEKAS, Belknap College, Center Harbor, New Hampshire 03226. $3; irregularly, 1 or 2 yearly. Founded 1962; sponsored by the Tolkien Society of America.

Major fields of interest: Imaginative literature in general with specialities in children's fantasy books, contemporary epic fantasy (especially Tolkien) and its sources. Also a little on Science Fiction. All types of articles desired, including satire of overserious criticism. Creative work also published.

Manuscript information: No length restrictions. Porter G. Perrin or University of Chicago style; footnotes at end of paper. 2 copies of Ms. preferred, though 1 is adequate. Report in 1 month.

Payment: None; 10 copies, additional at cost.

Copyright by TSA; rights to individual papers assigned to author.

NINETEENTH-CENTURY FICTION, 2319 Rolfe Hall, University of California, Los Angeles, California 90024. $8 and $10; quarterly. Founded 1945; sponsored by The University of California Press.

Major fields of interest: Nineteenth-century fiction in any aspect of scholarly inquiry including critical studies.

Manuscript information: Length may range from notes to articles of 20-25 pages. MLA style sheet. Report within 2 to 4 months.

Payment: 25 offprints.

Copyright by The University of California.

NINETEENTH CENTURY THEATRE RESEARCH, Department of English, University of Alberta, Edmonton, Alberta, Canada. $3 (individuals), $5 (institutions), Canadian funds; twice yearly. Founded 1973.

Major fields of interest: Nineteenth century theatre of the English-speaking world. Also, for example, foreign drama on London stage, etc. Scholarly emphasis; criticism accepted, but must be exceptional and preferably allied with scholarly research.

Manuscript information: About 5000 words, but flexible; merit decides. MLA style sheet; two copies needed for readers. Report in 1 to 2 months.

Payment: 25 offprints (subject to alteration).

Copyright policy: Author retains, but acknowledgement expected.

Bibliographical issue in September.

THE NORTH AMERICAN REVIEW, University of Northern Iowa, Cedar Falls, Iowa 50613. $6; quarterly. Founded 1815 (revived 1964);

sponsored by University of Northern Iowa. For unsolicited articles, query first; unsolicited creative work welcomed.

Major fields of interest: Fiction and poetry; reviews; literary, political, and current events subjects; "scholarly" pieces rarely used.

Manuscript information: Style demands only common sense and clarity. Footnotes avoided. Report in 1-3 months.

Payment: $10 per published page, minimum; poetry 50¢ a line. Offprints arranged with author at cost.

Copyright: Fiction and poetry, 1st N.A. Serial Rights; others, rights negotiated.

NORTH CAROLINA FOLKLORE, Box 5308, Raleigh, North Carolina 27607. $2; semi-annually (May and Nov.) with occasional special issues. Founded 1948; sponsored by the North Carolina Folklore Society and the School of Liberal Arts, North Carolina State University.

Major fields of interest: Collection of folklore, folklore studies, news about folklore activities, and artistic treatment of folklore materials.

Manuscript information: Articles of 500-2000 words are preferred. Report in approximately 2 weeks.

Payment: 3 copies of the issue.

Not copyrighted.

NORTHEAST FOLKLORE, B Stevens Hall South, University of Maine, Orono, Maine 04473. $2 for membership; annual. Members also receive the Society's Newsletter. Founded 1958; sponsored by Northeast Folklore Society and Department of Anthropology, UMO.

Major fields of interest: Folklore in original collections of songs and tales; also studies of material of folklore interest.

Manuscript information: Monographs of 75-150 pages preferred but shorter articles sometimes accepted if several on the same subject can be grouped together. MLA or American Anthropological Association style sheets; footnotes should be placed at the end of the article. Report in less than a month.

Payment: 25 copies of the issue.

Copyright by the Northeast Folklore Society.

NORTHWEST REVIEW, University of Oregon, Eugene, Oregon

97403. $1.50/issue. $4/yr. (3 issues). Founded 1957. Independent publication based at the University of Oregon.

Publishes poetry, fiction, art and reviews. Occasional special issues on the work of a particular author; occasional interviews or articles on what's happening on the literary scene, but these are generally planned and assigned; few unsolicited articles accepted.

No payment for contributions; 3 complimentary copies of the issue.

All contents copyrighted by the magazine; released to the *author only* on request. First North American rights.

NOTES AND QUERIES, Oxford University Press, Ely House, Dover Street, London W1X 4PH, England. £5; monthly. Founded 1849.

Major fields of interest: Literary and historical notes of any type: source materials, bibliographical notes, genealogy, lexicography, textual emendations, literary parallels, and readers' queries and answers.

Manuscript information: Articles should be short, although they may run to 3 or 4 printed pages, and in some cases, be published in parts.

No payment.

Copyright: Exclusive use of material until publication.

NOTES ON CONTEMPORARY LITERATURE, 550 N. White Street, Carrollton, Georgia 30117. $3.50; 5 times a year. Founded 1971; sponsored by West Georgia College.

Major fields of interest: Literature (American, English, Continental) written since 1940. Primarily brief explications, source studies, comparisons, etc.

Manuscript information: 1000 words or less (shorter notes preferred). MLA style sheet. Footnotes at end of article. 1 copy needed. Report in 2 weeks.

Payment: 2 offprints.

All issues copyrighted by co-editors, William S. Doxey and Benjamin W. Griffith.

Bibliographical issue in December.

NOTES ON MISSISSIPPI WRITERS. Box 433 Southern Station, Hattiesburg, Mississippi 39401. $2; 3 issues a year. Founded 1968;

sponsored by English Department, University of Southern Mississippi.

Major fields of interest: Mississippi writers. All types of articles accepted.

Manuscript information: Articles should be short, up to 20 typed pages. MLA style sheet; footnotes should be placed at end of article. Report in 2-3 months. Printing 2-6 months.

Payment: 10 offprints.

Not copyrighted, but can be on special request.

A bibliographical issue appears at various times.

NOTRE DAME ENGLISH JOURNAL, Department of English, University of Notre Dame, Notre Dame, Indiana 46556. $2.50; twice a year. Founded 1960; sponsored by Notre Dame English Association.

Major fields of interest: Critical articles in all areas of English and American literature. Compelling articles of a linguistic or bibliographic nature, as well as those reaching into other modern languages, are occasionally considered.

Manuscript information: Maximum 5000 words. MLA style sheet. One copy needed, but 2 will speed reply. Report usually within 5 to 8 weeks. Abstract (in correct MLA form) required upon article's acceptance.

Payment: 5 copies of issue and 10 to 20 offprints of article.

Copyright held by Notre Dame English Association; reassignment liberally granted.

NOTTINGHAM MEDIAEVAL STUDIES, The University, Nottingham, NG7 2RD England. £1 or $3 post free for annual issue of 100 pages on 1 September. Founded 1957; sponsored by The University, Nottingham. Most material is supplied by members of the University, although an occasional Ms. is accepted from outside the University.

Major fields of interest: Any study concerned with the language, literature, history, art, sociology, religion, etc., of the Middle Ages in Europe taking a very liberal interpretation of the term mediaeval to include late Classical and early Renaissance material.

Manuscript information: 25 pages of 600 words per page or 15,000 words the ideal length, although less is permissible. MLA style sheet; footnotes should be numbered consecutively throughout the article and appear at the bottom of the relevant page. Report within a month.

Payment: 50 offprints.

No copyright.

NOVEL: A Forum on Fiction, Box 1984, Brown University, Providence, Rhode Island 02912. $4.50, $10 for 3 years; 3 issues a year. Founded 1967; sponsored by English and Foreign Literature Departments of Brown University.

Major fields of interest: The novel in all ages, in all literatures. Articles are mainly critical, but the journal is open to any approach to fiction which proves lively and informative.

Manuscript information: Articles of 15-20 pages preferred; may not exceed 30. MLA style sheet; footnotes should be kept to minimum. Report in 3-6 months.

Payment: $50 for essays, $35 for review essays, $10 for short reviews; 3 free copies of issue; 20 copies of the issue may be purchased for $6.50.

NOVEL copyrights first appearance but gives author's copyright on request.

NUOVA ANTOLOGIA di lettere, arti e Scienze, Via Marcello Malpighi 2, 00161-Rome, Italy. Founded 1866; sponsored by the Società "La Nuova Antologia." Unsolicited Mss. not desired.

Major fields of interest: Ancient and contemporary letters, arts, and science. Creative material also published.

Manuscript information: Articles should run 10 pages in length.

Copyrighted.

OCCIDENT, Eshleman Hall, University of California, Berkeley, California 94720. $2; annually plus special issue. Founded 1881; sponsored by Associated Students University of California.

Major fields of interest: Fiction, poetry, literary and cultural criticism.

Manuscript information: No preference on length of article. MLA style sheet; footnotes should be incorporated into the article whenever possible. Report in 5 weeks.

Payment: 2 copies at request of writer.

Copyright released at author's request.

THE OHIO REVIEW, A Journal of the Humanities, 246 Ellis Hall, Ohio University, Athens, Ohio 45701. $5/year, $12/3 years, $2/single copy; 3 times a year. Founded 1958; sponsored by Ohio University.

Major fields of interest: Essays, poetry, short fiction, interviews, book reviews. Solid essays of general humanistic interest that attempt to cross disciplinary lines or view their subjects against a broad intellectual background.

Manuscript information: Prefer articles of 3000-10,000 words. MLA style sheet. Two copies of Ms. needed. Report usually in 8-10 weeks.

Payment: Copies, offprints, and (usually) token honorarium (currently $50 up for essays; $25 up for fiction; $10 up for poetry).

Copyrighted: reprint permission and fees negotiated with the editor.

OLD ENGLISH NEWSLETTER, Center for Medieval and Renaissance Studies, The Ohio State University, 320 Main Library, Columbus, Ohio 43210. Free to scholars; library rate $3; semi-annually. Founded 1966; sponsored by MLA, English Group 1, Old English. Except for news of general interest, material is solicited directly. Articles of pedagogical interest welcome, however.

Major fields of interest: Old English language and literature. Short articles; only short news items.

Manuscript information: MLA style sheet; report in 1 month.

Bibliography in the January issue.

ORAL ENGLISH, Le Moyne College, Syracuse, New York 13214. $1 (US individuals), $2 (foreign individuals), $3 (all libraries); multiple orders amounting to $5 or more may be discounted 20%. Quarterly, plus irregular supplements. Founded 1972.

Major fields of interest: Any oral approach to literature or composition. While our goal is pedagogical, our articles range from the pedagogical, through many kinds of criticism, to rather philosophical theory. "In the forseeable future we shall be needing well written, readable, thoughtful pedagogical articles for teachers beginning with oral approaches to literature and composition — especially adequately described classroom procedures that work."

Manuscript information: 1000-2500 words preferred; 3500 words ordinary maximum. Writers interested in doing a whole supplementary issue should inquire first. MLA style sheet, revised edition. One copy needed; if convenient 1 to 3 additional copies. Footnotes double-spaced on separate sheet. Report within a month, sooner if possible.

Payment: 20 copies of issue (more, within reason, if desired).

Copyrighted by editors, who do not foresee any situation in which they would not honor writers' requests gratis.

ORBIS LITTERARUM, Odense Universitet, Niels Bohrs Allé, DU-5000 Odense, Denmark. 150 kroner; quarterly. Founded 1943.

Major fields of interest: General and theoretical studies of European and American literature. Critical articles and studies in literary aesthetics preferred.

Manuscript information: Articles of 10-20 pages preferred. Report in 2-4 months.

Payment: 30 offprints.

Bibliographic issue in Vol. VII, 1950.

ORGANON, Eastern Washington State College, Cheney, Washington 99004. Quarterly. Founded 1970; sponsored by Graduate Council, EWSC.

Major fields of interest: General academic fields. Research, critical essays, creative pieces and poems.

Manuscript information: Style sheet: Campbell, Form and Style in Thesis Writing. One copy needed for readers. Report in 1 month.

Payment: None. Copies of journal provided.

All issues copyrighted.

OTHER SCHOLARS, 507 Fifth Avenue, New York, N.Y. 10017. $15; 3 times a year. Founded 1973.

Major fields of interest: "We publish works in the humanities and the sciences that present the information in new ways. We publish avant-garde reference works." A study of a single word, idea, genre, etc. that is exhaustively researched and presented in a new manner. First three issues were on pornography, schizophrenia, fascism.

Manuscript information: Unsolicited Mss. desired, "but query first." Each study must be at least 20,000 words. Two copies needed by readers. Report in 1 month.

Payment: 50 copies.
Copyright policy: at author's option.

OUTPOSTS, 72 Burwood Rd., Walton-on-Thames, Surrey, England. £1 ($5 United States); quarterly. Founded 1943; sponsored by Howard Sergeant.

Major fields of interest: Contemporary poetry and criticism. Critical or explication de texte articles preferred.

Manuscript information: Articles may be up to 2000 words. Time for report varies: between 1 and 2 weeks.

Payment by arrangement.

Copyright: First rights.

OVERLAND, G.P.O. Box 98a, Melbourne C.1, Australia 3001. $2 (Aust.); quarterly. Founded 1954.

Major fields of interest: Contemporary Australian writing, democratic in tone. Short stories, poetry, criticism, and features preferred. Concentration on Australian subjects.

Manuscript information: Articles of 1500 words preferred. Footnotes rarely used. Report in 2 months.

Payment by arrangement.

PAIDEUMA, A Journal Devoted to Ezra Pound Scholarship, 225 Stevens Hall, University of Maine, Orono, Maine 04473. $10 for 2 years; 3 times yearly. Founded 1972; sponsored by National Poetry Foundation, Inc.

Major fields of interest: Ezra Pound scholarship or closely related material. Biographical articles, *explication de texte*, source study. Bibliographical section in each issue.

Manuscript information: Length should be whatever a pointed subject demands. MLA style sheet. Report in about 2 months.

Payment: 5 copies of full journal.

Copyright by National Poetry Foundation, Inc.

PAPERS IN LINGUISTICS, Box 5677, Postal Station "L," Edmonton, Alberta, Canada. $15 per volume of 4 issues for faculty and organizations, $12 for individuals, $8 for students, plus $1 handling and shipping costs; irregularly (3-9 issues yearly). Founded 1969.

Major fields of interest: Theoretical linguistics. Original research and reviews of publications concerned with theoretical linguistics preferred. "The basic aim of the journal is to present before the linguistic community relevant current material in the shortest possible time."

Manuscript information: 10-25 pages, doublespaced. LSA style sheet; reference footnotes in text in parentheses, long and explanatory footnotes immediately following text. 2 copies of Ms. needed in camera-ready copy to be published by offset process. Report in 2 weeks; accepted material will appear in print within 6 weeks.

Payment: None; 3 copies of the issue.

Not yet copyrighted.

PAPERS OF THE BIBLIOGRAPHICAL SOCIETY OF AMERICA.
Business address P.O. Box 397, New York, N.Y. 10017. $15; quarterly. Founded 1904; sponsored by Bibliographical Society of America.

Major fields of interest: Articles and notes of bibliographical interest, chiefly in the literary field, and book reviews of similar material. Articles on printing and publishing history used.

Manuscript information: Articles up to 10,000 words and notes of from 200-3500 words preferred. MLA style sheet. Report within 3 months. Articles and notes should be accompanied by a 10-200-word abstract and addressed to William B. Todd, Editor, Department of English, University of Texas, Austin, Texas 78712. Book reviews should be addressed to Lawrence S. Thompson, Department of Classics, University of Kentucky, Lexington, Kentucky 40506.

Payment: 40 offprints of articles, 25 of notes, reviews supplied free.

Copyright by Bibliographical Society of America, but reassigned on request.

PAPERS ON LANGUAGE AND LITERATURE, Southern Illinois University, Edwardsville, Illinois 62025. $7; quarterly. Founded 1964; sponsored by the Department of English of Edwardsville Campus, Southern Illinois University.

Major fields of interest: Articles written by and for scholars and critics of language and literature in English. Literary history, analysis, stylistics, and evaluation, as well as original materials relating to belles lettres (letters, journals, notebooks and similar documents), are published. A section of briefer notes is in each issue. Representative titles: "Samuel Richardson's Early Literary Reputation in The Netherlands," "Strindberg's The Dance of Death and Edward Albee's Who's Afraid of Virginia Woolf?" PLL has initiated a significant series of papers on Anglo-American literary relations and on European relations with American writing.

Manuscript information: Chicago Manual of Style; footnotes at the end of the text. Original and 1 copy of the Ms. should be submitted.

THE PARIS REVIEW, 45-39 171 Place, Flushing, New York 11358. $4; quarterly. Founded 1953.

Major fields of interest: Creative writing. Also publishes interviews with writers.

Manuscript information: No restrictions on length. Report within 3 months.

Payment: $100-$200, depending on length.

PARNASSUS: POETRY IN REVIEW, 216 West 89th St., New York, N.Y. 10024. $7; semi-annual. Founded 1972.

Major fields of interest: Reviewing poetry books. No unsolicited Mss. desired.

Manuscript information: Length varies.

Payment varies.

PARTISAN REVIEW, Rutgers University, New Brunswick, New Jersey 08903. $5.50; student rate, $4.50; quarterly. Founded 1934.

Major fields of interest: Creative criticism of current literature, politics, poetry, and art; fiction and poetry published.

Manuscript information: Not responsible for unsolicited Mss. Return postage must be enclosed. Report in 5 months.

Payment: .015¢ per word for prose; 40¢ per line for poetry.

PAUNCH, c/o Arthur Efron, 123 Woodward Avenue, Buffalo, New York 14214. $4 for libraries, $3 for individuals; twice a year. Founded 1963; sponsored by Arthur Efron.

Major fields of interest: The concerns of the magazine will be (1) the body in literature; (2) problems in aesthetics, particularly in relation to Dewey's ART AS EXPERIENCE and Pepper's THE BASIS OF CRITICISM IN THE ARTS; (3) Literature in relation to the authority — and criminality — of the modern state; (4) reviews of new writing and a few new poems. The personal relation of the reader to the work of literature is an aspect of criticism close to PAUNCH. "The reader is likely to be a struggling human being: not someone ready to 'respond' in accordance with the latent values of the works of literature that are taught in universities, but someone who can only do that when an on-going process of self-analysis is made part of the experience itself."

Manuscript information: Any length. Report in a month or less during academic year.

Payment: 15 copies of the issue, plus small cash payment.

Copyright by editor.

PENSÉE, P.O. Box 414, Portland, Oregon 97207. $10 for 10 issues; quarterly. Founded 1966; sponsored by Student Academic Freedom Forum.

Major fields of interest: Interdisciplinary approach to catastrophism. Creative, non-scholarly material also published.

Manuscript information: 2000 words. Two copies needed by readers. Footnote material treatment: standard scientific. Report in 4 weeks.

Payment: Token honorarium.

Copyright policy: Flexible; reprint rights granted.

PERFORMANCE, 249 W. 13th St., New York, New York 10011. $9; bimonthly. Founded 1971; sponsored by New York Performance Foundation.

Major fields of interest: Contemporary theater, film. To a lesser extent, music, TV, dance. Some scholarly and documentary material. Radical social orientation. Best indication of type of articles preferred is partial list of contributors in first year of publication: Richard Gilman, Eric Bentley, Jan Kott, Todd Gitlin, Annette Michelson, Richard Pearce, Rochelle Owens, Ed Bullins, Peter Brook, the Becks, Richard Schecner, Joe Chaikin. Plays (new, or translations of previously untranslated work), film and TV scripts also published.

"We use photographs, and appreciate receiving good appropriate ones with mss."

Manuscript information: 12-25 manuscript pages. One copy needed by readers. Report from 2 weeks to 2 months.

Payment: 2-3¢ a word. 2 free copies; offprints at cost.

Copyright held by magazine unless special arrangements made.

THE PERSONALIST, c/o John Hospers, Editor, School of Philosophy, University of Southern California, Los Angeles, California 90007. $6; quarterly. Founded 1920; sponsored by the School of Philosophy, University of Southern California.

Major field of interest: Philosophy.

Manuscript information: MLA style sheet; footnotes are listed at the end of the article.

Payment: 3 copies of the issue.

Copyrighted; permission is given to reprint, provided the author approves.

PERSPECTIVE, Washington University P.O., St. Louis, Missouri 63130. $4; quarterly. Founded 1947.

Major fields of interest: Fiction, poetry, criticism (articles on modern — late 19th and 20th century — authors). Critical and intrepertative articles preferred.

Manuscript information: Prefer articles of 4000-5000 words, but would not reject longer Mss. MLA style sheet. Prefer no footnotes; if they are necessary, incorporate in text if possible; otherwise they should appear at end of article. Report in 1-2 months.

Payment: 5 copies; special rates for purchase of copies by contributors.

Copyright is held in name of magazine, but will be reassigned on request of author.

PHILOLOGICA PRAGENSIA, Liliova 13, 11645 Praha 1, Czechoslovakia. Kcs 32,- ($4); quarterly. Founded 1958; sponsored by Czechoslovak Academy of Sciences, Institute of Foreign Languages and Literatures.

Major fields of interest: All topics concerning Romance and Germanic Linguistics and Literatures. Contributions of scientific value are published. Articles are published in English, German, French, Spanish, Portuguese.

Manuscript information: Articles of up to 20 typewritten pages preferred.

Payment: 50 copies of articles.

From 1972 on each odd number includes a Czech supplement ČASOPIS PRO MODERNÍ FILOLOGII.

PHILOLOGICAL QUARTERLY, University of Iowa, Iowa City, Iowa 52242. $7.50, $14 for 2 years; quarterly. Founded 1922; sponsored by University of Iowa.

Major fields of interest: PQ is devoted to scholarly linguistic and literary studies. Its field embraces Ancient Greek and Latin as well as the modern European languages. Papers dealing with specific problems of interpretations in language or literature are generally preferred to studies in pure linguistic theory or aesthetics.

Manuscript information: Articles may vary from a few hundred words to 8000 words. MLA style sheet. Footnotes should be typed with double-spacing on separate sheets following the last page of the article; they should be numbered consecutively. Report time varies from a few days to 3 months; try to give report in 1 month.

Payment: None.

Copyrighted.

Bibliography: "The Eighteenth Century: A Current Bibliography" in July.

THE PHILOSOPHICAL REVIEW, 218 Goldwin Smith Hall, Cornell University, Ithaca, New York 14850. $5 for individuals, $8 for libraries; quarterly. Founded 1892.

Major fields of interest: All branches of philosophical investigation, including history of philosophy. Representative titles: "Jonathan Edwards on Free Will and Moral Agency," "Aesthetic Vision," "Hobbes' Concept of Obligation," and "Linguistic Relativity."

Manuscript information: Articles of 10-25 pages and discussions of 3-10 pages preferred. University of Chicago style manual.

Payment: 50 offprints.

PHILOSOPHY AND RHETORIC, 246 Sparks Building, University Park, Pennsylvania 16802. $10; quarterly. Founded 1968; sponsored by Pennsylvania State University Press.

Major fields of interest: Philosophical implications of rhetoric. Critical and critical-historical articles preferred.

Manuscript information: 15-20 double-spaced type written pages. 2 copies of Ms. Footnotes at end of article. Report in 3 months.

Payment: None; 25 offprints.

Copyright by Pennsylvania State University Press.

PHOENIX, Journal of the Classical Association of Canada, Trinity College, Toronto, Ontario, Canada M5S IH8; $10, $4 for students; quarterly. Founded 1946; sponsored by the Classical Association of Canada.

Major fields of interest: Greek and Latin literature, philosophy, history, general problems of classical archaeology; influence of the classics on later European literature. Ms. may be in English or French.

Manuscript information: Prefer articles of 5000-6000 words; notes of 1000-3000 words used. Footnotes printed at the bottom of the page; for format see "Notes for Contributors" printed at the beginning of volume 27 (1973). Report normally within 3 months.

Payment: 25 offprints.

Copyrighted; permission may be secured from editor for subsequent use of the material.

PHYLON, The Atlanta University Review of Race and Culture, 223 Chestnut Street, S.W., Atlanta, Georgia 30314; $4.50; quarterly. Founded 1940; sponsored by Atlanta University.

Major fields of interest: Broadly race and culture, American and worldwide; descriptive and interpretative comments on life of a country, an area, a people, a race, a sub-group, based on first-hand knowledge or reputable research; literature, art, and folk materials as they reflect these broad interests. Creative material used.

Manuscript information: Articles of not more than 8000 words preferred. University of Chicago style manual; 2 copies of the Ms. Notice of receipt sent immediately; report in 8 weeks.

Payment: 20-25 offprints; 2 copies of issue.

154

Copyright by Atlanta University and permission to quote is given by the magazine.

Bibliography in Fourth Quarter.

PLAYERS MAGAZINE, The Magazine of American Theatre, NIU Theatre, DeKalb, Illinois 60115. $5 and $8.50; bi-monthly. Founded 1923; sponsored by National Collegiate Players.

Major fields of interest: All aspects of American theater. Creative non-scholarly material published only if on American theater.

Manuscript information: Unsolicited Mss. desired only if accompanied by stamped self-addressed envelope. Approximately 6000 words. MLA style sheet. One copy needed by readers. Footnotes at end of article. Report time varies.

Payment: 5 offprints.

PLAYERS holds the copyright to all printed material.

PMLA (Publications of the Modern Language Association of America), 62 Fifth Avenue, New York, New York 10011. Regular $25, students $7, joint husband and wife $35, foreign $18; quarterly, with two supplementary issues (directory and program). Association founded 1883; publication founded 1884. Sponsored by the Modern Language Association of America; unsolicited Mss. from members only.

Major fields of interest: PMLA invites articles on the modern languages and literatures which are of significant interest to the entire membership of the Association. Articles should (1) employ a widely applicable approach or methodology; or (2) use an interdisciplinary approach of importance to the interpretation of literature; or (3) treat a broad subject or theme; or (4) treat a major author or work; or (5) discuss a minor author or work in such a way as to bring insight to a major author, work, genre, period, or critical method.

Manuscript information: Articles should be at least 2500 but not more than 12,500 words, written in English, and accompanied by an abstract on the standard form obtainable from the Editor. MLA style sheet should be followed. Report in 60 days.

Copyrighted.

The MLA International Bibliography of Books and Articles on the Modern Languages and Literatures is now a separate publication.

The MLA now also publishes the MLA Abstracts of Articles in Scholarly Journals.

POE STUDIES, English Department, Washington State University, Pullman, Washington 99163. $3; 2-3 times yearly. Founded 1968; sponsored by Washington State University.

Major fields of interest: Poe and his contemporaries. Gothicism.

Manuscript information: Articles under 5000 words preferred, but will take longer ones; no minimum length. MLA style sheet; documentation important, but as few footnotes as practical (parenthetical notes in text after first citation). Two copies of Ms. Report in 2-4 months.

Payment: 10 copies of the issue, minimum.

No copyright at present.

POET AND CRITIC, 210 Pearson Hall, Iowa State University, Ames, Iowa 50010. $3, $5 for 2 years; 3 times a year. Revived 1964; sponsored by Department of English, Iowa State University.

Major fields of interest: Trends and techniques in modern verse. Contributors of verse are sent copies of other poems accepted for the issue in which their verse will appear and asked for a brief critical comment on them. These comments are printed with the poems in the issue. Critical and scholarly articles are preferred.

Manuscript information: Articles of 2000-3000 words are preferred. Style generally that of either MLA or Chicago style sheets. Report within 4 to 6 weeks.

Payment: A cash prize is offered for the best poem in each issue. Other contributors receive copies.

POET LORE, 52 Cranbury Road, Westport, Connecticut 06880. $8; quarterly. Founded 1889; sponsored by Literary Publications Foundation, Inc. Editor-in-Chief, John Williams Andrews.

Major fields of interest: Any kinds of good poetry and verse drama. Unsolicited prose not published.

Manuscript information: Mss. to be typewritten, double-spaced. Footnotes rare. Report in 2-3 months.

Payment: 1 copy of the issue. Money prizes.

POETICS: International Journal for the Theory of Literature, Teun A. van Kijk, Department of General Literary Studies, University of Amsterdam, Amsterdam, Netherlands. 50 Dglds (individuals), 72 Dglds (institutions); about 4 isuues per year. Founded 1971.

Major fields of interest: theory of literature, linguistic study of literature, theoretical stylistics, discourse analysis and text grammar, interdisciplinary study of literature. The articles must have a dominantly theoretical character, with emphasis on explicitness and new methods in linguistics, logic and mathematics. No concrete analyses of particular texts are accepted.

Manuscript information: Any length to about 60 printed pages. Mouton style sheet. One copy needed by readers.

Payment: 25 offprints.

In principle the copyright is held by Mouton & Co., The Hague (publishers).

POETRY, 1228 North Dearborn Parkway, Chicago, Illinois 60610. $12; monthly. Founded 1912 by Harriet Monroe. Edited by Daryl Hine.

Major fields of interest: Poetry and reviews.

Payment: $1 a line for poetry plus 2 copies of the issue, $10 per page for prose plus 1 copy of the issue.

Manuscript information: Reply in 5-6 weeks.

THE POLISH REVIEW, 59 East 66th Street, New York, New York 10021. $8; quarterly. Founded 1956; published by the Polish Institute of Arts and Sciences in America.

Major fields of interest: Polish problems in the broadest sense of the word. Cultural and literary relations with the West, and particularly with the English-speaking peoples. Critical and biographical articles are desired as well as translations from Polish literary works into English. Representative titles: "Joseph Conrad: Some Polish Documents," "The Polish Short Story in English," "Poland's Past in English Historiography." Creative work also published.

Manuscript information: No specific length for articles. MLA style sheet; footnotes should be placed on a separate sheet. 2 copies of the Ms. Report in about a month.

Payment: Offprints by arrangement.

Copyright is held by the journal.

POPULAR MUSIC AND SOCIETY, Sociology Department, Bowling Green State University, Bowling Green, Ohio 43403. $6; quarterly. Founded 1971; sponsored by Department of Sociology.

Major fields of interest: Studies of pop music — art aspects. Must be scholarly. Everything except opinion papers. Creative non-scholarly material published in review section.

Manuscript information: 10 to 20 pages. MLA style sheet. Two copies needed by readers. Report in 1 week to 2 months.

Payment: 25 offprints.

Copyright held by editor.

PRAIRIE SCHOONER, 201 Andrews Hall, University of Nebraska, Lincoln, Nebraska 68508. $4.50; quarterly. Founded 1927; sponsored by the University of Nebraska Press and English Department.

Major fields of interest: The magazine is primarily a literary journal, publishing poetry, short stories, reviews, and articles in each issue. Anything written too "academically" is not accepted.

Manuscript information: Prefer articles of approximately 1500-3000 words. Any style sheet; footnotes placed at the bottom of the page, but rarely used. Report usually within 4 weeks.

Payment: 2 copies of the issue and 10 tearsheets. Yearly prizes.

Copyright held by University of Nebraska Press; transferred to author upon request.

THE PRINCETON UNIVERSITY LIBRARY CHRONICLE, Princeton University Library, Princeton, New Jersey 08540. $7.50; 3 issues yearly. Founded 1939; sponsored by Friends of the Princeton University Library.

Major fields of interest: Records the acquisition by the Princeton Library of noteworthy books, manuscripts, and other material; surveys the Library's special collections; describes in detail important or interesting items in the possession of the Library, and publishes articles based on such items; publishes articles of general bibliographical, literary, and historical interest related in some way to the materials in the Library.

Manuscript information: Articles of 10-25 pages preferred. MLA style sheet (with some variations); footnotes double-spaced at the end of the article. Report usually within 1 month.

Payment: 5-10 copies of the issue.
Copyrighted.

PROCEEDINGS OF THE AMERICAN ANTIQUARIAN SOCIETY, 185 Salisbury Street, Worcester, Massachusetts 01609. $15; twice yearly. Founded 1812; published by American Antiquarian Society. Unsolicited Mss. not desired.

Major fields of interest: American history and bibliography. Contents are papers read at the Society's meetings, bibliographies, and documents.

Payment: 30 offprints.

PROOF: THE YEARBOOK OF AMERICAN BIBLIOGRAPHICAL AND TEXTUAL STUDIES, University of South Carolina Press, Columbia, S.C. 29208. $20; annually. Founded 1971; sponsored by University of South Carolina Press.

Major fields of interest: American bibliographical and textual studies. PROOF emphasizes essays on the theory and practice of bibliography and textual criticism and on printing, publishing, and bookselling history.

Manuscript information: Consult recent issue of PROOF for style. Two copies needed by readers. Footnotes double-spaced at end of article following PROOF style. Report in 1-2 months.

Payment: $50-$75 plus 50 offprints.

Copyrighted by journal.

PROSE, 6 St. Luke's Place, New York, N.Y. 10014. $3; twice yearly. Founded 1970.

Major fields of interest: Belles lettres. "High" style in writing. Subject matter not important, although tendency is toward the literary and the arts. Creative non-scholarly material also published.

Manuscript information: Unsolicited Mss. not desired. Please query first. 3000 to 6000 words. One copy needed by readers. Report in 2 weeks.

Payment: $500 on acceptance for publication. Up to 20 copies of magazine.

Copyright under Prose Publishers Incorporated, reverts to author on publication.

THE PSYCHOANALYTIC REVIEW, 150 West 13th Street, New York, New York 10011. $14; quarterly. Founded 1913; sponsored by National Psychological Association for Psychoanalysis.

Major fields of interest: Psychoanalytic essays, clinical and applied; book reviews; psychoanalytic interpretations of literature, history, biography, etc. Some creative work also published.

Manuscript information: 12-35 double-spaced, typewritten pages. See journal for style; keep footnotes to minimum or include in Notes and References. 3 Ms. copies needed. Report in 1-2 months.

Payment: None; offprints may be ordered prepaid.

Copyright by the journal.

PUBLICATION OF THE AMERICAN DIALECT SOCIETY, Center for Applied Linguistics, 1611 North Kent Street, Arlington, VA 22209. $12.50 — includes subscription to *Publications* (2 issues per year), *Newsletter* (3 issues per year), and *American Speech* (4 issues per year). No student dues rate. Founded 1889. Copies are available from the University of Alabama Press. Contributors must be members.

Major fields of interest: The study of the English language in North America, together with other languages influencing it, or influenced by it; regionalisms and linguistic geography; place names; usages; non-English dialects; new words; proverbial sayings. Articles on general grammar without dialect emphasis or articles on literary figures not known as dialect writers not accepted.

Manuscript information: No given length; excluding notes, any length up to monograph. MLA style sheet; footnotes are placed at the end of the article or monograph chapters. Report within 6 months.

Payment: 5 copies.

Copyrighted.

PUCRED, Box 382, San Francisco, California 94101. $3.50; quarterly. Founded 1972.

Major fields of interest: No restrictions. Parodies of critical and scholarly approaches; satire. Creative non-scholarly material also published.

Manuscript information: 2-5 pages. PUCRED style sheet. One copy needed by readers. Report in 1 week.

Payment: 5 copies of complete issue.
Copyright by the journal, free to author.

THE QUARTERLY JOURNAL OF SPEECH, Robert L. Scott, Department of Speech — Communication, University of Minnesota, Minneapolis, Minnesota 55455. $12.50 for 4 issues (February, April, October, December). Founded 1915; sponsored by the Speech Association of America.

Major fields of interest: All areas of speech, drama, and communication with no restrictions as to type of article preferred. Recent titles: "The Rhetoric of Confrontation," "Toward a Theory of Interpretation."

Manuscript information: Articles vary in length; rarely over 6000 words. Complete documentation desired. Footnotes should be numbered consecutively and placed on a separate sheet at the end of the article. The identity of the author should be revealed *only* on the title page. Report within 2 months.

No payment.
Copyright by the Speech Association of America.

QUARTERLY REVIEW OF LITERATURE, 26 Haslet Avenue, Princeton, New Jersey 08540. $5; quarterly. Affiliated with the Creative Arts Program of Princeton University.

Major fields of interest: "In addition to poems, short stories and distinguished translations, the QRL features longer pieces: plays, novellas and long poems. The QRL also devotes Special Issues to the study of one writer."

QUARTET, 1119 Neal Pickett Dr., College Station, Texas 77840. $1; quarterly. Founded 1962; independent, non-profit, tax-exempt incorporation. Editor-owner: Richard Hauer Costa.

Major fields of interest: The creative arts — music, literature, painting, sculpture, photography. Short stories 4500 words and under. Poems welcome (but face delay in seeing print due to heavy backlog). All submissions to the College Station, Texas, address. Critical articles and reviews assigned. Art work, photography welcomed.

Manuscript information: Report in 6-8 weeks.

Payment: Nominal unless grant stipulates authors get portion of subsidy.

Copyright by the magazine; reprint permission available.

QUEEN'S QUARTERLY, Queen's University, Kingston, Ontario, Canada. $6.25; $15.50 for 3 years; 4 issues yearly. Founded 1893; sponsored by Queen's University, published by McGill, Queen's University Press.

Major fields of interest: General articles on international affairs, education, economics, philosophy, politics, science, social sciences, literature, reviews, short stories, poetry and book reviews. Articles should be aimed at a wide range of readers with a correspondingly wide range of interests.

Manuscript information: Approximately 3000 words the preferred length. Report in not more than 1 month.

Payment: $3 per printed page plus 2 copies of the issue. Offprints may be purchased by contributor for a nominal sum, deductible from the honorarium.

Author retains copyright.

QUEST, 148 Mahatma Gandhi Road, Bombay-1, India. Inland Rs.12/-, Foreign $6/-. Founded 1955; sponsored by Indian Committee for Cultural Freedom.

Major fields of interest: Critical and analytical articles on QUEST facet of Indian life; short stories and poems.

Manuscript information: Articles of 3000-4000 words. Typed, double-spaced. Footnotes kept to a minimum, at the end of the manuscript. Two copies needed by readers. Report in 8 weeks.

Payment: Rs.150/- per article.

RACKHAM LITERARY STUDIES, 4019 Modern Language Building, University of Michigan, Ann Arbor, Michigan 48104. $1/issue; free to UM graduate students; 2 issues per academic year; Fall and Spring. Founded 1970; sponsored by Rackham School of Graduate Studies and the departments of literature at the University of Michigan.

Major fields of interest: Language and literature — no period restrictions. Reviews and critical studies; short scholarly notes;

translations of poems and prose excerpts; bibliographies. Short translations only.

Manuscript information: Articles must be written in English. Notes: 1-5 pages; articles and reviews: maximum 30 pages. MLA style sheet. One copy needed by readers; manuscripts are not returned. Report in 1-2 months. Contributors must be graduate students, but need not be subscribers.

Payment: Three free copies of issue.

Copyrighted; permission to quote or reprint freely granted.

RLS carries running index of dissertations-in-process at the University of Michigan.

RE: ARTES LIBERALES, School of Liberal Arts, Stephen F. Austin State University, Nacogdoches, Texas 75961. $3; twice yearly (Fall and Spring). Founded 1968; sponsored by School of Liberal Arts.

Major fields of interest: Anthropology, geography, history, languages, literature, philosophy, political science, psychology, religion, sociology. Poetry, short stories, short plays also published.

Manuscript information: Articles should be under 10,000 words. MLA style sheet. Report in 1 to 2 months.

Payment: None. No offprints, but 3 copies of the journal.

RECHERCHES ANGLAISES ET AMERICAINES. 22, rue Descartes, Strasbourg 67000, France. 20 francs; 1 issue a year. Founded 1967; sponsored by Institut d'Anglais/Université des Lettres et Sciences Humaines, Stras. II.

Major fields of interest: Anything concerning American and British literature and civilization. Critical articles (no book reviews); each issue is devoted to a definite subject (for instance: the Theater, Southern Novelists, le Fantastique, etc.).

Manuscript information: Maximum number of pages; 20 (typed, double spaced). MLA style sheet. Two copies preferred for readers. Report time variable. Footnotes should be typed on a separate sheet.

Payment: None.

RECOVERING LITERATURE: A JOURNAL OF CONTEXTUALIST CRITICISM. Box 672, La Jolla, California 92037. $4.50; 3 times a year. Founded 1972; independent.

Major fields of interest: Critical articles on literary works from a contextualist point of view. "The best way to see our fields of interest is by reading the magazine."

Manuscript information: Any length article will be considered. Two copies needed by readers. Report in a month or more. Footnotes: "We tend to print the author's style."

Payment: Copies of the magazine; offprints by arrangement.

Copyright by magazine; reprint rights freely granted.

RED BUFFALO. 124 Winspear Avenue, Buffalo, N.Y. 14214. $4; quarterly. Founded 1971; sponsored by Program in American Studies, SUNY, Buffalo.

Major fields of interest: Issues topical.

Manuscript information: MLA style sheet. One copy needed by readers. Prefer inquiries before submitting unsolicited manuscripts. Report in several months.

Payment: None. Offprints as required, within reason.

RENAISSANCE AND MODERN STUDIES, The University, Nottingham, NE7 2RD, England. $4; annually. Founded 1957; sponsored by University of Nottingham. Unsolicited Mss. not desired; publishes primarily research by Faculty and research students of the University of Nottingham.

Major fields of interest: Humanities and social sciences generally, but with emphasis on English studies and history.

Manuscript information: Articles of about 10,000 words. Oxford University Press style sheet; footnotes (modified O.U.P. standards) appear at foot of page. Report in 2-3 months.

Payment: None; 24 offprints.

Copyright remains with author.

RENAISSANCE AND REFORMATION. CRSS, Victoria University, Toronto 5, Canada. $3 (Cdn); 3 times a year. Founded 1964; sponsored by Toronto, R & R Colloquium, C.R.R.S. of Victoria University.

Major fields of interest: Renaissance and Reformation studies — all disciplines. Critical articles, source studies, bibliographical, interdisciplinary articles.

Manuscript information: 10-15 page articles preferred. Revised edition of MLA style sheet. One copy needed by readers. Report in 1 week.

Payment: None.

Copyright by Toronto Renaissance and Reformation Colloquium.

RENAISSANCE DRAMA, Department of English, Northwestern University, Evanston, Illinois 60201. Price varies each year: Vol. 4 cost $10; annual volume. Founded 1964; sponsored by Northwestern University.

Major fields of interest: Renaissance drama. We interpret the chronological limits of the Renaissance liberally, and space is available for essays on precursors, as well as the utilization of Renaissance themes by later writers. All types of articles are welcome, although an annual topic does restrict the range somewhat.

Manuscript information: 20-40 Ms. pages, although we do publish longer articles. MLA style sheet. One copy needed, 2 if possible. Report time varies widely. Unsolicited Mss. desired, but most of our articles are on an announced topic.

Payment: 25 offprints.

RENAISSANCE PAPERS, English Department, University of North Carolina, Chapel Hill, North Carolina 27514. $3; annually. Founded 1954; sponsored by Southeastern Renaissance Conference. Contributors must be subscribers; papers to be printed are selected from those read at the program of the annual meeting.

Major fields of interest: Restricted to Renaissance interests (all fields).

Manuscript information: Articles of 10 pages preferred. MLA style sheet. Report in 2 months.

Payment: None; offprints available free, at least at present. Copyrighted.

RENAISSANCE QUARTERLY (formerly **RENAISSANCE NEWS**), 1161 Amsterdam Avenue, New York, New York 10027. $12.50 for individual membership in the Renaissance Society of America, $16 for institutions; quarterly, plus the annual STUDIES IN THE RENAISSANCE. Founded 1948; sponsored by the Renaissance Society of America.

Major fields of interest: All aspects of Renaissance culture, with special emphasis on articles of cross-disciplinary appeal. Reviews of current scholarly books.

Manuscript information: Maximum of 20 double-spaced pages, plus notes. MLA style sheet. Report in 1-3 months.

Bibliography in each issue.

RESEARCH IN AFRICAN LITERATURES, 2609 University, 320, The University of Texas at Austin, Austin, Texas 78712. $6 for 1 yr.; $11 for 2 yrs.; $15 for 3 yrs.; semi-annually. Founded 1970; sponsored by African and Afro-American Research Institute, University of Texas.

Major fields of interest: Literatures of or about Africa in any language; oral as well as written literatures. Does not publish creative writing, impressionistic literary criticism, translations, or unanalyzed collections of folklore texts. Especially welcomed are "theoretical, historical, and biographical articles; surveys of published research on a single topic; conference reports; bibliographies, discographies, filmographies, and lists of the holdings of unique collections of primary material; descriptions of university courses and degree programs; notes on works in progress; and reviews of recent critical and scholarly books."

Manuscript information: No restrictions on length. MLA style sheet. Prefer 2 copies of Ms. Report in 1 week to 2 months.

Payment: 6 copies of journal for articles, 2 for reviews; more on request.

Copyrighted.

RESEARCH IN THE TEACHING OF ENGLISH, 310 W. Delaware, Urbana, Illinois 61801. $12 for 3 years; 3 times yearly. Founded 1967; sponsored by NCTE.

Major fields of interest: As indicated by title of journal — reports of research, analyses of research problems, critiques of research.

Manuscript information: 5000-10,000 words preferred. Submit 2 copies of Ms. Send stamped self-addressed envelope for the journal's own style sheet. Report in 1-2 months.

Payment: None; 4 copies of the issue, reprints at cost.

Copyright by NCTE; author's permission necessary to reprint.

Bibliography (extensive) in each issue.

RESEARCH OPPORTUNITIES IN RENAISSANCE DRAMA, David Bergerson, ed., Department of English, Louisiana State University, New Orleans, La. 70122. Free; annually. Founded 1955.

Major fields of interest: English and Continental drama of the Renaissance; Medieval drama (a supplement each year). Prefer checklists, suggestions for research.

Manuscript information: No restrictions on length. MLA style sheet. Report in 1 month, usually.

Payment: 6 copies of the issue.

Copyrighted.

RESEARCH STUDIES (A quarterly publication of Washington State University), Washington State University, Pullman, Washington 99163. $4; quarterly. Founded 1929.

Major fields of interest: Contemporary (late-eighteenth century and after) literature, history, philosophy, sociology, anthropology. Emphasis on speculative analysis and cultural commentary.

Manuscript information: Articles usually not longer than 20 pages. Report in 2 weeks to 1 month.

Not copyrighted.

RESOURCES FOR AMERICAN LITERARY STUDY, Department of English, Virginia Commonwealth University, Richmond, Virginia 23220. $8; twice a year. Founded 1971; sponsored by Virginia Commonwealth University and University of Maryland. Business office: Department of English, University of Maryland, College Park, Maryland 20742.

Major fields of interest: Primary resources in the field of American literary study, e.g., bibliographical essays, annotated checklists, unpublished letters and manuscripts, catalogues of special collections, indices to literary magazines. Restricted to American literary study.

Manuscript information: About 50 pages maximum. MLA style sheet. Two copies needed by readers. Footnotes placed at bottom of page. Report in about 2 months.

Payment: None. Offprints available at cost.

Copyrighted.

RESTORATION AND 18th CENTURY THEATRE RESEARCH, Loyola University, 820 N. Michigan Ave., Chicago, Illinois 60611. $3; twice yearly. Founded 1962; sponsored by Loyola University.

Major fields of interest: Restoration and 18th-century drama and theater. All material relating to drama, stage, theater, actors, ballet, opera or bibliographies for the period is used. Interpretations of plays not desired.

Manuscript information: Under 5000 words the most desirable length. MLA style sheet; footnotes at the end of the article. Report in 3-6 months.

Payment: 5 copies of the magazine.

Copyright by Loyola University. Permission necessary to reproduce the article.

REVIEW OF ENGLISH STUDIES, c/o Clarendon Press, Oxford, England. £4.50 ($12.25); quarterly (February, May, August, November). Founded 1925; published by Oxford University Press.

Major fields of interest: English literature of all periods and English language, especially with reference to literary texts or problems.

Manuscript information: Articles should not exceed 7000 words; 5000 words the best length. "Guide to Contributors" is available on application. Footnotes should be placed at the end of the article. Report within a month.

Payment: 25 offprints.

Permission required for reprinting (usually given).

REVIEW OF NATIONAL LITERATURES, Perboyre Hall, St. John's University, Jamaica, New York 11439. $5; semi-annually. Founded 1970; sponsored by St. John's University.

Major fields of interest: "Each issue will focus on a national culture, or, more particularly, on a representative theme, author, literary movement, or critical tendency, in an effort to provide substantial and concentrated materials for comparative study."

Manuscript information: Articles commissioned. No unsolicited manuscripts accepted.

REVISTA IBEROAMERICANA, University of Pittsburgh, Pittsburgh,

Pennsylvania 15213. $8, $3 in Latin America; minimum of 4 issues a year. Founded 1938; sponsored by Instituto Internacional de Literatura Iberoamericana.

Major fields of interest: Latin American literature, all genres. Occasional articles of linguistic or comparative interest. Articles are generally in Spanish or Portuguese.

Manuscript information: Articles of 15-25 pages preferred. MLA style sheet.

REVUE BELGE DE PHILOLOGIE ET D'HISTOIRE, 4, boulevard de l' Empereur, Brussels 1000, Belgium. 900 B. fr; quarterly. Founded 1920; sponsored by Societé pour le progrès des études philologiques et historiques.

Major fields of interest: All fields of modern languages and literatures. Critical articles and source studies preferred.

Manuscript information: Prefer articles of 20-30 pages in length. Report within 1 month.

Payment: 40 offprints.

Bibliography in each volume.

REVUE DE LITTÉRATURE COMPARÉE, J. Body, Faculté des Lettres et Sciences Humaines, Tours, France. NF 45; quarterly. Founded 1921; sponsored by Marcel Bataillon and Jacques Voisine.

Major fields of interest: Historical and esthetic relationships and comparisons of authors, works, styles, and themes of different countries and epochs. Studies must be comparative in nature.

Manuscript information: 10 to 25 printed pages. Footnotes should be placed at the bottom of each page. Publication within 12 months.

Payment: 30 offprints.

REVUE DE LOUISIANE-LOUISIANA REVIEW. Professor Léandre Page, P.O. Box 3936, Lafayette, Louisiana 70501. $8; 2 issues a year. Founded 1871; sponsored by State of Louisiana — Governor — Council for the Development of French in Louisiana.

Major fields of interest: Bilingual review — French and English. Literature, Language (French), History (Louisiana). (Academic and vulgarised.) Critique, essay, biography, tale, story, study, etc. Creative non-scholarly material also published.

Manuscript information: 15 pages maximum. Typed, double space. Two copies needed by readers.

Copyright by CODOFIL.

REVUE DE L'UNIVERSITÉ D'OTTAWA, 550 rue Cumberland, Ottawa, Ontario, Canada K1N 6N5. $7.50; quarterly. Founded 1931; sponsored by the University of Ottawa Press.

Major fields of interest: University subjects. Articles on general culture preferred.

Manuscript information: Articles of 10 pages.

Payment: None; 25 offprints.

Bibliography bound with each number.

RICE UNIVERSITY STUDIES, Rice University, Houston, Texas 77001. Quarterly. Founded 1912; sponsored by The Rice University. Articles are usually written by members of The Rice University faculty or visiting lecturers.

RIVERSIDE QUARTERLY. Box 40, University Station, Regina, Canada. $2 for 4 issues; published irregularly. Founded 1964.

Major fields of interest: Science-fiction and fantasy. Critical articles. Creative non-scholarly material also published.

Manuscript information: MLA style sheet. One copy of manuscript needed by readers. Report in 2 weeks.

Payment: In copies. No offprints.

Copyright policy: All copyrights revert to the author.

RIVISTA DI LETTERATURE MODERNE E COMPARATE, viale Mazzini 46, 50132 Florence, Italy. $11.25; quarterly. Founded 1945. Unsolicited Mss. not desired.

Major fields of interest: General and critical articles on modern literatures (to the exclusion of Italian literature) and on comparative literature.

Manuscript information: Articles should be from 15 to 20 typed pages in length.

Payment: 20 offprints.

Bibliographical issue annually.

ROMANCE NOTES, Dey Hall, Chapel Hill, North Carolina 27514. $8 for Vol. XIV (1972-73), 3 issues: Autumn, Winter, and Summer; Founded 1959; sponsored by the University of North Carolina.

Major fields of interest: All periods of the Romance languages and literatures. Notes on English and American literatures must show a definite association with one of the Romance languages and literatures.

Manuscript information: Only notes accepted, 6 typewritten pages or less the required length. MLA style sheet. Report in about 2-6 months.

No payment.

ROMANCE PHILOLOGY, 2321 Dwinelle Hall, University of California, Berkeley, California 94720. $12 for individuals; $6 for graduate students; $18 for institutions; quarterly. Founded 1947; sponsored by The University Press. Contributors must be subscribers and should query the journal before submitting unsolicited Mss.

Major fields of interest: Any phase of early Romance literature or Romance literatures and languages, from late Antiquity to the early Renaissance.

Manuscript information: Articles may range in length from the short monograph to, occasionally, notes. MLA style sheet for literary studies; special rules for linguistic studies; foreign usage for articles written in foreign languages. Report normally within a few weeks.

Payment: 100 offprints of articles; 25 tearsheets of long reviews.

Copyright by The University of California Press.

ROMANIC REVIEW, 518 Philosophy Hall, Columbia University, New York, New York 10027. $7.50; quarterly. Founded 1909; sponsored by the Department of Romance Languages of Columbia University.

Major fields of interest: Articles relating to Romance literatures with no chronological limitations; very general surveys are not encouraged. Mss. in English or in French.

Manuscript information: Articles may be up to 25 typed pages in length. MLA style sheet; footnotes should be double-spaced on a separate sheet and numbered consecutively. Report within 3 months during academic year; publication within 2 years.

Payment: 2-10 copies of the issue (depending on whether publication is an article or book review); others at discount. Offprints may be purchased.

Copyright by Columbia University Press.

SADAKICHI HARTMANN NEWSLETTER, Dr. Richard Tuerk, Managing Editor, Department of English, East Texas State University, East Texas Station, Commerce, Texas 75428. $2.50; 3 times a year. Founded 1969; sponsored by Department of English, East Texas State University.

Major fields of interest: Art, art criticism, literature, literary criticism, cultural history, intellectual history related to activities and writings of Sadakichi Hartmann and figures associated with him. Creative non-scholarly material possibly published also.

Manuscript information: Up to 10 double-spaced, typewritten pages. If longer, they could be run in installment. MLA style sheet. Two copies needed by readers. Report within 3 months, usually immediately.

Payment: 10 offprints.

Copyright policy: Each issue is copyrighted in the name of Wistaria Hartmann Linton.

SALMAGUNDI, Skidmore College, Saratoga Springs, New York 12866. $6; quarterly. Founded 1965; sponsored by Skidmore College.

Major fields of interest: Humanities and the Social Sciences. Prefer "high-brow critical and biographical" studies. Poems, stories, and plays also published.

Manuscript information: Articles may be from 2000-15,000 words. MLA style sheet. Report in 1-3 months.

Payment varies; from $100-$250.

SATIRE NEWSLETTER, State University College, Oneonta, New York 13820. $2; semi-annually. Founded 1963.

Major fields of interest: Satire, criticism, reviews, bibliography, original verse, sketches. Especially interested in articles about satire in literatures outside the Anglo-American tradition as well as about satire in art, music, and other forms of creative expression.

Manuscript information: Articles under 15 pages are preferred.

MLA style sheet; footnotes should be placed at the end of the article. Report within 1-3 months.

Payment: 2 copies of the issue.

Not copyrighted.

Bibliographical section irregularly.

SATURDAY REVIEW, 380 Madison Avenue, New York, N.Y. 10017. $9; weekly. "Unsolicited manuscripts cannot be returned unless accompanied by a properly addressed envelope bearing sufficient postage."

SCANDINAVIAN STUDIES, c/o Harald Naess, Department of Scandinavian Studies, 1306 Van Hise Hall, University of Wisconsin, Madison, Wisconsin 53706. $15; quarterly. Founded 1911; sponsored by the Society for the Advancement of Scandinavian Study.

Major fields of interest: Scholarly articles on Scandinavian languages and literature; comparative literature; comparative linguistics, history and social science.

Manuscript information: 25 typewritten pages the maximum length. Report within 6 weeks at most.

Payment: 5 copies of the issue.

Bibliography appears annually.

SCHOLARLY PUBLISHING: A JOURNAL FOR AUTHORS & PUBLISHERS, University of Toronto Press, Toronto M5S 1A6, Canada. $10; quarterly. Founded 1969; sponsored by the University of Toronto Press.

Major fields of interest: Any material related to the publishing of scholarly works.

Manuscript information: 1500-5000 word range preferred. Limit number of footnotes as far as possible; placed at end of article. Report in 3 weeks (if accepted as submitted).

Payment: Varies with length of article; 100 offprints free; additional offprints may be purchased at commercial rates.

Copyright by the publisher.

SCIENCE AND SOCIETY, 30 East 20th Street, New York, New York 10003. $6 for individuals; $11 for institutions; quarterly. Founded 1936; sponsored by Science & Society, Inc.

Major fields of interest: "To promote the exploration, in the broadest way, of the relationship between Marxist philosophy and the social welfare."

Manuscript information: Articles should range from 3000-6000 words in length. Style manual of The University of Chicago Press. Report in 6-8 weeks.

Payment: Offprints may be ordered at contributor's expense.

SCOTTISH INTERNATIONAL REVIEW, 23 George Square, Edinburgh EH8 9LD, Scotland. $4; 40 pages monthly except June and July. Founded 1968; receives financial support from Scottish Arts Council.

Major fields of interest: Twentieth century literature, music, cinema, etc., with direct or indirect relevance to Scotland. Also publishes comments on current affairs in Scotland. Open to short stories and poetry.

Manuscript information: Articles of 2000-3000 words preferred. Prefer 3 copies of Ms. Footnotes should be kept to a minimum; when required, printed at the foot of the appropriate column. Report in 6-8 weeks.

Payment: £4 per 1000 words for prose. For poetry: £2.10 for up to 30 lines, rising through £5 for 50 lines or over.

Unless otherwise specified, copyright rests with the author on condition of due acknowledgment of publication.

SCOTTISH STUDIES, 27 George Square, Edinburgh, EH8 9LD, Scotland. £2 ($6) semiannually. Founded 1957; sponsored by School of Scottish Studies, University of Edinburgh.

Major fields of interest: Scottish regional ethnology, folklore, folk tales and music, national culture, custom and belief, place names, settlement history, venacular history, etc. Source studies and critical reviews preferred. Contributions must have a bearing on Scotland.

Manuscript information: Articles of 5000-10,000 words preferred. Footnotes should be incorporated in the text if possible and typed on a separate sheet; bibliographical references on yet another sheet.

"Work cited in the list of references should be confined to those quoted in text, unless a formal bibliography is featured as part of the article. Avoid lengthening references by adding comments. Arrange the references in alphabetical order. When an author is cited for publications in different years, arrange references chronologically. Cite references briefly in brackets in text itself by author, year of publication and relevant page number, e.g. (Watson 1926: 431). Provide fuller description in the list of references, giving name of author in capitals as it appears on title page of book or at end of article, italicising titles of books and journals and putting titles of articles in journals or Festschriften in inverted commas.

WATSON, WILLIAM J.
  1926 *History of the Celtic Place-Names of Scotland.*
       Edinburgh
"Note the following:—
(i) Quote full pagination of articles.
(ii) Author cited for more than one publication in any one year, put (a), (b), etc., before individual references.

OSBORNE, R. H.
  1956a "Internal Migration in England and Wales, 1951."
        Advancement of Science 12:424-43.
  1956b *"Scottish Migration Statistics:* A note." Scottish
        Geographical Magazine 72:153-159."
Payment: 25 offprints; further offprints at low rate.
Copyright lies with School of Scottish Studies, University of Edinburgh, and each inidividual author.
Annual Bibliography included in November issue.

THE SCRIBLERIAN AND THE KIT-CATS, Temple University, Philadelphia, Pennsylvania 19122. $3 ($4 outside US); semi-annually. Founded 1968.

Major fields of interest: Original members of Scriblerus Club and subsequent scholarship about them, their associates the Kit-cats and Dryden. Will consider bibliographical, textual, biographical, critical, and source studies. Articles must be brief. Book reviews are solicited but will accept unsolicited ones.

Manuscript information: Articles up to 600 words. MLA style sheet; footnotes are published at the end of the article. Report within 1 month.

Payment: Up to 5 copies.

Copyrighted; material may be reprinted with permission of the journal and the author.

Each issue contains bibliography.

SEMIOTICA, 516 E. Sixth Street, Bloomington, Indiana 47401. $11; quarterly. Founded 1969; the organ of the International Association of Semiotic Studies, sponsored by International Council for Philosophy and Humanistic Studies and the International Social Science Council.

Major field of interest: Any field in which the notion of the sign is recognized and discussed.

Manuscript information: A SEMIOTICA style sheet is available. Report immediately.

Payment: 25 offprints; others at cost.

THE SERIF: Kent State University Library Quarterly, Kent State University Libraries, Kent, Ohio 44242. $6; quarterly. Founded 1964; sponsored by Kent State University Libraries.

Major fields of interest: Essays on bibliographical and book collecting subjects, notes on bibliographical problems, indexes, checklists, bibliographies.

Manuscript information: MLA style sheet; footnotes should be placed at end of the Ms. Report in 1 month.

Payment: 5 copies of the journal.

Copyright by the Kent State University Libraries.

SEVENTEENTH-CENTURY NEWS, English Department, University of Wisconsin-Milwaukee, Milwaukee, Wisc. 53211. Subscriptions to English Department, Pennsylvania State University, University Park, Pa. 16802. $2, $8 for 5 years; quarterly. Founded 1942; sponsored by the Milton Society, the 17th-Century English Section of MLA, Pennsylvania State University, University of Rochester, University of Oklahoma, Bowling Green University, University of Michigan-Dearborn, University of Wisconsin-Milwaukee.

Major fields of interest: All aspects of 17th-century culture, excluding Shakespeare, in all countries, with particular emphasis on literature in English. Full-length articles not acceptable. Short notes, queries, book reviews, abstracts of published work, surveys of scholarship in a particular field, and bibliographies are invited.

Manuscript information: Length should be 750 words at most. MLA style sheet. Footnotes used sparingly; incorporate reference material in the text. Query in advance preferred. (English and European subjects to J. Max Patrick, English Dept., University of Wisconsin-Milwaukee; American subjects to H. T. Meserole, English Dept., Pennsylvania State University.) Report within 1 month.

Payment: 10 copies of the issue.

Books for review, on English and European subjects, should be sent to Professor J. Max Patrick, English Dept., University of Wisconsin-Milwaukee; on American, to Professor Harrison T. Meserole, English Dept., Pennsylvania State University.

THE SEWANEE REVIEW, The University of the South, Sewanee, Tennessee 37375. U.S. and foreign: $7 per yr., $13 for 2 yrs.; quarterly. Founded 1892; published by the University of the South.

Major fields of interest: Short stories of high quality, verse, reviews, critical articles on literature and the arts.

Manuscript information: 2000-10,000 words. Footnotes should be held to a minimum. Report within 6 weeks.

Payment: $10-$12 per page for prose; 60¢ per line for poetry. Payment on publication.

Copyright held by journal for author's protection.

SHAKESPEARE-JAHRBUCH, Dr. Günther Klotz, managing editor, 102 Berlin, Berolinastrasse 9, DDR. 12, - M; annually. Founded 1864; sponsored by Deutsche Shakespeare-Gesellschaft.

Major fields of interest: Shakespearian studies, studies of Shakespeare's time and of his contemporaries, Shakespeare's reception today. Critical, analytical articles preferred. Articles may be in German or in English.

Manuscript information: 15-30 pages of Ms. copy. Footnotes at end of article. Two copies of Ms. needed. Report in 6 weeks.

Payment: 12,-M per printed page; up to 25 offprints.

Copyright by the author.

THE SHAKESPEARE NEWSLETTER, University of Illinois at Chicago Circle, Chicago, Illinois 60680. $2 for 6 issues. Founded 1951; published and edited by Louis Marder.

Major fields of interest: All forms of Shakespeareana. Shakespeare drama, historical criticism, etc. Creative material published, but only if historically oriented. No pure criticism.

Manuscript information: Length varies from less than 1 column of 600 words to a maximum of 3 columns covering a "broad aspect intensively." MLA style sheet. Footnotes should be held to a minimum and should be included in the text if at all possible. Report within a month.

Payment: Several copies of the issue on request.

No copyright.

SHAKESPEARE QUARTERLY, The Folger Shakespeare Library, 201 East Capitol Street, Washington, D.C. 20003. $10, $12 foreign; quarterly. Founded 1950; sponsored by The Folger Shakespeare Library.

Major fields of interest: Shakespeare, his life, times, theatre, etc. Reviews of Shakespeare studies and editions, Shakespeare festivals, and the London and New York productions. Critical, biographical, explications, and source study articles preferred.

Manuscript information: 15-20 typed pages. MLA style sheet; abstract in PMLA style should accompany Ms. Report in 2-6 months.

Payment: None; 5 copies for articles, 3 for notes, 1 for reviews.

Copyright by The Folger Shakespeare Library.

Bibliography in Summer number.

SHAKESPEARE STUDIES, University of South Carolina, Columbia, S.C. 29208. $14.95; annually. Founded 1965; sponsored by The Center for Shakespeare Studies.

Major fields of interest: Shakespeare and the age of Shakespeare. Critical, scholarly articles used.

Manuscript information: No restrictions on length. University of Chicago style. Report in 2-6 months.

Payment: 1 volume plus 50 offprints.

Copyright by The Center for Shakespeare Studies.

SHAKESPEARE SURVEY, Cambridge University Press, Cambridge, England. Price varies; issued annually. Founded 1948.

Major fields of interest: Critical articles on Shakespeare.

Manuscript information: 4000-5000 words the preferred length. Long quotations should be single-spaced and indented. Except where there are special reasons, quotations of Shakespeare are made from the Globe edition, and line references should be given. Reference form should follow this pattern: e.g., *Henry V*, iv, iii, 25. Footnotes should be placed at the end of the text, and their numbering should run consecutively throughout. Expressions such as 'First Folio' should be written in full. Capital initials should be used for reference to a specific Quarto or Folio; lower case for general reference. In book title references, indicate place of publication only if it is other than London. References to book volumes should be in small Roman numerals. Titles of articles should be indicated by single quotes. Christian names may be omitted after the first reference.

Payment: 25 offprints.

Copyright by the publisher.

SHAKESPEAREAN RESEARCH AND OPPORTUNITIES, English Department, Graduate Center, City University of New York, 33 W. 42nd Street, New York, N.Y. 10036. $5; institutions, $10; annually. Founded 1965.

Major fields of interest: Shakespeare: Renaissance, especially Renaissance intellectual contexts. Prefer "bibliographies, check lists, anything which will aid or stimulate Shakespearean studies."

Manuscript information: Accept full-length articles and notes. MLA style sheet; 2 Ms. copies. Report at once.

Payment: Number of offprints "to be determined."

SHANTIH, P.O. Box 125, Bay Ridge Station, Brooklyn, New York 11220. $1.25/issue; 4 for $5; 2-4 times a year. Founded 1970; sponsored by CCLM.

Major fields of interest: Modern international writings and art. Critical-journalistic articles, creative non-scholarly material also.

Manuscript information: Short articles of 1000-2500 words. MLA style sheet. One copy needed for readers. Report in 1 month.

Payment: Any number of offprints desired.

Copyright policy: Self-copyrighted.

THE SHAVIAN: THE JOURNAL OF THE SHAW SOCIETY, 125 Markyate Road, Dagenham, Essex, RM8 2LB, England. $3.50; 1 or 2 times a year. Founded 1953; sponsored by The Shaw Society (England).

Major fields of interest: Bernard Shaw — life and work, his contemporaries and influences, past and present impact and evaluations. Types of articles: critical, biographical, reviews, news and notes of theater and film, scholarly bibliographical studies, etc. Creative non-scholarly material also published.

Manuscript information: Up to 1000 words; larger text as occasional papers. Three copies needed by readers. Report in 3 months. Return if postage forwarded. Footnotes at end of text.

Payment: 6 offprints.

Copyright vested in Shaw Society; freedom to use on application and if given full acknowledgment.

Irregular bibliographical issue.

THE SHAW REVIEW, S-234 Burrowes Building, The Pennsylvania State University, University Park, Pennsylvania 16802. $5; 3 issues yearly (January, May, and September). Founded 1951; published by the Pennsylvania State University Press.

Major fields of interest: Bernard Shaw: his life, works, and impact, including his relations to his contemporaries and his continuing influence upon literature and thought.

Manuscript information: 5000 word maximum except upon extraordinary circumstances. MLA style sheet; footnotes preferred at the end of the Ms. Unpublished Ms. material used in an article should have written prior clearance for publication from the writer, estate, library, or other owner of the rights or of the property. Report in about a month.

Payment: 10 copies of the issue.

Each issue copyrighted by the magazine.

SHENANDOAH: THE WASHINGTON AND LEE UNIVERSITY REVIEW, Box 722, Lexington, Virginia 24450. $4, $7 for 2 years; quarterly. Founded 1949; sponsored by Washington and Lee University.

Major fields of interest: Fiction, poetry, literary criticism, interviews, literary biography and autobiography, reviews.

Manuscript information: No established length, perhaps 1500-5000. Footnotes discouraged. Report normally within 8 weeks.

Payment: Contributors' copies, plus arranged payments.
Copyrighted by SHENANDOAH.

SILLIMAN JOURNAL, School of Journalism, Silliman University, Dumaguete City, Philippines. $8; quarterly. Founded 1954; sponsored by Silliman University.

Major fields of interest: Articles in the humanities and sciences.

Manuscript information: Articles of 20-30 double spaced typewritten pages preferred. 2 Ms. copies needed. Report in 2 months.

Payment: 25 reprints and 1 copy of journal.

Articles may be reprinted with credit given to journal as source. Bibliographies in second and fourth quarters.

SINCLAIR LEWIS NEWSLETTER, English Department, St. Cloud State College, St. Cloud, Minnesota 56301. $1; once or twice yearly. Founded 1969; sponsored by the School of Arts and Sciences, St. Cloud State College.

Major fields of interest: Sinclair Lewis and writers associated with him.

Manuscript information: 2000 words or under. MLA style sheet; footnotes at end of Ms. 2 copies of Ms. Report in 2 months.

Payment: 5 copies of the journal.

Copyright remains with the journal.

SLAVONIC AND EAST EUROPEAN REVIEW, University of London, School of Slavonic and East European Studies, London W.C.1E 7HU, England. £4 or $13.50 for 4 issues. Founded 1922; sponsored by the University of London School of Slavonic and East European Studies.

Major fields of interest: Languages, literature, and history of the countries of East, Central and Slavonic Europe (excluding Germany).

Manuscript information: Articles should be 6000-8000 words in length. Footnotes should be placed at the bottom of the page or at the end of the article, and numbered consecutively throughout. Contributors should obtain the journal's instruction sheet which contains details of Ms. preparation and a table of transliteration. Report within 2 months.

181

Payment: 50 offprints; additional at a nominal cost.
Copyright remains with the journal.

SMALL PRESS REVIEW, 5218 Scottwood Rd., Paradise, California 95969. $3.50; quarterly. Founded 1966.

Major fields of interest: News, reviews, features of Small Press books and little magazines. Lists all books and magazines received; up-dates annual Directory of Little Magazine and Small Presses.

Manuscript information: Articles of 1000-3000 words preferred. Footnotes discouraged. Report in 2 weeks.

Payment: 1¢ a word or by arrangement; as many copies as needed. Copyrighted.

THE SMITH, 5 Beekman St., New York, N.Y. 10038. $7; 2 book format issues yearly plus at least 6 special issues. Founded 1964.

Major fields of interest: A general magazine. "While the editors publish the work of specialists which is relevant to everyman, the magazine is devoted to no hobbyhorse, petty specialties or vested interests." Accepts "articles providing fresh, important perspective on literary trends and accomplishments." Creative materials used.

Manuscript information: Articles are usually from 500-2000 words but sometimes as long as 10,000 words. Footnotes are discouraged; editors favor references included in the text. Report usually in less than 6 weeks.

Payment: Modest and by arrangement, from $15/50 depending on quality/length; 3 copies of the magazine.

First North American serial rights only.

SOCIETY FOR THE STUDY OF MIDWESTERN LITERATURE NEWSLETTER, 240 Ernst Bessey Hall, Michigan State University, East Lansing, Michigan 48823. $1 dues; 3 times a year. Founded 1971; sponsored by Society for the Study of Midwestern Literature.

Major fields of interest: Midwestern literature. Reviews, notes, queries, short essays, check lists, bibliographies. Bibliographical issue published. Contributors must be members.

Manuscript information: 200-500 words. MLA style sheet. One copy needed for readers. Report in 2 weeks.

Payment: None.
Copyrighted by the Society.

SOUNDINGS, An Interdisciplinary Journal, Box 6309, Station B, Vanderbilt University, Nashville, Tenn. 37235. $7; quarterly. Founded 1967; sponsored by Society for Religion in Higher Education and Vanderbilt University.

Major fields of interest: "Search for new ways to be scholars in our time, for our time. Bold, competent articles that highlight insights, findings, issues in diverse fields of study which disclose humane concerns."

Manuscript information: Articles of about 3000 words preferred. MLA style sheet; footnotes should be placed at end of article, explanatory notes at bottom of page. Two Ms. copies needed.

Payment: 10 free copies of issue.

Copyright by SOUNDINGS.

THE SOUTH ATLANTIC QUARTERLY, Box 6679, College Station, Durham, North Carolina 27708. $6; quarterly. Founded 1902; sponsored by the Duke University Press.

Major fields of interest: Critical articles on public affairs, literature, history, government, and the arts.

Manuscript information: 3500 words or less. Chicago manual of style. Report usually within 1 month.

Copyright by the Duke University Press.

THE SOUTH CAROLINA REVIEW (comes out in lieu of certain issues of FURMAN STUDIES but does not supersede the STUDIES), Department of English, Furman University, Greenville, South Carolina 29613. $2, $3.50 for 2 years; twice yearly (November and May). Founded 1968; sponsored by Furman University.

Major fields of interest: Creative writing (fiction, personal essays, poetry); literary criticism and scholarship, especially about Southern writers; cultural, social, political issues. Short stories, personal essays, and poems preferred.

Manuscript information: 10 to 20 Ms. pages. MLA style sheet or whatever is appropriate to material; footnotes preferably in text. Report in 2-4 weeks.

Payment: 6 copies of the issue.

Copyright assigned to author on request. [See also FURMAN STUDIES.]

THE SOUTH DAKOTA REVIEW, Box 111, University Exchange, Vermillion, South Dakota 57069. $4; quarterly (Sept., Dec., March, May). Founded 1963; sponsored by the College of Arts and Sciences, University of South Dakota.

Major fields of interest: American literature; Western American literature, culture, and history; if material is non-American, 20th century preferred. Emphasis is on regional matters, generally the Great Plains. Critical, historical, and general cultural articles preferred. Style should be good informal American English, neither too popular nor too pompous; aim is toward a literate but not stuffy magazine. Creative work also published.

Manuscript information: Articles should be 1000 to 2500 words for "Comments and Reviews" (used only occasionally), 3000 words for average pieces, 5000-7000 words occasionally. MLA style sheet; incorporate footnotes into text if possible; prefer no footnotes. Report usually in 2 weeks, especially for rejects.

Payment: 1-4 copies of the issue.

Copyright held by magazine, but released automatically on request from the author.

SOUTHERLY, English Department, Sydney University, New South Wales, Australia. $5.33 Australia, $6 U.S.A.; quarterly. Founded 1939; sponsored by English Association (Sydney). Subscriptions to: Wentworth Press, 48 Cooper St., Surty Hills, N.S.W. 2010, Australia.

Major fields of interest: Australian literature. Critical and scholarly material also published.

Manuscript information: Articles of 15-17 typed pages preferred. MLA style sheet. Footnotes should be numbered consecutively and placed at the foot of each page. Report in 2 months.

Payment: Payment is made, but no offprints are given.

Copyright is vested in author; material may be republished with acknowledgment.

SOUTHERN FOLKLORE QUARTERLY, c/o Roger M. Thompson, University of Florida, Gainesville, Florida 32601. $6.50; quarterly. Founded 1937; sponsored by The University of Florida and the Folklore Section, South Atlantic Modern Language Association.

Major fields of interest: Folklore as used by literary authors, critical studies of folklore, occasional collections of folklore and general folklore material.

Manuscript information: MLA style sheet.

Payment: Offprints may be purchased by contributor.

Authors control requests to reprint.

Annual folklore bibliography occupies the entire September issue.

SOUTHERN HUMANITIES REVIEW, 9090 Haley Center, Auburn University, Auburn, Alabama 36830. $4; quarterly (Winter, Spring, Summer, Fall). Founded 1967; sponsored by Auburn University, in cooperation with the Southern Humanities Conference.

Major fields of interest: Scholarly-critical essays (of relatively broad appeal) on all humanistic studies (literature, theology, philosophy, history, music, etc.), plus poetry short fiction, personal essays. Critical, scholarly, biographical, historical, explication de texte, etc., articles preferred.

Manuscript information: Articles of 3500-5000 words; poems should not exceed 2 pages. MLA style sheet. Report in 4-6 months.

Payment: 20 offprints, 2 copies of the issue to essayists and fiction writers, 1 copy to poets and book reviewers.

Copyright registered by issue; permission to reprint generally granted on request.

Index in #4 of each volume.

THE SOUTHERN LITERARY JOURNAL, Greenlaw Hall, University of North Carolina at Chapel Hill, North Carolina 27514. $5; twice yearly. Founded 1968; sponsored by the English Department, University of North Carolina.

Major fields of interest: Restricted to essays on the literature of the South; can use *nothing* else.

Manuscript information: MLA style sheet. Report in 1-2 months.

Payment: $5 per printed page.

Copyright by the magazine.

THE SOUTHERN QUARTERLY, Box 78, Southern Station, Hattiesburg, Mississippi 39401. $3; quarterly. Founded 1962; sponsored by University of Southern Mississippi. Unsolicited Mss. not desired;

185

contributions presently restricted to faculty and graduate students of University of Southern Mississippi.

SOUTHERN REVIEW, English Department, University of Adelaide, Adelaide, South Australia 5000. $4.50 (Aust.); 3 times yearly. Founded 1963; sponsored by University of Adelaide.

Major fields of interest: English, American and Commonwealth Literature. Critical, comparative, interdisciplinary articles preferred. Creative work also published.

Manuscript information: Medium to long articles preferred. MLA style sheet. Report in 3 months.

Payment: None for articles, $5 for short poems; offprints: 20 of articles, 10 of reviews or poems. (Extras obtainable if paid for.)

Copyright vested in authors.

THE SOUTHERN REVIEW, Drawer D, University Station, Baton Rouge, Louisiana 70803. $5 for 1 yr.; $9 for 2 yrs.; quarterly. Founded July 1935; published under co-editorship of Cleanth Brooks and Robert Penn Warren from 1935 to 1942; first issue of the new series appeared in January 1965. Sponsored by Louisiana State University.

Major fields of interest: Creative writing, criticism of modern literature; Southern literature and history; history of ideas and sociology.

Manuscript information: Essays should be 4000 to 10,000 words; fiction, 4000 to 8000; poetry, 1 to 4 pages. Chicago Style Manual; original copy of Ms.; no footnotes. Reports in 1 to 2 months.

Payment: 3¢ a word for prose; $20 a page for poetry; offprints at cost.

Copyright: First American serial rights.

SOUTHERN SPEECH JOURNAL, Department of Speech, University of North Carolina, Chapel Hill, N.C. 27514. $10; quarterly. Founded 1935; sponsored by Southern Speech Communication Association.

Major fields of interest: Communicative disorders, radio-TV-film, interpretation, theatre, speech education, and generally contributions of a quantitative or behavioral approach. Critical and quantitative articles preferred, with some preference given to topics of a Southern flavor.

Manuscript information: 4000 words. MLA style sheet; footnotes double-spaced at end of Ms., no use of *Ibid.*, etc., unnumbered first footnote identifying the author(s). 2 copies of Ms.; original on heavy bond paper with carbon on light weight or xerox copy paper. A 100-word summary should be included to introduce the Ms.; subheads needed to divide Ms. Report in 6-8 weeks.

Payment: None; 3 offprints.

Copyrighted; permission to reprint must be given by author.

Bibliography in Fall issue.

SOUTHWEST REVIEW, Southern Methodist University, Dallas, Texas 75275. $4; quarterly. Founded 1915; sponsored by Southern Methodist University.

Major fields of interest: Critical articles on contemporary American literature. Articles should be directed at the general reader. Creative material also published.

Manuscript information: Around 3000 words the preferred length. University of Chicago style manual. Footnoting should be eliminated as much as possible; when used, place at the bottom of the page. Report in 12 weeks.

Copyright by Southern Methodist University Press, publisher of the magazine. Permissions and copyright assignments given readily, since copyright is held in trust for the contributor.

SOUTHWESTERN AMERICAN LITERATURE, Box 13646, N.T. Station, Denton, Texas 76203. $3; 3 times a year. Founded 1969; sponsored by Southwestern American Literature Association.

Major fields of interest: Articles and book reviews on Southwestern literature and folklore. Scholarly pieces about Southwestern writing and writers. Critical, biographical, survey, genre articles, etc.

Manuscript information: Articles: 15-20 typewritten pages; book reviews: 2-3 typewritten pages. MLA style sheet. One copy needed by readers. Report in 60 days. Footnotes at end of article.

Payment: 2 copies of journal.

SAL retains copyright; reprint privileges available to writer upon request.

SOVIET STUDIES IN LITERATURE, 901 North Broadway, White Plains, New York 10603. $60; quarterly. Founded 1964; published by International Arts and Sciences Press. Unsolicited Mss. not desired.

Major fields of interest: The journal contains unabridged translations of the best critical articles and studies selected from Soviet literary publications.

SPECTRUM, P.O. Box 14800, Santa Barbara, California 93107. Published once a year in the spring. Founded 1957; sponsored by the students Literary Association in conjunction with the Office of Public Information in UCSB.

Major fields of interest: Poetry, short stories.

Manuscript information: Prefer stories of under 5000 words. Any poetry. Return in 1-2 months.

Submission must be copyright free.

SPECULUM, 1430 Massachusetts Avenue, Cambridge, Massachusetts 02138. $18; quarterly. Founded 1926; sponsored by the Mediaeval Academy of America.

Major fields of interest: Mediaeval (roughly 500 to 1500 A.D.). Critical and source study articles are preferred.

Manuscript information: Articles of 6000-12,000 words preferred. MLA style sheet; footnotes should be double-spaced on sheets separate from text. Report in 6 months.

Payment: Authors are charged for offprints.

Copyright by the Mediaeval Academy of America.

SPEECH MONOGRAPHS, c/o Thomas M. Scheidel, Department of Communication Arts, University of Wisconsin, Madison, Wisconsin 53706. $12.50 for 4 issues (March, June, August, November). Founded 1934; sponsored by the Speech Association of America.

Major fields of interest: Research in all areas of communication, with emphasis on oral communication, theatre, broadcasting, and film.

Manuscript information: Articles vary considerably in length. MLA style sheet; footnotes should be typed on separate pages at the end of the Ms. Report in 2 months on the average.

No payment: 25 free reprints and additional ones may be ordered.

Copyright by the Speech Association of America.

SPENSER NEWSLETTER, Department of English, University of Western Ontario, London, 72, Canada. $3 with invoicing, $2 without invoicing ($3 for 2 years without invoicing), $1 for individual copies, 3 times a year. Founded 1970; sponsored by the Department of English.

Major fields of interest: News of Spenser studies. Reviews and notices of books about Spenser, abstracts of articles in journals, news of conferences, work in progress, etc. Interested in current publications and works in progress in the field of Spenser studies.

Manuscript information: MLA style sheet. Report in several weeks.

SPOKEN ENGLISH, 32 Roe Lane, Southport, Lancashire, England. 30/-; 3 times yearly (May, September, January). Founded 1968; sponsored by English Speaking Board.

Major fields of interest: All aspects of spoken English and oral communication. Desire accounts of practical, experimental work with children and adults in the field of spoken English. Creative work can also be considered.

Manuscript information: Length of articles varies (from 1500-3000 words roughly). Time needed for report depends on circumstances; all Mss. considered and replied to immediately.

Payment: None; offprints may be ordered.

Copyrighted.

STECHERT-HAFNER NEWS, 866 Third Avenue, New York, New York 10022. Free to library customers; monthly September-May; yearly index $2. Founded 1946; sponsored by Stechert-Hafner, Inc.

Major fields of interest: The library world, foreign books, bookselling, serials, periodicals, modern library techniques, authors' bibliographies. Readers are mainly librarians of college, university, and large public libraries, government departments, industrial organizations, scientific associations. Authoritative, but not oppressively scholarly material desired.

Manuscript information: Articles of 1800 words preferred; any recognized style sheet. Immediate report from reader.

Payment: $25; 20 copies of the issue.

STEINBECK QUARTERLY (formerly STEINBECK NEWSLET-
TER), English Department, Ball State University, Muncie, Indiana
47306. $3; quarterly. Founded 1968; sponsored by Ball State Univers-
ity and John Steinbeck Society.

Major fields of interest: John Steinbeck and related subjects. All
types of articles except biographical desired.

Manuscript information: Articles of 5-10 pages preferred. MLA
style sheet; footnotes should be placed at end of article. 3 copies
(original plus 2 Xerox copies) of Ms. needed. Report in 1 month.
Unsolicited articles must be accompanied by a letter.

Payment: 5 copies of issue for article; 3 for reviews.

Copyright by editor.

Occasional bibliographical issue; usually first issue of the year.

STEPPENWOLF, Box 55045, Omaha, Nebraska 68155. $2, $3 outside
North America and England; annually. Founded 1965.

Major fields of interest: Poetry, interpretative essays; scholarly
studies. Most space is given over to modern poetry. Authors of articles or commentaries should query the editors before sending Ms.

Manuscript information: No set length limitations for articles.
MLA, University of Chicago, or other style sheets acceptable, if clarity
of presentation is maintained; footnotes appear at end of article.
Report usually in 1 week, at times 3-4 weeks. Any material translated
into English must be accompanied by a copy of the work in its original language.

Payment: 2 copies of issue.

Copyright by editors; reprint rights or transfer of copyright must
be obtained in writing from the editors.

STUDI AMERICANI, Edizioni di Storia e Letteratura, Via Lancellotti
18, Rome, Italy. 3500-6000 Lire for the annual volume. Founded 1955.

Major fields of interest: American literature and history.

Manuscript information: Articles of about 25 typewritten pages
preferred. Mss. must reach editor within the month of December.
Report after 2 months.

Payment: 1000 Lire per printed page; 30 offprints.

STUDIA LINGUISTICA: Revue de Linguistique Générale et Comparée, c/o Professor Bertil Malmberg, Lunds Universitets, Institution

för Linguistik, Kävlingevägen 20, 22240 Lund, Sweden. 15 Swedish Crowns; semi-annually.

Major fields of interest: General and comparative linguistics. Articles must be in German, English, Spanish, or French. Report in about 1 month; perhaps longer during vacation.

Payment: 50 offprints.

STUDIA NEOPHILOLOGICA, c/o Professor Bengt Hasselrot, Gropgränd 2A, Uppsala, Sweden. $13.50 for 2 issues (June and December). Founded 1928; sponsored by Professors of English, French and German.

Major fields of interest: English, German, and French language and literature. Articles preferably should be critical, philological, or source studies and written in English, French, or German.

Manuscript information: 10 to 20 pages in length. Avoid abbreviations like Sok, NoB. Place titles of works quoted at the bottom of the page, not in the text. Titles of books should be underlined (italics), except when preceded or followed by a quotation in italics. In this case do not use a comma before or after the title of the work quoted, nor between title and a single numeral. If the title of a work is followed by the name of the journal in which it appeared, the name of the journal is not italicized. When quoting special word forms, use italics. However, Latin words from which later forms are derived should be printed in spaced-out type (e.g., faire f a c e r e). Translations of words quoted should be within single quotation marks (e.g., faire 'make'). Put a comma between author's name and title of work, before a numeral indicating part of a work, before place of publication, before date of publication, and before p. (page) or S. (Seite). Editors ask that contributors find as concise a form as possible for their contributions. Report within 1 month.

Payment: 50 offprints of articles, 25 of reviews.

Liberal copyright policy.

STUDIES IN AMERICAN FICTION, Department of English, Northeastern University, Boston, Mass. 02115. $3; twice a year. Founded 1973; sponsored by Northeastern University.

Major fields of interest: American fiction. Scholarly and critical articles of all types. Occasional annotated bibliographies.

Manuscript information: 1-25 pages. MLA style sheet. Two copies needed by readers. Report in 3 months.

Payment: 10 offprints.

Copyright by Journal unless otherwise arranged.

STUDIES IN AMERICAN HUMOR, Jack Meathenia, Editor, Department of English, Southwest Texas State University, San Marcos, Texas 78666. $5, $3 student; 3 times a year (Spring, Fall, Winter). Founded 1973.

Major fields of interest: Devoted exclusively to the study and explication of humor in American literature. Articles may deal with any significant aspect of humor in American literature, or pertain to the authors of humorous literature, from the colonial to the contemporary. All types of well-written, knowledgeable articles accepted. In all instances, scholarship and readability are prerequisite. Original creative work and folklore studies will not be accepted. An occasional special issue will be devoted to a single topic, the work of an individual author, or even a particular book. Suggestions for topics for the special issues, as well as names of scholars to treat them, are always welcome. News notes — reports of research, publications, meetings, etc. — are also invited.

Manuscript information: Approximately 10-15 pages (3000-5000 words). MLA style sheet. Two copies needed by readers. Footnotes on a separate sheet at end of article. A short biographical sketch should accompany each manuscript. Report in 6 to 8 weeks.

Payment: 2 copies of the issue and 10 offprints. Additional offprints available at cost.

Copyrighted by STUDIES IN AMERICAN HUMOR.

STUDIES IN BIBLIOGRAPHY, c/o Fredson Bowers, Editor, Box 467, Route 8, Charlottesville, Virginia 22901. $10 to members, $15 to non-members for annual issue. Founded 1947; sponsored by the Bibliographical Society of the University of Virginia.

Major fields of interest: Textual criticism, publishing history, analytical and historical bibliography.

Manuscript information: No length preference. MLA style sheet. See current issues for footnote treatment. Report within 1 month.

Payment: About 20 offprints.

No copyright policy.
Bibliographical issue annually.

STUDIES IN BLACK LITERATURE, Department of English, Mary Washington College, Fredericksburg, Virginia 22401. $7; 3 times yearly (February, June, October). Founded 1970; sponsored by Mary Washington College.

Major fields of interest: Afro-American literature, African literature. Critical, analytical, interpretive, source-study, etc., articles preferred.

Manuscript information: Up to 5000 words. MLA style sheet. 2 copies of the Ms. Report in 2-4 weeks, or less.

Payment: copies of the issue.

Copyright in name of Raman K. Singh, Editor.

Bibliography is future possibility.

STUDIES IN BROWNING AND HIS CIRCLE, Box 6336, Baylor University, Waco, Texas 76706. $5; 2 issues yearly. Founded 1973; sponsored by Armstrong Browning Library.

Major fields of interest: Robert & Elizabeth Barrett Browning. Issues will include review of the year's research on Robert and Elizabeth Barrett Browning, book reviews of all books concerning the Brownings and their circle, research in progress, notes and queries, unpublished letters and poems, desiderata, checklists of acquisitions of research material by libraries throughout the world, announcements of library exhibits, catalogues, speeches, symposiums, and the like. Articles of a strictly critical nature or explications of the text of individual poems are not solicited.

Manuscript information: MLA style sheet.

Payment: 10 offprints.

Copyright by the Library.

Bibliographic checklist in each issue.

STUDIES IN BURKE AND HIS TIME, c/o Dr. Steven R. Phillips, Department of English, Alfred University, Alfred, New York 14802. Three issues yearly.

Major fields of interest: All aspects of the period 1750-1800 in America, Great Britain, and Europe, as well as Edmund Burke's life, thought, continuing influence, or milieu, and ideas which support or oppose Burke. In addition, the journal publishes review essays and book reviews on scholarly work in the later half of the eighteenth century.

Manuscript information: House style. Report within 60-90 days.

STUDIES IN CONTEMPORARY SATIRE, Department of English, Alliance College, Cambridge Springs, Pennsylvania 16403. $3 (individual copies and back issues available at $1.50); 2 times a year. Founded 1972.

Major fields of interest: Contemporary satire in graphic art, poetry, fiction, drama, non-fiction, music, film. Critical studies and creative non-scholarly material published. Graphic art also published.

Manuscript information: 10 typed pages. Footnotes at end of article. Graphics: 4¾" x 7" preferred. Report in 1-2 months.

Payment: 7 offprints.

Copyrighted.

STUDIES IN ENGLISH, University of Mississippi, University, Mississippi 38677. $2; annual issue. Founded 1959; sponsored by Department of English, University of Mississippi. Unsolicited Mss. not desired.

Major fields of interest: English and American language and literature.

Manuscript information: MLA style sheet.

STUDIES IN ENGLISH LITERATURE, c/o Carroll Camden, Editor, Rice University, Houston, Texas 77001. $8 (individuals), $10 (libraries, U.S. and Canadian), $3 (individual copies); quarterly. Founded 1960; sponsored by Rice University.

Major fields of interest: 4 issues each year as follows: (Winter) Non-dramatic Prose and Poetry of the English Renaissance, (Spring) Elizabethan and Jacobean Drama, (Summer) Restoration and Eighteenth Century, (Autumn) Romantic and Victorian. Emphasis is on scholarly articles — historical research, critical essays, etc.

Manuscript information: MLA style sheet. 2 copies of the Ms. preferred but not required. Articles should be 12-24 pages in length, including footnotes. Report within 2 months.

Payment: 25 offprints.

Copyrighted.

Each issue contains a review article covering the significant scholarship of the year in the area of the issue's concentration.

STUDIES IN ENGLISH LITERATURE, 18 Makamachi, Shinjuku-ku, Tokyo, Japan 162. 3000 yen; 3 times a year, of which 1 is English Number. Founded 1919; sponsored by The English Literary Society of Japan.

Major fields of interest: No restrictions. Contributors must be subscribers.

Manuscript information: Less than 25 typed pages. MLA style sheet. Two copies needed by readers. Report in about 3 months.

Payment: 20 free offprints.

Copyright by The English Literary Society of Japan.

STUDIES IN PHILOLOGY, Department of English, University of North Carolina, Chapel Hill, North Carolina 27514. $10; 5 times a year. Founded 1906; sponsored by The Uuiversity of North Carolina.

Major fields of interest: Languages and literatures, classical, medieval, and modern, without restriction as to periods or fields. Historical criticism and linguistic studies preferred.

Manuscript information: 10 to 25 printed pages in length. MLA style sheet. Carbon copies will not be read. Footnotes should be numbered consecutively throughout and may be placed on separate pages at the end of the article or inserted in the text after the line containing the index reference number. They should not be placed at the bottom of the page. Report may take 30 to 60 days, depending upon the character of the article and the time of year; summer may require a longer period.

Payment: 20 offprints.

Copyrighted.

Texts and Studies number December each year.

STUDIES IN ROMANTICISM, 236 Bay State Road, Boston, Massachusetts 02215. $7.50; quarterly. Founded 1961; sponsored by the Graduate School of Boston University.

Major fields of interest: Romanticism in the following fields: Comparative literature, economic history, English, fine arts, Germanic literatures, history of religion and church history, history of science, music, philosophy, Romance literatures, Scandinavian literatures, and Slavic literatures.

Manuscript information: Articles should be under 12,000 words in length. MLA style sheet; footnotes should be double spaced at end of Ms. Report within 3 or 4 months.

Payment: 4 copies of the issue.

Copyright by Trustees of Boston University.

STUDIES IN SCOTTISH LITERATURE (SSL), English Department, University of South Carolina, Columbia, South Carolina 29208. $5; quarterly. Founded 1963.

Major fields of interest: Articles of Scottish literary interest in the broadest sense are the concern of the journal.

Manuscript information: 5000 to 8000 words the desired length. No prescribed style sheet; footnotes should be kept to a sensible minimum. Report within 6 months.

Payment: 20 offprints and one copy of the issue for articles; 10 offprints and one copy of the issue for "Notes and Documents" section; 5 offprints for reviews.

Copyright is held by editor; permission to reprint always granted.

STUDIES IN SHORT FICTION, c/o Frank L. Hoskins, Jr., Newberry College, Newberry, South Carolina 29108. $8; quarterly. Founded 1963; sponsored by Newberry College.

Major fields of interest: Short fiction, all periods; major critical articles and notes such as explication de texte preferred.

Manuscript information: Maximum length for articles 2250 words, including footnotes; notes 750 words. MLA style sheet; footnotes at foot of page. Report in 5-6 weeks.

Payment: 2 copies of the issue.

Bibliographical issue in the Summer number.

STUDIES IN THE HUMANITIES, 111B Leonard Hall, Indiana University of Pennsylvania, Indiana, Pennsylvania 15701. $3; twice yearly (Winter and Summer). Founded 1969; sponsored by Indiana University of Pennsylvania.

Major fields of interest: The broad area of the humanities — literature, language, theater, films. Most articles are critical studies, but source and biographical studies and explications are welcome.

Manuscript information: 4000 words maximum. MLA style sheet; double-column format with footnotes. Separate bibliographies for each article not published. Report in up to 6 months.

Payment: None; 3 copies of the issue; 100 reprints (minimum) may be purchased from printer.

Copyright by IUP.

STUDIES IN LINGUISTICS, c/o Dr. George L. Trager, Editor, Department of Anthropology, Northern Illinois University, DeKalb, Illinois 60115. $6 to agents and individuals if paid in advance; $7.50 if invoice is required; 4 numbers to each volume (usually 2, 3, or 4 numbers in a single issue, plus Occasional Papers. Founded 1942.

Major fields of interest: Anthropological structural linguistics.

Manuscript information: Length varies from short articles or reviews to articles of 25 pages or so. Longer contributions are published as Occasional Papers. Charts, diagrams, etc., should be drawn or typed at the point where they should appear, or they may be made into separate pages. Footnotes not used; references in text to author and date (and if necessary, page), with a terminal bibliography; quotation and discussion of material referred to should be an integral part of the text. The Editor may suggest changes to conform to this format. Decision to publish usually made quickly.

Payment: Occasional Papers must have total cost of publication provided by subvention or other outside source; royalties and other payments (including repayment of costs) are arranged individually. 50 offprints of articles, 25 of reviews are provided free to contributors; additional copies at cost.

STUDIES IN THE LITERARY IMAGINATION, c/o Paul G. Blount, Editor, English Department, Georgia State University, Atlanta, Georgia 30303. Semi-annually. Founded 1968; sponsored by English Department, Georgia State University. Unsolicited Mss. not desired.

Major fields of interest: Literature and language (general) and related topics, such as history, biography. Each issue is planned by a specialist who consults with authors for specific contributions.

Manuscript information: No restrictions on length. MLA style sheet; footnotes at bottom of page.

Payment: 10 offprints, plus an additional 10 upon request.

Copyrighted, but an author may apply for and hold his own copyright for his contribution.

STUDIES IN THE NOVEL, North Texas State University, Denton, Texas 76203. $4; quarterly. Founded 1969; sponsored by North Texas State University.

Major fields of interest: All aspects of the novel. Scholarly and critical articles preferred.

Manuscript information: No policy on length. MLA style sheet. Report in 60 days usually.

Payment: 2 copies of journal.

Copyright retained by STUDIES IN THE NOVEL.

STUDIES IN THE RENAISSANCE, 1161 Amsterdam Avenue, New York, New York 10027. $12.50 for individual membership in Renaissance Society of America, $16 for institutional memberships; annually. Founded 1954; sponsored by Renaissance Society of America.

Major fields of interest: All phases of the Renaissance. Articles should be of interest in more than one field of specialization; special studies in a single field are less desirable.

Manuscript information: 25-40 pages preferred. MLA style sheet; footnotes at end of Ms. Report in 1-3 months; journal accepts or rejects on a current basis and does not allow a backlog to accumulate.

STUDIES IN THE TWENTIETH CENTURY, P.O. Box 12, Troy, New York 12181. $4; twice a year. Founded 1968.

Major fields of interest: Scholarly and critical articles concerning the art and literary movements of the twentieth century, and their philosophies.

Manuscript information: Fairly long articles. MLA style sheet. One copy needed by readers. Report within 2 weeks. Footnotes at end of article, "and not many of them."

Payment: 3 copies and 25 offprints.

STYLE, English Department, University of Arkansas, Fayetteville, Arkansas 72701. $5; students $3; single issue $2; 3 times a year. Founded 1967; sponsored by the University of Arkansas.

Major fields of interest: All aspects of style. Critical articles preferred.

Manuscript information: No restrictions on length. MLA style sheet. 2 copies of Ms. needed. An abstract is required. Report within 3 months.

Payment: 15 offprints.

Copyrighted.

Bibliographical issue in Winter.

SUB-STANCE, A Journal of Theory and Literary Criticism, 748 Van Hise Hall, University of Wisconsin, Madison, Wisconsin 53706. $4 regular, $3 student; $8 institutions; 3 times a year (Fall, Winter, Spring). Founded 1971; sponsored by Department of French and Italian of the University of Wisconsin.

Major fields of interest: Recent trends in literary theory, particularly emphasizing development in the last decade in France. Also linguistic theory and American developments. Issues have included studies of Ponge, Beckett, Barthes, Ricardou, poetic functions of language, literature and psychoanalysis, theories of poetics, Beyond Structuralism, contemporary French poetry, etc.

Manuscript information: MLA style sheet (but somewhat flexible on format). Articles usually 10-20 pages. Report in 1 or 2 months.

Payment: inquire about details.

Copyrighted.

SYMPOSIUM, 210 H. B. Crouse Hall, Syracuse University, Syracuse, New York 13210. $8 for 4 issues. Founded 1946; sponsored by the Department of Romance Languages, Syracuse University.

Major fields of interest: Modern foreign literatures. Articles dealing with English and American literature are published only if some sort of comparative approach is used.

Manuscript information: No special length required, minimum length: 15 double-spaced typed pages. MLA style sheet; footnotes should be placed at the end of the article. Report in up to 1 month.

Payment: 5 copies of the issue.

Articles may not be reprinted elsewhere, in whole or in part, without the written permission of the publisher, Syracuse University Press.

THE TAMARACK REVIEW, Box 159, Station K, Toronto 12, Ontario, Canada. $5; quarterly. Founded 1956.

Major fields of interest: Canadian poetry and stories. Some articles and reviews of literary books.

Manuscript information: Articles may range from 2000-10,000 words in length. Report within 1 month.

Payment: About 1½¢ per word and 2 copies of the issue.

Copyright remains with the author.

TENNESSEE FOLKLORE SOCIETY BULLETIN, Box 234, Middle Tennessee State University, Murfreesboro, Tennessee 37130. $2 for students, $3 for other individuals, $4 for institutions; quarterly. Founded 1935; sponsored by the Tennessee Folklore Society. Mimeographed.

Major fields of interest: Any aspects of folklore, folk arts and crafts, folk song, or folk life and customs (including folk speech). Particular interest is in the South, especially in Tennessee, but geographical limits are not set on the material published in the magazine. Articles may be of any type, including reports of folklore collections.

Manuscript information: Articles of 100-1500 words preferred, but longer papers and short notes also used. MLA style sheet should be observed. Pedantic detail in footnotes not encouraged, but footnotes may be used to offer incidental discussion and to convey information of interest not directly related to the text. Report usually within a week.

Payment: 3 copies of the issue.

Copyright by the magazine.

TENNESSEE STUDIES IN LITERATURE, Richard Kelly, editor, McClung Tower 306, University of Tennessee, Knoxville, Tennessee 37916. $5 for annual issue. Founded 1956; sponsored by the University of Tennessee.

Major fields of interest: Scholarly and critical articles on English and American literature, and other literary studies (German, French, etc.). Occasional special issues.

Manuscript information: Papers should be no longer than 8000 words or 5 printed pages. MLA style sheet; footnotes at the end of the article. Report within 3 months; receipt of Mss. promptly acknowledged.

Payment: 50 offprints.

Copyright by the University, but authors usually allowed to reprint.

TENNYSON RESEARCH BULLETIN, Tennyson Society, Tennyson Research Centre, City Library, Lincoln, England. $4.50 individual membership in Tennyson Society, $6 institutional; annually. Founded 1967.

Major fields of interest: Tennysoniana, publications, research, news items, etc.

Manuscript information: Approximately 2000-3000 words; notes must be listed at end and referred to by number in text. Longer articles (minimum 10,000 words) may be considered for publication as monographs.

Copyright by The Tennyson Society.

TESOL QUARTERLY, Maurice Imhoof, Editor, Education 309, Indiana University, Bloomington, Indiana 47401. $10; quarterly (March, June, September, December). Founded 1967; sponsored by Organization of Teachers of English to Speakers of Other Languages.

Major fields of interest: English language, linguistics, language learning, etc., as related to teaching English as a second language or as a second dialect. Critical and scholarly articles, reports of experiments, review of materials and books in the field, etc., preferred.

Manuscript information: 10-15 typewritten pages. MLA style sheet; footnotes typed directly below the line to which referred. 3 copies of Ms. needed. Report in 2-3 months.

Payment: None; 25 offprints.

Copyright belongs to the quarterly, but author's permission needed to reprint.

TEXAS STUDIES IN LITERATURE AND LANGUAGE, P.O. Box 7822, University Station, Austin, Texas 78712. $8 for individuals, $10 for institutions. Founded 1959; sponsored by The University of Texas.

Major fields of interest: The humanities, with emphasis on literature, language, philosophy, and fine arts. Articles may be critical, textual, bibliographical or explication. Treatment of material should be scholarly rather than popular.

Manuscript information: 3000-6000 words, though there is no set limit. MLA style is followed generally. Report ordinarily within 3 months.

Payment: 50 offprints and 1 free issue.

Copyright by The University of Texas Press. Contributors usually have the right of quotation under the general rule of scholarly criticism; in the rare instances where such a rule does not apply, contributors are expected to clear the privilege of quoting with copyowners.

THEATRE ANNUAL, Hiram College, Hiram, Ohio. $2; annually. Founded 1942; sponsored by Faculty-Student Association.

Major fields of interest: Restricted only to theatre; all types of articles considered.

Manuscript information: 2000-3000 words. MLA style sheet. Report in 2-4 weeks.

Payment: 10 copies of the issue.

Copyright by the editor.

THE THEATRE JOURNAL, Alfred E. Rickert, Editor, Department of English, SUNY-Oswego, Oswego, New York 13126. $1 per issue; 2 issues a year. Founded 1960; sponsored by New York State Theatre Association.

Major fields of interest: Theater and drama. No restrictions on types of articles. Each issue includes a play not previously published.

Manuscript information: 1000-6000 words. MLA style sheet. One copy needed by readers. Report in 60 days.

Payment: 2 author's copies of the journal.

Copyright policy: Periodical is copyrighted. Playwrights retain complete rights to plays published by THE THEATRE JOURNAL.

THEATRE NOTEBOOK, 103 Ralph Court, Queensway, London W2 5HU, England. 30/-; quarterly. Founded 1945.

Major fields of interest: The history and practice of the British theater. The journal is concerned strictly with the study of the theater, not with the study of the drama.

Manuscript information: Articles should be from 2000-4000 words in length. Report in about 1 month.

Payment: 6 copies of the issue.

THEATRE QUARTERLY, 39 Goodge St., London W1P 1FD, England. $8 (individuals), $12 (institutions); quarterly. Founded 1971; sponsored in association with the Commission for a British Theatre Institute.

Major fields of interest: Theater and other performing arts, historical and contemporary, in all countries. Emphasis on performance, not literary criticism. Leaning towards popular theater. Historical and contemporary material tends to be descriptive with critical tone, e.g. reconstructions of famous productions of past, surveys or accounts of individual careers (playwrights, directors, performers) or theater movements, or countries. Occasional critical reassessments of individual plays and playwrights. Creative non-scholarly material also published.

Manuscript information: 3000 to 8000 words, longer if needed by subject. Style sheet supplied on request; 1 copy needed by readers. Typed, double spaced, footnotes at end of articles. Send stamped addressed envelopes or International Reply Coupons. Report time varies.

Payment: $35 to $75 per article. Three complimentary copies; offprints at cost.

Copyright policy: First serial rights only.

Companion periodical "Theatrefacts" includes current bibliography; quarterly with TQ.

THEATRE RESEARCH/RECHERCHES THÉATRALES, 14 Woronzow Road, London N.W.8, England; Mss. should be submitted to one of the joint editors, Department of Drama, University of Glasgow, Scotland, and the Department of Drama, University of Manchester, Great Britain. 20 Swiss Francs; 2 issues yearly. Founded 1958.

Major fields of interest: Research into the history of the theater in all countries written from a comparative point of view. Bilingual: English and French.

Manuscript information: Articles should be from 2000-5000 words in length. Report within 1 month.

Payment: 10 copies of the issue.

THEATRE STUDIES, Department of Theatre, The Ohio State University, Columbus, Ohio 43210. Issued once a year, during Summer Quarter. Founded 1954; sponsored by The Ohio State University Department of Theatre. Unsolicited Mss. not desired.

Major fields of interest: Theatre history. Articles desired only on request of the editor since the aim of the publication is the reporting of research activities within The Ohio State University Theatre Collection.

THEATRE SURVEY, c/o Atillio Favorini and George E. Bogusch, Managing Editors, Department of Speech and Theatre Arts, University of Pittsburgh, Pittsburgh, Pennsylvania 15260. $5; semi-annually. Founded 1960; sponsored by the American Society for Theatre Research, in association with the Division of Humanities, University of Pittsburgh.

Major fields of interest: Theater history.

Manuscript information: 15 printed pages the preferred length. Report in approximately 3 months.

Copyright by the journal.

THOREAU JOURNAL QUARTERLY, P.O. Box 551, Old Town, Maine 04468. $4 to members, $6 to subscribers; quarterly. Founded 1968; sponsored by Thoreau Fellowship, National and International.

Major fields of interest: Any subject related to Thoreau interests — literature, philosophy, conservation, Indians, etc. Can include Emerson, Hawthorne Alcott, Sanborn, if Thoreau-oriented. Articles on "Civil Disobedience" used only if they have literary leaning. Creative material also used.

Manuscript information: Maximum length for articles 1800 words; short items of 300 words also used. Report in 1 month.

Payment: 2 copies for longer articles, 1 for shorter ones; reprints may be ordered at cost.

Not copyrighted.

THOREAU SOCIETY BULLETIN, State University College, Genesco, New York 14454. $2; quarterly. Founded 1941; sponsored by The Thoreau Society, Inc.

Major fields of interest: Henry David Thoreau, his life and his works.

Manuscript information: The shorter the article, the better, with a probable maximum of 2000 words. MLA style sheet; no footnotes preferred, but if essential, they should be kept to a minimum. Report almost immediately.

Payment: 20 copies given on request.

No copyright.

THOTH, Department of English, Syracuse University, Syracuse, New York 13210. $3, institutions; 3 issues per year. Founded 1959; sponsored by Syracuse University.

Major fields of interest: English and American literature. Critical, scholarly, and bibliographic articles preferred.

Manuscript information: Articles should be no longer than 30 typed pages. MLA style sheet; footnotes at bottom of printed page. Report in about 4 months.

Payment: 6 copies.

Copyright by Syracuse University, returnable to the author.

Note: Manuscripts are accepted from any graduate student or ABD in an accredited graduate school in the U.S. or Canada.

THOUGHT, A Weekly Review of Politics and the Arts, 35 Netaji Subhas Marg, Delhi-6, India II ISSN 0040 6449. $7.50; weekly. Contributors must be subscribers.

Major fields of interest: Current politics, literature, and the arts. Creative material also published.

Manuscript information: Articles should be 1300-1600 words in length.

Payment: By arrangement.

THOUGHT, Fordham University Press, Box L, Fordham University, Bronx, New York 10458. $10; quarterly. Founded 1926; sponsored by Fordham University.

Major fields of interest: "There are no restrictions." The journal is interested in learning and culture in all fields. Articles should not, however, reflect an anti-Catholic, anti-Christian viewpoint. Scholarly articles on subjects of permanent value and contemporary interest are desired. The "technical" should be avoided since the journal is a quarterly of general interest; also "since it is academic it avoids the popular." Poetry occasionally used.

Manuscript information: Articles should range from 5000-11,000 words. University of Chicago style manual; footnotes may be placed at the foot of the page or at the end of the article, but in either case must be numbered consecutively throughout. Report in 1 to 2 months.

Payment: 25 bound reprints.

Copyright by the magazine unless special arrangements are made in particular cases.

THE TIMES LITERARY SUPPLEMENT, Printing House Square, London E.C.4, England. $26 air freight; weekly. Founded 1902; sponsored by Times Newspapers, Ltd. Unsolicited Mss. considered, but available space is limited.

Major fields of interest: Articles making fresh literary discoveries or emendations to accepted notions concerning trends or authors. All reviews are commisioned by the editor. Bibliographical articles published each week. Poetry also used.

Manuscript information: Articles should be 800-3000 words in length.

TOPIC, Washington and Jefferson College, Washington, Pennsylvania 15301. $2; semi-annually. Founded 1960; sponsored by Washington and Jefferson College.

Major fields of interest: Some field of the liberal arts provides the topic for each issue, which is devoted to a single topic, such as philosophy, literature, psychology, history, economics, etc. Articles should be analytical or expository, relating to the issue's topic, scholarly in content, but intended for readers outside a given discipline.

Manuscript information: Articles should be 2500-4000 words in length, and manuscripts of the April issue should be received by January 15 preceding; for the October issue, by July 15 preceding.

Footnotes acceptable, but restraint requested. Report within 6 months.

Copyright by the College.

TRADITIO, Studies in Ancient and Medieval History, Thought, and Religion, Fordham University Press, Box L, Fordham University, Bronx, New York 10458. $13.50; annually. Founded 1943; sponsored by Fordham University Press.

Major fields of interest: Medieval studies; critical editions and definitive studies preferred.

Manuscript information: No length restrictions. Own style sheet is required. Two copies of Ms. preferred. Footnotes should be typed, double-spaced on separate sheets. Submissions received at beginning of March, decision reported by end of October.

Payment: For longer articles, a copy of the volume and 25 free offprints. For shorter articles, 25 free offprints.

Not all volumes copyrighted.

TRANSACTIONS OF THE CAMBRIDGE BIBLIOGRAPHICAL SOCIETY, University Library, Cambridge, England. £2; annual issue. Founded 1949; sponsored by the Society. Query editors before sending Mss.

Major fields of interest: Bibliography with some Cambridge connection, for example, dealing with Mss. or printed books in the Cambridge libraries or books printed at Cambridge or by Cambridge authors. Contributions of general bibliographical interest will also be considered. Enumerative bibliographies from full-dress treatment to check lists are desired as well as historical bibliography; histories of libraries, bookselling, publishing, bookbinding, book collecting, printing, type founding, palaeography, and catalogues of Mss., etc.

Manuscript information: Editors should be queried, but in general, articles over 10,000 words difficult to accommodate, although they may be printed in instalments. Separate monographs are possible for long Mss. Footnotes should be typed separately at the end. Formula for references can be checked in previous issues.

Payment: 25 offprints; more at author's expense.

Copyright assigned to the Society, but permission to reprint is usually given after an interval.

TRIQUARTERLY, 101 University Hall, Northwestern University, Evanston, Illinois 60201. $7; 3 times yearly, with occasional supplements. Founded 1964; sponsored by Northwestern University.

Major fields of interest: Arts, letters, and opinion. Creative material of primary interest.

Manuscript information: Articles should be "as brief as is consistent with comprehensibility." MLA style sheet; footnotes are placed at end of article whenever possible; when not possible, notes are indicated in text by asterisks, then placed at the bottom of the appropriate page. Report in approximately 6 weeks.

Payment: "Sometimes."

Blanket copyright of issue; assignment on request.

T. S. ELIOT NEWSLETTER, English Department, Ross 766-S, York University, Downsview, Ontario, Canada M3J 1P3. $5 for 4 issues; twice a year.

Major fields of interest: T. S. Eliot and Eliot-related figures. "All reviews by invitation, but we are always interested in hearing from Eliot scholars about their projects, publications, etc. Also notes and queries."

Manuscript information: "Short abstracts, research and project particulars, notes and queries, bibliographical information — less than 300 words preferably. Any standard form of presentation." Two copies needed by readers. Report in 8 to 10 weeks. "Please avoid using footnotes."

Payment: 1 copy of newsletter.

Copyright retained by the newsletter, unless a mutually agreeable special arrangement is made.

TULANE STUDIES IN ENGLISH, English Department, Tulane University, New Orleans, Louisiana 70118. Founded 1949; sponsored by Tulane University. Unsolicited Mss. not desired. Contributors are members of the English Faculty of Tulane University.

Major fields of interest: English and American literature from Beowulf to the present.

THE TWAINIAN, Mark Twain Research Foundation, Perry, Missouri 63462. $5 for annual membership; bi-monthly. Founded 1939.

Major fields of interest: Life and writings of Mark Twain. Source studies should contain new information only. Sample copy available upon request.

TWENTIETH CENTURY LITERATURE, William McBrien, Editor, Hofstra University, Hempstead, New York 11550. $6 (individuals), $8 (institutions); foreign: $7 (individuals), $9 (institutions); single copies, $2 plus 50¢ postage; quarterly. Founded 1955.

Major fields of interest: Scholarly and critical articles, plus bibliography, on twentieth-century literature. Explication per se not published, but welcome when it is part of a larger scholarly or critical discussion.

Manuscript information: No required length. Footnotes should appear at the end of the article. Report within 2 to 3 months.

Payment: 25 offprints; additional offprints may be ordered at cost.

Special provision may be made for copyright on occasion.

Current Bibliography, a major feature of every issue, annotates periodical articles dealing with 20th-century literature.

UNDER THE SIGN OF PISCES: ANAIS NIN AND HER CIRCLE, Richard Centing, OSU Libraries, 1858 Neil Avenue, Columbus, Ohio 43210. $2; quarterly. Founded 1970; sponsored by The Ohio State University.

Major fields of interest: Twentieth century modern literary history relating to the expatriates of the thirties: Anais Nin, Henry Miller, et. al. Reports on Nin's personal appearances; reviews of books on the literary thirties, checklists of criticism about the circle.

Manuscript information: 1000 words preferred. No style sheet preferred: informal. One copy needed by readers. Report in 2 weeks. Footnotes at end of article. Use glossy photographs (previously unpublished).

Payment: One copy of newsletter.

Author retains copyright.

UNIVERSITIES QUARTERLY, 10 Great Turnstile, London WC IV 7HJ, England. £2.50; quarterly. Founded 1946.

Major fields of interest: Higher education and topics of importance in universities, e.g., fundamental questions of curricula, methods of teaching and administration, etc. The quarterly "publishes authoritative and controversial articles with the purpose of spreading the discussion of ideas about universities and higher education throughout all the universities in the world."

Manuscript information: Articles should be from 1500 words in length.

Payment: 25 offprints.

UNIVERSITY OF DAYTON REVIEW, University of Dayton, Dayton, Ohio 45409. Free, 3 issues a year. Founded 1964; sponsored by the University of Dayton.

Major fields of interest: Emphasis is on the humanities and interdisciplinary studies. Accepts articles suitable for both the general and specialist reader.

Manuscript information: Articles normally limited to 6000 words. MLA style sheet; footnotes should be placed at end of article. 2 copies of Ms. needed. Report in approximately 1 month. Note: long quotations should be double-spaced.

Payment: 5 offprints; more on request.

UNIVERSITY OF TORONTO QUARTERLY, University of Toronto Press, Toronto, Ontario M5S 16A, Canada. $8; quarterly. Founded 1930.

Major fields of interest: The humanities in general. Articles should be critical or biographical in nature.

Manuscript information: 6000 words the preferred length. MLA style sheet.

Payment: On publication.

Author retains copyright, but permission to quote must be obtained from both University of Toronto Press and author.

Bibliographical issue in July.

UNIVERSITY OF WINDSOR REVIEW, Windsor, Ontario, Canada. $2.50 plus 10¢ postage; biannually. Founded 1965; sponsored by University of Windsor.

Major fields of interest: Literature, history, political science, social sciences, art. Some poetry and fiction published. Contemporary stressed. Articles should not be "too narrow and not on areas already done to death."

Manuscript information: Prefer articles of 2500-3500 words. MLA style sheet; notes should be placed at end. Report in approximately 1 month.

Payment: 2 copies of issue plus 20 offprints.

Copyright remains with author. First serial rights only.

Bibliographical material in first issue of each volume.

THE USE OF ENGLISH, Chatto and Windus Educational, Park Street, St. Albans, Hertfordshire, England. £1.50; quarterly (May, September, November, February); sponsored by Chatto and Windus Educational.

Major fields of interest: The magazine is designed for readers concerned with the teaching of English at any level. The theory and practice of English teaching and the study of texts is stressed. Recent titles: "English in Crisis," "Graffiti in the Classroom," "Novel Approaches: Teaching *The Catcher in the Rye*," "Crisis of Culture." Creative material also used.

Manuscript information: Articles should be from 1500-3000 words in length. Footnotes should be avoided.

Payment: £4 per 1000 words.

VIATOR: Medieval and Renaissance Studies, Center for Medieval and Renaissance Studies, Los Angeles, California 90024. Subscription price not set; annually. First volume 1970; sponsored by UCLA Center for Medieval and Renaissance Studies.

Major fields of interest: Medieval and Renaissance studies A.D. 300-1600, including Byzantium and Islam. Documented, scholarly contributions, especially inter-cultural and inter-disciplinary.

Manuscript information: No preference on length. Use style in *Traditio;* footnotes are at end of article, numbered in sequence, typed, double spaced. Prefer 2 copies of Ms. Style sheet published at end of volumes 2 onward. Time lapse is 12 to 18 months.

Payment: 25 offprints.

Copyright by University of California Press.

THE VICTORIAN NEWSLETTER, c/o William E. Buckler, New York University, New York, New York 10003. $3, $5 for 2 years; published twice a year in Fall and Spring. Sponsored by English X Group of MLA.

Major fields of interest: Victorian literature in all phases, from studies of individual authors to notes and brief articles on specific phases of Victorian literature. "A Guide to Research Materials on the Major Victorians" includes Ms. information for individual authors.

Manuscript information: Articles vary in length from about 7500 words to short notes and "brief articles." Documentation desired where necessary, and footnotes should be listed at the end of the article. Report in 2 months in most cases.

Selected annotated current bibliography of Victorian studies in every issue.

VICTORIAN PERIODICALS NEWSLETTER, Department of English, University College, Toronto, Ontario M5S 1A1, Canada. $3 individual, $5 institutional; quarterly. Founded 1968; sponsored by the Research Society for Victorian Periodicals.

Major fields of interest: Victorian periodicals. Brief notes and queries, critical and scholarly articles and reviews published.

Manuscript information: 1200-2000 words. MLA style sheet; footnotes included in text where possible, otherwise on separate sheet at end of article. 2 copies of Ms. needed. Report in 1 month.

Bibliographical items appear regularly, but not as regular issue.

VICTORIAN POETRY: A CRITICAL JOURNAL OF VICTORIAN LITERATURE, 129 Armstrong Hall, West Virginia University, Morgantown, West Virginia 26505. $6 individual, $8 institution, $3 student rate; quarterly. Founded 1962; sponsored by West Virginia University.

Major fields of interest: Victorian literature (British). Critical articles preferred; explications welcomed for Notes section; others considered if valuable to readers.

Manuscript information: No length restrictions within reason. MLA style sheet; footnotes should be kept to a minimum and incorporated into text whenever possible. 2 copies (1 carbon) of Ms. requested. Abstracts required for articles ten pages or longer. Report usually within 3 months.

Payment: 5 copies of the issue; offprints at cost.

Copyright by West Virginia University; permission to reprint granted on terms stated in PMLA.

VICTORIAN STUDIES, Indiana University, Bloomington, Indiana 47401. $7 for individuals, $12 for institutions; quarterly (September, December, March, and June). Founded 1957; sponsored by Indiana University.

Major fields of interest: Scholarly and critical studies of English culture of the Victorian Period (c. 1830-1914) in any phase.

Manuscript information: No length restrictions other than that very long articles (over 30 typed pages) must justify their length. MLA style sheet. 2 copies of the Ms. needed. Footnotes should be typed separately at the end of the paper. Report within 2 or 3 months.

Payment: 2 free copies. $15 for 50, $25 for 100 offprints.

Bibliographical issue in June.

THE VIRGINIA QUARTERLY REVIEW, One West Range, Charlottesville, Virginia 22903. $7, $12 for 2 years; quarterly. Founded 1925; sponsored by The University of Virginia.

Major fields of interest: General literature and topics of discussion aimed at the general reader and not the specialized scholar. Creative material also published.

Manuscript information: Articles of 2000-7000 words preferred. No footnotes are used. Report within 2 weeks whenever possible.

Payment: $5 per page of 350 words for prose; 50¢ per line for poetry, payable on publication.

Copyright by the quarterly; assigned to author on request.

VISIBLE LANGUAGE (formerly THE JOURNAL OF TYPOGRAPHIC RESEARCH), c/o The Cleveland Museum of Art, Cleveland, Ohio 44106. $11; quarterly. Founded 1967.

Major fields of interest: Research on the visual media of language expression, and relation to content; descriptive bibliography; concrete poetry.

Manuscript information: No restrictions on length, but prefer compact articles. An Author's Guide for the organization, preparation, and submission of manuscripts is available from the editor.

Footnotes are placed at the end of the article. 3 Ms. copies needed. Report in 1-2 months.

Payment: Complimentary subscription for 1 year; 20 free offprints, additional at 20¢ each.

THE VISVA-BHARATI QUARTERLY, The Editor, P.O. Santiniketan, Dist. Birbhum, West Bengal, India. $4; quarterly. Founded 1923; sponsored by Visva-Bharati University.

Major fields of interest: Literature, Literary Criticism, Cultural Studies, Music, Dance, Drama, Philosophy, Religion, and Mysticism, History, Economics, Current Affairs, Poetry (serious), Biography, Translated stories and articles of general cultural interest. Critical, biographical and articles of general interest preferred. The journal "invites collaboration of writers, scholars and artists of different countries who, through disinterested pursuit of knowledge or creation or contemplation of beauty, are adding to the cultural heritage of Man." Also publishes creative work.

Manuscript information: Articles not to exceed 7000 words, "neatly typed in double space on one side of the paper with liberal margins" on 34 x 21 cm. paper. Footnotes in 8 point on each page; "whenever diacritical marks are used, an alternative spelling without diacritical marks should also be indicated." Report in 3 months.

Payment: Indian Rs.25 minimum, Rs.50 maximum, or adjusted as a subscription of the journal." 20 offprints and a copy of the journal free.

Copyright by the journal which "reserves the exclusive right to reprint and publish, or to permit other journals and organizations to print, publish, and/or to permit and to grant permission for taking microfilms of the materials used in this journal, in full or in part thereof." Any royalty received will be shared equally by journal and author.

A WAKE NEWSLETTER, Department of Literature, University of Essex, Wivenhoe Park, Colchester, CO4 3SQ, England. £2; every 2 months. Founded 1962.

Major fields of interest: Studies of James Joyce's *Finnegans Wake*.

Manuscript information: Articles from brief notes to a maximum of about 4000 words accepted. Style of presentation immaterial; footnotes at end of article. Report as soon as possible; speed of publication is important aim.

Payment: None; 2 copies of the issue normally supplied, more on request.

WALT WHITMAN REVIEW, c/o William White, Director, American Studies, Wayne State University, Detroit, Michigan 48202. $4, $7 for 2 years; quarterly. Founded 1955; sponsored by Charles E. Feinberg, Detroit, Michigan.

Major fields of interest: Articles, notes, and book reviews on Walt Whitman. Also criticism, interpretation, comments on the literary reputation, unpublished prose and poetry of Whitman, and biographical data.

Manuscript information: Articles should range from 500-3500 words in length. Modified MLA style sheet; avoid footnotes if possible. Receipt of Mss. acknowledged; report almost immediately; publication within 18 months.

Payment: 3 copies of the issue.

Copyright by Wayne State University Press.

WASCANA REVIEW, c/o Managing Editor, English Department, University of Saskatchewan, Regina Campus, Regina, Sask., Canada S4S 0A2. $2.50; 2 issues yearly (May and November). Founded 1966.

Major fields of interest: Critical articles, short fiction, and poetry especially desired. Range of interest is open, not restricted to any period.

Manuscript information: 1000-6000 words. MLA style sheet preferred, but not required; footnotes at the end of the article. Report in 4-6 weeks. Poetry: 4-100 lines.

Payment: $3 per page for prose, $10 per poem; 2 copies of the magazine, additional copies at $1 per copy.

Copyright by the magazine, permission to reprint if acknowledged that it first appeared in WASCANA.

Cumulative index of material published in WASCANA planned.

WEST COAST REVIEW, Simon Fraser University, Burnaby 2 (Vancouver), B.C., Canada. $6; 4 times yearly. Founded 1965; sponsored by West Coast Review Publishing Society.

Major fields of interest: Modern avant-garde fiction, poetry, music, photography, drawings, book reviews, bibliographies.

Manuscript information: 1000-3000 words for fiction, no restrictions on length of verse. Clear, typed Mss. desired; footnotes on separate sheet at end of article. 2 copies of Ms. needed. Report in 4 weeks.

Payment: $5 to $25; 2 copies of the issue.

Copyright by the magazine, released to author on request if full credit is given the REVIEW.

Continuing bibliography in each issue.

WESTERN AMERICAN LITERATURE, English Department, Colorado State University, Ft. Collins, Colorado 80521. $6; quarterly (Spring, Summer, Fall, Winter). Founded 1965; sponsored by Western Literature Association.

Major fields of interest: American Literature in and about the American West. Literary history, criticism, bibliography, and book reviews preferred.

Manuscript information: 15-25 pages preferred. MLA style sheet, footnotes at end of article. 1 copy of Ms. needed. 2 preferred. Report in 4 months.

Payment: None; 100 offprints.

Copyrighted.

Bibliography in February issue.

WESTERN FOLKLORE, Folklore and Mythology Group, UCLA, Los Angeles, California 90024. $10; quarterly. Founded 1942; sponsored by The University of California.

Major fields of interest: (in order of preference) Folklore of the West, folklore of general interest from all over America, world folklore (theoretical material only). Articles should stay within these fields and not involve "literary folklore" or astrology and kindred subjects. Folklore collectanea, annotated, where possible tracing individual items over large spans of time and space, is desirable.

Manuscript information: 3000-4000 words the preferred length. MLA style sheet or University of Chicago style manual; footnotes should be consecutive at the end of the article and double-spaced. Report within 1 month.

Payment: Some offprints.

Permission to use the material must be given in writing and will usually be granted for publication in scholarly but not in commercial journals.

WESTERN HUMANITIES REVIEW, Spencer Hall, University of Utah, Salt Lake City, Utah 84112. $5; quarterly. Founded 1947.

Major fields of interest: Articles in history, philosophy, art history and criticism, the relationship between science and the humanities, all fields of literary scholarship and literary criticism. Articles should take a broadly humanistic point of view. Close explications of texts not desired. Creative material also published.

Manuscript information: Articles of 3000-5000 words; shorter notes sometimes used. MLA style sheet, with modifications; footnotes on the final page, but other treatment is acceptable. Report usually within a few weeks; publication within a year.

Payment: Short stories and articles: up to $100; poems: to $35; book reviews: $25.

Copyright by the journal, but permission to reprint freely granted.

WESTERN REVIEW, Western New Mexico University, Silver City, New Mexico. $2, $1 single copy; twice yearly. Founded 1964; sponsored by Western New Mexico University.

Major fields of interest: The Humanities — literature, philosophy, art, history, economics, music, and creative writing. Types of work preferred: brief articles, not so specialized as to lack reader appeal; creative writing — poems, short stories, glossy photographs of art works, drawings of cover designs. Highly technical material excluded.

Manuscript information: Articles should be short, 800 to 1500 words. MLA style sheet and footnote form, giving author, title, publisher, place of publication, and date. Report usually within 1 to 2 months, unless earlier decision is requested.

Payment: None; 6 copies of issue.

Copyright by the journal; permission to reprint elsewhere freely given.

WILLIAM AND MARY QUARTERLY, A Magazine of Early American History, Box 220, Williamsburg, Virginia 23185. $8; quarterly.

Founded 1892; third series, 1944; published by the Institute of Early American History and Culture.

Major fields of interest: American history and culture in the First British Empire and U.S. to 1815 periods. Recent titles: "An Economic Interpretation of the American Revolution," "Will and Intellect in the New England Mind." Each issue contains a Notes and Documents section and Reviews of Books.

Manuscript information: Maximum length for articles is 10,000 words. MLA style sheet; footnotes should be typed separately at the end of the article. Report within 3 months.

Payment: 90 offprints, 1 year's subscription.

Copyright held by the magazine but transferred to the author upon request.

WOMEN'S STUDIES: AN INTERDISCIPLINARY JOURNAL, Department of English, Queens College, Flushing, New York 11364. Three times a year. Founded 1972.

Major fields of interest: Interdisciplinary/feminist criticism in all fields. All types of articles preferred. Poetry, fiction, book and film reviews also published.

Manuscript information: 20 page articles preferred. MLA style sheet. Three copies needed by reader.

Payment: 50 offprints.

Gordon and Brach retains copyright.

WORD: Journal of The International Linguistic Association (formerly the Linguistic Circle of New York), Department of English, Clark University, Worcester, Mass. 01610. $10 for 3 issues. Founded 1943; published by the International Linguistic Association.

Major fields of interest: General linguistics; studies of importance to the theory or methodology of linguistics, without restriction to particular language families.

Manuscript information: 2000-50,000 words. Contributors should consult previous issues of the journal for general style. Report within 2-3 months. Published in English.

Payment: 100 reprints; additional at cost.

THE WORDSWORTH CIRCLE, Department of English, Temple University, Philadelphia, Pennsylvania 19122. $4 (1 yr.), $7 (2 yrs.), $9

(3 yrs.); quarterly. Founded 1969; sponsored by Temple University.

Major fields of interest: Wordsworth, during first year of publication; Coleridge the second; Hazlitt, De Quincey, Lamb, Southey, minor poets, and popular writers in successive years. From first issue, however, information on all figures in the first generation English Romantics will be published. Will accept brief notes, queries, reports on papers, meetings, research in progress, auctions, exhibitions, library collections and special events. One issue each year will consist of a forum based upon responses of particular scholars to a topic of mutual interest.

Manuscript information. Short notes to articles of 5000 words accepted. MLA style sheet. Report in 4-6 weeks.

Payment: None; probably no offprints. Annual prize essay.

Annual review issue, containing reviews in all fields of the first generation English Romantics; each summer beginning 1973.

WORKS, AMS Press, 56 East 13th Street, New York, New York 10003. $5; quarterly. Founded 1967; sponsored by AMS Press.

Major fields of interest: Poetry, fiction, drama, translation, and criticism.

Manuscript information: Any length of article, any style sheet; footnotes on page where cited. Report in 4-8 weeks.

Payment: 25¢ a line for poetry, $50-$150 for prose and drama depending on quality and length; 2 copies of the issue.

Copyrighted; reprint rights revert to author with stipulation that it be mentioned that the material first appeared in WORKS.

WORLD LITERATURE WRITTEN IN ENGLISH (formerly CBCL NEWSLETTER), c/o Robert McDowell, Editor, Department of English, University of Texas at Arlington, Arlington, Texas 76010. $2; available on exchange basis to libraries; twice yearly. Founded 1962; sponsored by Group 12, Modern Language Association.

Major fields of interest: Literature in English apart from British-U.S. Interviews, reviews, bibliography and criticism related to "new" literatures in English preferred.

Manuscript information: MLA style sheet. Report in 30 days.

No payment.

No copyright.

THE YALE REVIEW, Box 1902A, Yale Station, New Haven, Connecticut 06520. $6; quarterly. Founded 1911; sponsored by Yale University.

Major fields of interest: Critical articles on topics of interest to the intelligent nonspecialist — politics, economics, the arts, etc. Short stories and poems are also published.

Manuscript information: Articles may range from 2500-5000 words in length. No scholarly apparatus permitted (no footnotes, bibliography, etc.). Report may take as long as 3 or 4 months.

Payment to contributors.

Copyright retained by the magazine unless transfer is requested.

YALE/THEATRE, Box 2046, Yale Station, New Haven, Connecticut 06520. $5.50, 2 yrs.: $10.50; tri-annually. Founded 1968; sponsored by Yale School of Drama.

Major fields of interest: All aspects of the theatre. Criticism, reviews, interpretations, and plays preferred ". . . tend not to focus on pieces of scholarly research." Mss. of plays, "with permission, will be placed in our drama library for directors seeking new work to produce."

Manuscript information: 3000-12,000 words. MLA style sheet. Report in 6 weeks.

Payment: None; 5 offprints, more on request.

Copyrighted.

YALE UNIVERSITY LIBRARY GAZETTE, Yale University Library, New Haven, Connecticut 06520. $6; quarterly. Founded 1926; sponsored by Yale University Library.

Major fields of interest: Material connected with the Yale Library or Yale University, or research done at the Yale Library.

Manuscript information: 1500-3000 words the preferred length. General style of the Yale University Press should be followed. 2 copies of the Ms. (original and carbon) needed. Footnotes should be reduced to the essential minimum. Report within 2 weeks.

Payment: 2-10 copies of the issue.

No copyright unless a special case is involved.

YEARBOOK OF COMPARATIVE AND GENERAL LITERATURE, Comparative Literature Office, Ballantine Hall 402, Indiana University, Bloomington, Indiana 47401. $5; annually. Founded 1951; since 1961 sponsored by the Comparative Literature Program at Indiana University.

Major fields of interest: Literary theory, news of the fields of comparative literature; reviews of recent translations; annual bibliography of scholarly and critical works in comparative literature, annual list of translations into English.

Manuscript information: Length determined by subject. MLA style sheet, including footnote treatment. Report in 3 months.

Copyright through the Comparative Literature Program at Indiana University.

YEATS STUDIES. Final information not available. Query Professor Norman H. MacKenzie, Department of English, Queen's University, Kingston, Ontario, Canada.

ZEITSCHRIFT FÜR ANGLISTIK UND AMERIKANISTIK, VEB Verlag Enzyklopädie, Leipzig, German Democratic Republic, Gerichtsweg 26. M 7,50 per copy; quarterly. Founded 1953.

Major fields of interest: Any aspects of English or American language or literature.

Manuscript information: 20 to 30 typewritten pages. Articles may be in either English or German. Footnotes should be grouped at the end of the article. Report in about 5-6 weeks.

Payment: 25 offprints; about 16 M per printed page.

Copyright by VEB Verlag Enzyklopädie.

INDEX

Entries are by title under major subject headings. Periodicals listed as *GENERAL* include studies in several fields

225

Field
Florida Quarterly
Georgia Review
Iowa Review
Journal of Modern Literature
Il Letterato
Litterair Paspoort
Malahat Review
Modern Drama
Modern Fiction Studies
Modern Poetry Studies
Modernist Studies
Mosaic
Neue Deutsche Literatur
Neueren Sprachen
New American Review
Notes on Contemporary Literature
Occident
Outposts
Paris Review
Partisan Review
Performance
Perspective
Poet and Critic
Poet Lore
Renaissance and Modern Studies
Revue Belge
Rivista di Letterature Moderne
    e Comparate
South Dakota Review
Southern Review (U.S.A.)
Studies in Contemporary Satire
Twentieth Century Literature
University of Windsor Review
West Coast Review

DICKENS, CHARLES
Dickens Studies Annual
Dickens Studies Newsletter
Dickensian
DICKINSON, EMILY
Emily Dickinson Bulletin
Higginson Journal of Poetry
DOYLE, SIR ARTHUR CONAN
Baker Street Journal

DRAMA AND THEATER
Adam
Comparative Drama
Drama & Theatre
Drama Review (TDR)
Dramatics
Educational Theatre Journal
Modern Drama
Newsletter, American Society for
    Theatre Research
Nineteenth Century Theatre
    Research
Performance
Players Magazine
Quarterly Journal of Speech
Renaissance Drama
Research Opportunities in
    Renaissance Drama
Restoration and 18th Century
    Theatre Research
Southern Speech Journal
Speech Monographs
Theatre Annual
Theatre Journal
Theatre Notebook
Theatre Quarterly
Theatre Research
Theatre Studies
Theatre Survey
Yale/Theatre
DREISER, THEODORE
Dreiser Newsletter

ENGLISH LITERATURE (*see also*
CONTEMPORARY LITERATURE;
LITERATURE GENERAL;
MEDIEVAL STUDIES; RENAIS-
SANCE STUDIES; VICTORIAN
STUDIES; *and individual entries*
for BACON, BLAKE, BRONTËS,
BYRON, BROWNING, BURKE,
CARLETON, CONRAD, DICKENS,
DOYLE, ELIOT, GISSING, GRAVES,
HOPKINS, JOHNSON, JOYCE,
KEATS, KIPLING, LAWRENCE,

MILL, MILTON, MORRIS, SHAKESPEARE, SHAW, SHELLEY, SPENSER, TENNYSON, TOLKIEN, WAUGH, WORDSWORTH, WOLLENSTONECRAFT)
  Anglia
  Antigonish Review
  Eighteenth-Century Studies
  ELH
  English
  English Language Notes
  English Literature in Transition
  English Miscellany
  English Studies
  English Studies in Africa
  Enlightenment Studies
  Essays in Criticism
  Études Anglaises
  Furman Studies
  Huntington Library Quarterly
  Iowa English Yearbook
  Johnsonian Newsletter
  Journal of English and Germanic
    Philology
  Journal of Narrative Technique
  Literary Criterion
  Literary Monographs
  Massachusetts Studies in English
  New Rambler
  Nineteenth-Century Theatre
    Research
  Notre Dame English Journal
  PMLA
  Recherches Anglaises et
    Americaines
  Restoration and 18th Century
    Theatre Research
  Review of English Studies
  Scriblerian
  Seventeenth-Century News
  Southern Review (Australia)
  Studies in English Literature
  Thoth
  Zeitschrift für Anglistic und
    Americanistik

ELIOT, T. S.
  T. S. Eliot Newsletter
EUROPEAN LITERATURE
  Adam
  American-Scandinavian Review
  Ariel
  Books Abroad
  Bulletin of Hispanic Studies
  Canadian Modern Language
    Review
  Deutsche Vierteljahrsschrift . . .
  Essays in Criticism
  Forum Italicum
  French Studies
  Germanic Review
  Hispanic Review
  Insula
  Italica
  Journal of English and Germanic
    Philology
  Journal of European Studies
  Modern Fiction Studies
  Mediterranean Review
  MLN
  Modern Language Quarterly
  Modern Language Review
  Moderna Sprak
  Monatshefte für Deutschen . . .
  Neue Deutsche Literatur
  Neueren Sprachen
  Neuphilologische Mitteilungen
  Philologica Pragensia
  Polish Review
  Romance Notes
  Romance Philology
  Romanic Revue
  Scandinavian Studies
  Slavonic and East European
    Review
  Studia Neophilologica
  Symposium
  Theatre Research
EXPLICATION
  Canadian Modern Language
    Review

Green River Review
Harper's Magazine
Harvard Theological Review
Hermanthena
Horizon
Hudson Review
Humanities Association Review
Illinois Quarterly
Journal of Ethnic Studies
Kansas Quarterly
Listener
Listening
Massachusetts Review
Meanjin Quarterly
Michigan Academician
Michigan Quarterly Review
Midwest Quarterly
Modern Age
Month
Nation
National Review
New England Review
New Leader
New Orleans Review
New Republic
New Statesman
North American Review
Northwest Review
Ohio Review
Other Scholars
Partisan Review
Phylon
Popular Music and Society
Quartet
Queen's Quarterly
RE: Artes Liberales
Recovering Literature
Revue de l'Université d'Ottawa
Rice University Studies
Salmagundi
Saturday Review
Scholarly Publishing
Science & Society
Sewanee Review
Shenandoah
Silliman Journal

Small Press Review
Smith
Soundings
South Atlantic Quarterly
Southern Humanities Review
Southern Quarterly
Soviet Studies in Literature
Spectrum
Steppenwolf
Thought
Topic
Triquarterly
University of Dayton Review
University of Windsor Review
Visva-Bharati Quarterly
Wascana Review
West Coast Review
Works
Yale Review
GRAVES, ROBERT
    Focus on Robert Graves
GISSING, GEORGE
    Gissing Newsletter

HARTMANN, SADAKICHI
    Sadakichi Hartmann Newsletter
HAWTHORNE, NATHANIEL
    Hawthorne Journal
    Nathaniel Hawthorne Journal
HEMINGWAY, ERNEST
    Fitzgerald/Hemingway Annual
    Hemingway Notes
HISTORY OF IDEAS
    American Documentation
    Biblioteque d'Humanisme ...
    Castrvm Peregrini
    Denver Quarterly
    Deutsche Vierteljahrsschrift ...
    Journal of the History of Ideas
    PMLA
HOPKINS, G. M.
    Hopkins Research Bulletin

INTERDISCIPLINARY STUDIES
    Clio
    Eighteenth-Century Studies

Enlightenment Essays
ETC.
Feminist Studies
Furman Studies
Hartford Studies in Literature
Journal of Ethnic Studies
Journal of European Studies
Journal of Medieval and
  Renaissance Studies
Michigan Quarterly Review
Ohio Review
Soundings
University of Dayton Review
Women's Studies
IRISH LITERATURE
  Colby Library Quarterly
  Dublin Magazine
  Éire-Ireland
  Irish University Review
  Journal of Irish Literature
  Long Room
  Yeats Studies

JOHNSON, SAMUEL
  Johnsonian Newsletter
  New Rambler
JOYCE, JAMES
  James Joyce Quarterly
  Wake Newsletter

KEATS, JOHN
  Keats-Shelley Journal
  Keats-Shelley Memorial Bulletin
KIPLING, RUDYARD
  Kipling Journal

LAWRENCE, D. H.
  D. H. Lawrence Review
LEWIS, SINCLAIR
  Sinclair Lewis Newsletter
LIBRARY JOURNALS
  Bodleian Library Record
  Books at Brown
  Bulletin of the John Rylands
    Library

Bulletin of the New York Public
    Library
  Colby Library Quarterly
  College and Research Libraries
  Harvard Library Bulletin
  Huntington Library Quarterly
  Journal of Rutgers University
    Library
  Library Chronicle
  Library Chronicle of University of
    Texas
  Long Room
  Newberry Library Bulletin
  Princeton University Library
    Chronicle
  Serif
  Yale University Library Gazette
LINGUISTICS, SEMANTICS,
LANGUAGE, PHILOLOGY
  American Documentation
  American Speech
  Anglia
  Anthropological Linguistics
  Anthropos
  AUMLA
  Canadian Journal of Linguistics
  Costerus
  ETC.
  Forum Italicum
  General Linguistics
  Germanic Review
  Glossa
  International Journal of American
    Linguistics
  International Journal of
    Psycholinguistics
  International Review of Applied
    Linguistics
  Journal of English Linguistics
  Journal of Literary Semantics
  La Monda Lingvo-Problemo
  Language
  Language and Speech
  Language and Style
  Language in Society

Language Learning
Lingua
Lingua e Stile
Linguistic Reporter
Linguistics
Meta
Morehead State University Bulletin
Applied Linguistics
Names
Newsletter of American Dialect
Society
Papers in Linguistics
Philological Quarterly
Philosophy and Rhetoric
Publication of American Dialect
Society
Romance Philology
Scandinavian Studies
Semiotica
Spoken English
Studia Linguistica
Studies in Linguistics
Sub-stance
TESOL Quarterly
Texas Studies in Literature and
Language
Word
LITERATURE, GENERAL
Agenda
American Notes & Queries
Antigonish Review
Archiv für das Studium ...
Ariel
Arizona Quarterly
Arkham Collector
Arlington Quarterly
AUMLA
Ball State University Forum
Bonniers Litterära Magasin
British Book News
Bulletin MMLA
Bulletin of the New York Public
Library
Bulletin RMMLA
California English Journal

Cambridge Quarterly
Canadian Author & Bookman
Canadian Modern Language
Review
Carleton Miscellany
Castrvm Peregrini
CEA Critic
Chicago Review
CLA Journal
Colby Library Quarterly
Concerning Poetry
Costerus
Critical Quarterly
Critical Review: Melbourne
Criticism
Dalhousie Review
Dekalb Literary Arts Journal
Delta
Descant
Diacritics
ELH
English Language Notes
English Quarterly
English Record
Essays in Criticism
Essays in Literature
Explicator
Extrapolation
Far-Western Forum
Florida Quarterly
Four Quarters
Furman Studies
Genre
Georgia Review
Hartford Studies in Literature
Hollins Critic
Hudson Review
Humanities Association Review
Huntington Library Quarterly
Japan Quarterly
Journal of English and Germanic
Philology
Journal of Modern Literature
Journal of Narrative Technique
Journal of Popular Culture

Language and Style
Language of Poems
Literary Criterion
Literary Half-Yearly
Literary Review
Literature in Wissenschaft ...
Litterair Paspoort
London Magazine
Massachusetts Review
Massachusetts Studies in English
Michigan Quarterly Review
MLN
Modern Language Quarterly
Modern Language Review
Modern Philology
Moderna Sprak
Mundus Artium
Neueren Sprachen
Neuphilologische Mitteilungen
New York Times Book Review
Niekas
Nineteenth-Century Fiction
Northwest Review
Notes & Queries
Notre Dame English Journal
Novel
Nuova Antologia
Papers on Language and
  Literature
Perspective
Philologica Pragensia
Philological Quarterly
PMLA
Poetry
Prairie Schooner
Prose
Quarterly Review of Literature
Rackham Literary Studies
Research in African Literatures
Revue Belge de Philologie ...
Satire Newsletter
Seventeenth-Century News
Southern Humanities Review
Stechert-Hafner News
Studia Neophilologica
Studies in English

Studies in Philology
Studies in Romanticism
Studies in Short Fiction
Studies in the Humanities
Studies in the Literary
  Imagination
Studies in the Novel
Style
Tennessee Studies in Literature
Texas Studies in Literature and
  Language
Thoth
Times Literary Supplement
Tulane Studies in English
University Review
University of Toronto Quarterly
Virginia Quarterly Review
Western Humanities Review
Western Review
LONDON, JACK
  Jack London Newsletter

MARK TWAIN (*see* CLEMENS)
MARKHAM, EDWIN
  Markham Review
MEDIEVAL STUDIES
  Annuale Mediaevale
  Chaucer Review
  Chronica
  Classica et Mediaevalia
  Comitatus
  Journal of Medieval and Renais-
    sance Studies
  Mediaeval Studies
  Medievalia et Humanistica
  Medium Aevum
  Modern Philology
  Nottingham Mediaeval Studies
  Old English Newsletter
  Research Opportunities in
    Renaissance Drama
  Speculum
  Traditio
  Viator
MILL, J. S.
  Mill News Letter

MILTON, JOHN
  Milton Quarterly
  Milton Studies
MORE, SIR THOMAS
  Moreana
MORRIS, WILLIAM
  Journal of William Morris
    Society

NIN, ANAIS
  Under the Sign of Pisces

O'CONNOR, FLANNERY
  Flannery O'Connor Bulletin

PEDAGOGICAL STUDIES
  California English Journal
  Canadian Modern Language
    Review
  CEA Critic
  CEA Forum
  College Composition and
    Communication
  College English
  Convergence
  English Journal
  English Quarterly
  English Record
  Exercise Exchange
  Extrapolation
  Freshman English News
  Illinois English Bulletin
  Iowa English Yearbook
  Journal of Aesthetic Education
  Journal of English Teaching
    Techniques
  Leaflet
  Literatur in Wissenschaft ...
  Modern Language Journal
  Monatshefte für Deutschen ...
  Neueren Sprachen
  Oral English
  Research in Teaching of English
  TESOL
  Universities Quarterly
  Use of English

POE, EDGAR ALLAN
  Poe Studies
POUND, EZRA
  Paideuma
PSYCHOLOGY AND LITERATURE
  American Imago
  Literature and Psychology
  Psychoanalytic Review

RENAISSANCE STUDIES
  Baconiana
  Bibliotheque d'Humanisme &
    Renaissance
  Comitatus
  English Literary Renaissance
  Erasmus in English
  Journal of Medieval and Renais-
    sance Studies
  Medievalia et Humanistica
  Renaissance and Modern Studies
  Renaissance and Reformation
  Renaissance Drama
  Renaissance Papers
  Renaissance Quarterly
  Research Opportunities in
    Renaissance Drama
  Seventeenth-Century News
  Studies in English Literature
  Studies in Philology
  Studies in the Renaissance
  Viator

SCOTTISH STUDIES
  Scottish International Review
  Scottish Studies
  Studies in Scottish Literature
SHAKESPEARE, WILLIAM
  Shakespeare-Jahrbuch
  Shakespeare Newsletter
  Shakespeare Quarterly
  Shakespeare Studies
  Shakespeare Survey
  Shakespearean Research and
    Opportunities
SHAW, GEORGE BERNARD
  Independent Shavian

Shavian
Shaw Review
SHELLEY, PERCY BYSSHE
Keats-Shelley Journal
Keats-Shelley Memorial Bulletin
SOUTHERN LITERATURE AND
CULTURE
Alabama Review
Appalachian Journal
Georgia Review
Mississippi Quarterly
Notes on Mississippi Writers
South Carolina Review
Southern Literary Journal
Southern Quarterly
Southern Review
Southern Speech Journal
SPENSER, EDMUND
Spenser Newsletter
STEINBECK, JOHN
Steinbeck Quarterly

TENNYSON, LORD ALFRED
Tennyson Research Bulletin
THEORY (*see* AESTHETICS AND
THEORY)

THOREAU, HENRY DAVID
Thoreau Journal Quarterly
Thoreau Society Bulletin
TOLKIEN, J. R. R.
Niekas

VICTORIAN STUDIES
Studies in English Literature
Victorian Newsletter
Victorian Periodicals Newsletter
Victorian Poetry
Victorian Studies

WAUGH, EVELYN
Evelyn Waugh Newsletter
WELSH LITERATURE
Anglo-Welsh Review
WHITMAN, WALT
Calamus
Walt Whitman Review
WOLLSTONECRAFT, MARY
Mary Wollstonecraft Newsletter
WOMEN STUDIES
Feminist Studies
Mary Wollstonecraft Newsletter
Women's Studies